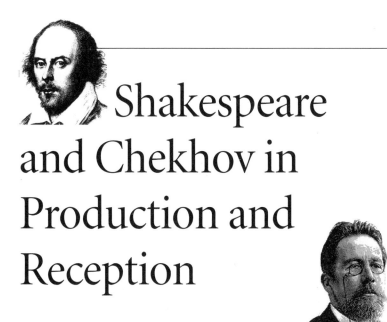

Shakespeare and Chekhov in Production and Reception

Studies in

THEATRE HISTORY & CULTURE

Edited by Thomas Postlewait

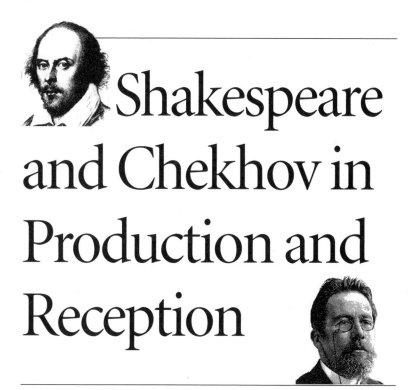

Shakespeare and Chekhov in Production and Reception

THEATRICAL EVENTS AND THEIR AUDIENCES

John Tulloch

University of Iowa Press

Iowa City

University of Iowa Press, Iowa City 52242

Copyright © 2005 by the University of Iowa Press

All rights reserved

Printed in the United States of America

Design by Richard Hendel

http://www.uiowa.edu/uiowapress

The University of Iowa Press is a member of Green Press
Initiative and is committed to preserving natural resources.

Printed on acid-free paper

Library of Congress Cataloging-in-Publication Data

Tulloch, John.

Shakespeare and Chekhov in production and reception:
theatrical events and their audiences / by John Tulloch.

    p.   cm.—(Studies in theatre history and culture)

Includes bibliographical references and index.

ISBN 0-87745-926-6 (cloth)

1. Shakespeare, William, 1564–1616—Dramatic production.
2. Chekhov, Anton Pavlovich, 1860–1904—Dramatic production.   3. Chekhov, Anton Pavlovich, 1860–1904—Stage
history.   4. Shakespeare, William, 1564–1616—Stage history.
5. Theater audiences.   I. Title.   II. Series.

PR3091.T85 2005

792.9′5—dc22   2004058012

05 06 07 08 09 C 5 4 3 2 1

To Rob Jordan,

who encouraged me

to bring television and

theatre studies together

CONTENTS

PREFACE

This book is about theatrical events, in particular, productions of Shakespeare and Chekhov in mainstream theatre, and their audiences. As a book of case studies, it represents a methodological exploration into theatre production and audience research over several years. In line with Norman Denzin and Yvonna Lincoln's postmodernist and ethnographic emphasis on local "tales from the field," it is a book of local case studies, most of them based on detailed ethnographic and qualitative research at theatres and among audiences in different countries. But it is also a book that chooses to select (and value) continuing production histories of Shakespeare and Chekhov that engage with current globalizing trends.

Two very different intellectual traditions face off here. My background as a sociologist is in media and cultural studies, and for many colleagues internationally a book on "Shakespeare" and "Chekhov" (even in inverted commas!) will be much less welcome than one on *The Simpsons*, *Batman*, or *Star Trek*. They are not interested in "high culture," except as an endlessly dismissed and residual category of humanism. On the other hand, there are the more traditional Chekhov scholars like Laurence Senelick (see chapter 4) who do still believe in artistic genius, authorship, and aesthetic value and write rather well about it but who tend to dismiss both the "arbitrary line readings" of "what might be called post-modern performances" and the "didactic discourses" of an "activist message" (1997, 301, 320, 322). Certainly, Senelick's comments about the "soap operatics of the usual American production" or the "pure Hollywood" vulgarity of some postglasnost Russian productions of Chekhov as well as his remarks about "fashionable literary theory" would confirm cultural studies scholars in their worst prejudices (1997, 304, 355).

But I happen to enjoy Hollywood, soap opera, and popular science fiction as well as many live theatre productions of Chekhov and Shakespeare and sometimes want to write about them. Over the years I have worked on a number of "ethnographies of production" in television as well as conducting television audience research and analysis. My pleasures in live theatre performance have led me even further, into fascination with the "liveness" of theatrical event and its audience.

Methodologies of theatre audience research are a major focus here. The book does not represent one position methodologically, any more than the theory aspect of the book represents one position, though in both cases I hope that the different theories and methods are made to cohere with one another by way of the case studies.

The methodologies I focus on vary for three reasons. The first is the qualitative/quantitative principle. For many years, cultural/media studies more or less rejected quantitative work, even in audience research, and it is only in the last decade or so that there have been strong calls for some mixing of the two. The second reason is pragmatic. Theatres vary in the access they will allow, so different case studies necessarily had different methodologies. For example, *The Free State* study at the Theatre Royal, Bath, was intended to have both qualitative and quantitative data, to be accessed in part by way of the theatre's audience tracking system. However, late concerns at the theatre forced me to come up with an alternative. This was to ask for respondents to *The Cherry Orchard* survey (picked up on seats at the theatre) to make themselves available, if interested, for interviews about *The Free State*, which many of them had recently seen. I then made sure that I got both long interview and survey data in my subsequent piece of theatre audience research at the Q Theatre in Penrith, New South Wales. The third reason is developmental. My own audience ideas have developed over several years with each case study. For example, post-coded qualitative responses to the Theatre Royal, Bath, *The Cherry Orchard* case study could be used as multiple-choice questions for the next survey at the Q Theatre and so on.

Thus, my inclusion of different audience methodologies in different chapters is deliberate but also to some extent a matter of happenstance, which has necessarily led to a strongly reflexive theme in this book. I have tried to examine consistently what it means to employ this or that methodology to this or that study or what the advantages may be in doing so. This is an ongoing narrative of the book.

And if methodology is meant to be developmental but reflexively systematic in this book, theory is meant to provide a map of places we will visit when it is appropriate to do so for research reasons. This is not intended to be a metatheory book, but I do try to bring theories together from fields that seldom get together. Nor, though, is the theory simply eclectic. My own position here is, broadly, cultural materialist, with a strong emphasis on the material conditions of both production and reception, and this theoretical position has undoubtedly influenced the theatre case studies included here.

Two particular conceptual maps (which are not theories, as such) are drawn on to provide a structure for the book. My own cultural/media studies production/audience research background is developed to provide one (sequential) kind of map. This focuses on the relationship between spectator positions constructed (sometimes in contradiction) during production and on the social audience readings that take place among actual audiences. The original Australian Research Council Large Grant research (which I conducted with Associate Professor Tom Burvill of Macquarie University, Sydney), which is represented in part 2 of the book, contained extensive work on other aspects of this sequencing, including rehearsals analysis at the American Repertory Theater, Boston, analysis of newspaper reviews of Chekhov productions, a production study of Adrian Noble's *The Cherry Orchard* at Stratford-upon-Avon, England, and a survey of all book and refereed journal academic criticism of Chekhov's short stories and plays that had appeared in English over a twenty-five-year period prior to the research. There has been space for little or nothing of these analyses here, though much of the production/audience work does appear in part 2.

The second aspect of the conceptual map draws on theatrical event research that has been conducted with colleagues in the International Federation of Theatre Research's Theatrical Event working group. Over the last ten years this group has developed a range of concepts in this post-performance theory field. In particular, I have drawn in part 3 on Willmar Sauter's recent work. This has not been intended to take his particular problematic (or that of another Theatrical Event colleague, Peter Eversmann) as an end point, any more than the risk modernity / postmodernity contrast in the introduction (and part 1) of the book is meant to finalize that particular epistemological debate. Rather, all four sections in the introduction are articulated there to suggest theoretical areas of relevance to the topic, which will be revisited when the case studies make that appropriate. Similarly, Sauter's four segments of the theatrical event are useful signposts by way of which I can take my own thinking further.

Part 2 of the book would have been impossible without the intellectual and practical involvement in the Australian Research Council (ARC) research of Tom Burvill. Tom conducted a number of the interviews quoted here, attended several weeks of rehearsals of *The Seagull* at Belvoir

Street Theatre in Sydney, and engaged with me in each stage of the research (including the extensive analysis of Chekhov academic critical paradigms, which is hardly represented here). That ARC research project took a number of years, was conducted in three different countries, and was complicated, both theoretically and practically. Yet I enjoyed it enormously because of the subject, because of Tom Burvill's involvement, and because of the many Chekhov scholars who gave generously of their time toward it. I only regret that there is not space here to draw more on what they said about Chekhov in criticism and performance and on how they said it.

ACKNOWLEDGMENTS

My debt is great to very many people, both those who were a professional part of the theatrical events described here and the many audience members interviewed for this book.

My primary thanks is to Tom Burvill, who was my co-researcher in the "Chekhov: In Criticism, Performance and Reading" Australian Research Council Large Grant funded project which underpins two chapters of this book. Tom not only did the rehearsal observations and interviews for Belvoir Street Theatre's *The Seagull* analyzed here, some of the interviews for Eyre/Griffiths's *The Cherry Orchard* productions, interviewed with me some of the student audience groups who watched that production, conducted production observation and interviews of RSC's *The Cherry Orchard* (which gets much less space than I would have liked in this book), discussed with me over many months — together with our excellent research assistant Andrew Hood — the "Chekhov: In Criticism" part of the project (which also finds little space for discussion here), but also co-authored with me some early pieces related to the project. He is overall a wonderful colleague on a project that carried us far and wide in search of productions, critics, and audiences. I also want to thank the Australian Research Council, without whose support those chapters could not have been written.

The kind of research reported on here requires considerable theatre access — to their professional staff, both on and off stage, as well as to their audiences. I am enormously grateful to professional performers, as well as the technical and marketing staff, at the Q Theatre, Penrith, New South Wales; the Belvoir Street Theatre, Sydney, Australia; the New Theatre, Newtown, Sydney, Australia; the Royal Shakespeare Company, Stratford-upon-Avon, England; the Theatre Royal, Bath, England; the English Touring Theatre; the American Repertory Theater, Boston, USA, and to television performers and technical professionals associated with the Richard Eyre/ Trevor Griffiths productions of *The Cherry Orchard* at Nottingham Playhouse and on BBC 1 Television, so many of whom were interviewed, while only some are quoted here. In the case of the ART,

Boston, an entire chapter on the rehearsal process of Simone Federman's production of *The Three Sisters* was omitted from this book for reasons of space, mainly because we had very little audience data for that production, unlike all the others that are covered here (though Tom Burvill and I have published a short piece on it elsewhere). I acknowledge what is missing as well as what is here because so many people gave of their time in interviews, were patient with us in watching rehearsals and performances, and only some of them are directly represented in the pages that follow.

Two artistic directors gave us a special degree of access, amounting to nearly being an "ethnography" of production. Very special thanks, then, are due to Mary-Anne Gifford of the Railway Street Theatre Company at Penrith (and the company's general manager Dallas Lewis) and to Neil Armfield at Belvoir Street Theatre, Sydney. Considerable access to actors and other theatre professionals was also provided by Adrian Noble at the Royal Shakespeare Company and by Ron Daniels and Robert Brustein at the ART, Boston, whom I thank heartily for making the productions discussed here (and others too briefly discussed) such an enjoyable experience. Key interviews about their productions came from Janet Suzman, Richard Eyre, and Trevor Griffiths, all of whom found time for me in very busy schedules. Working with professional theatre people and television people provides access to a unique mix of creativity, intelligence, and professionalism which in turn provides a real buzz for researchers of the live event, and can be gained in no other way than "being there." So my thanks to all of you.

Another crucial category of acknowledgments, given the theatre audience focus of this book, covers the various audiences interviewed and surveyed. These range from students in theatre and Russian studies courses at universities in the USA, Australia, and the UK; school students in Western Sydney, Penrith, and the Blue Mountains, New South Wales; the Friends of the Other Places at Stratford-upon-Avon, England; and the University of the Third Age in Sydney, Australia, together with audience members surveyed and interviewed at all the theatres mentioned above. My policy in the book has been to withhold the real names of audience members quoted, on grounds of ethics committees' preferences, but many of those interviewed will recognize their enormous contribution to this book. Special thanks are also due to teachers and principals who allowed me access to their school students, to lecturers at numerous universities who did the same, and to the very many international Chekhov and

Shakespeare scholars interviewed, of whom only Laurence Senelick and Peter Holland are represented (again too briefly) here. The same is true of many newspaper theatre reviewers interviewed — their role, and that of university critics, in making meanings for audiences of Shakespeare and Chekhov in production still has, largely, to be written.

Finally, my thanks go to Rob Jordan, who has been a mentor to me through many years of writing about film, television, and theatre, and to whom this book is dedicated.

Part One

Introduction

1
DEFINING THEATRICAL EVENT AND AUDIENCE RESEARCH

Two casual observations of theatre audiences help introduce the project for this book. They are both of teenagers watching performances of Shakespeare. One was in 1999 at the Barbican Theatre, London, for a performance of *The Tempest*. The other was in 2001 at the Q Theatre, Penrith, New South Wales, where a production of *Much Ado about Nothing* was running.

The Barbican is a large theatre space and, until recently, the London home of the Royal Shakespeare Company. As such, it could afford quite lavish productions and spectacular effects, and the Barbican's *The Tempest* certainly achieved these. The production had been well reviewed, and seats were hard to come by. I only managed to get a seat at the very edge of the gods for the very last matinee performance.

There were a number of school parties present. In fact, I was surrounded by students in the very back row, high up and far from the stage. Six schoolgirls who had even more extreme seats than I did were clearly bored. Throughout the first half they chatted to each other, staring challengingly at me when I occasionally got distracted and looked across at them. By the opening of the second half, one was reading a romance novel and the others had resorted to their Walkmans and were waving their arms to the sound of their own music, which could just be heard by other close-by audience members.

Academics like myself who have worked for a long time in media and cultural studies have got used to celebrating this kind of incident as resistant reading. These teenage girls were alienated from the entire high-cultural event. Sitting uncomfortably, brought here by their teachers to see valued theatre that was playing their A-level (school-leaving certificate) set text, they brought with them into the theatre space (and also into my leisure space) their own popular cultural performance. Their body language indicated at different times a mixture of distraction (from the play but not from their music), of provocation, and of "doing what they shouldn't" as they outstared my gaze at them. This composite of everyday popular music and performative body language became an alternative entertainment event that was sometimes hard to ignore.

In accord with feminist cultural theory (e.g., McRobbie 1984), it would be both plausible and appropriate to consider the ways that these girls were transforming this play of "patriarchal colonization" (Bennett 1996, 125), *The Tempest*, into their own everyday pleasures, especially their enjoyment in opposing the dominant male gaze of a "legitimate" theatregoer. This kind of resistant reading analysis has been enormously important in cultural studies and obviously could be taken much further in this case, for example, in terms of the girls' gender, ethnicities (three black, one Asian, two white), class, cultural capital, and habitus. Cultural studies writers over the years have made great play between the paralleling of school structures and broader societal structures that were often highlighted by way of these resistant readings of media texts.

However, I agree with Pertti Alasuutari, who argues in *Rethinking the Media Audience* that the theory of resistant reading too often entraps us in false or inadequate dichotomies:

> It is important to notice that the celebration of the active viewer . . . [and] resistance through mass culture is still fixed to the idea that the consumption of (mass) culture has to be legitimated. Reading romances or watching a television serial is granted a legitimation by showing that it is somehow valuable and useful. . . . While the older highbrow/lowbrow distinction was totally based on criteria set by the cultural product, the new conception sets criteria according to the way a product is consumed. It is a move away from the sphere of aesthetics to the political, or one could say that it politicizes the aesthetics of

everyday life, but it is nevertheless a reproduction of the hierarchical notion of culture. (1999, 11)

This is nicely put because it captures precisely the way in which not so much as "legitimate" theatregoer but rather as researcher/observer I was perceiving the six girls at the Barbican: in terms of a *political* legitimation of their performance in the continuing context of a high/popular culture dichotomy. To put it bluntly, it was all too easy for me at that moment to reach for the rather simplistic response of "Well, the Barbican brings this on itself via the high cultural space, architecture, and class-ostension (and ostentation) of its performance."

But what if we want to get beyond that dichotomy of high/popular culture altogether? Alasuutari, in moving toward his third-generation notion of audience analysis, insists that "it is no way necessary to think that pleasure must be instrumentalised" (1999, 11). To assume that teenagers' pleasures at the theatre are likely to lie in a politics of resistance (since surely they are not going to *enjoy* their teacher-prescribed, high-cultural text) is to devalue the pleasures that many young people (alongside much older people like myself) can, in fact, get at a Shakespearean theatrical event.

This observation introduces my second theatre audience anecdote. In February 2001 I was sitting in the back row of a semicircle of seats clustering around the small thrust stage of the Q Theatre in Penrith, New South Wales. Again it was a matinee performance, and again I was alongside five or six schoolgirls. On this occasion the entire theatre audience was composed of school parties, and the young people were sitting very close (even when in the back row) to the actors playing *Much Ado about Nothing* onstage.

This time, though, the girls were not bored, and at the end of the performance the entire audience of young people erupted in pleasure (which is not to say they weren't laughing, humming, dancing to the music, and chuckling to each other about individual performers during the show). At the end, the girls next to me were on their feet, clapping, whistling, and cheering. And the same thing happened at that evening's performance with an audience mainly of adults but that again had some school students, dressed now as stylish late teens going out for the evening, not in their school uniforms.

My two anecdotes introduce my project for this book, which is (1) to offer a cultural studies approach to the relations of theatre history, production, and audience within the emerging concept of the theatrical event; (2) to provide a first application of third-generation audience theory and methodology from media/cultural studies to two of Western theatre's major canonical institutions; (3) to examine the continuing history of Chekhov and Shakespeare as a series of stories currently and locally told in the context of a blurring of academic genres; and (4) to emphasize a poststructuralist focus on local tales from the field even while talking about theatre as a globalized leisure industry within risk and postmodernity. Because these aims need examination of some key concepts and problems, I will enlarge on each in turn.

The Theatrical Event

The concept of theatrical event is a relatively new one in theatre and cultural studies. In part, it is centered in current research and publication by a multidisciplinary team working within the International Federation for Theatre Research (of which both Willmar Sauter and Peter Eversmann, mentioned below, are members). But it has also arisen in the work of theatre audience theorist Susan Bennett. Because of the particular emphasis of this book on theatre audiences, I will begin with her analysis of the theatrical event.

In *Theatre Audiences* Bennett provides a processual approach to cultural studies that combines an analysis of performance with audience: "Theatre as a cultural commodity is probably best understood as a result of its conditions of production and reception . . . and a key area for further research is the relationship between the two for specific cultural environments, for specific types of theatre" (1997, 106). Although Bennett doesn't directly focus on the theatrical event, she does discuss the relationship between theatrical event and the local, situated context. Speaking about differences between regional and urban theatres, Bennett argues that "these different theatres create different kinds of events for the audience and, in their diversity, maintain occasion and place as signals for art which are heterogeneous and flexible" (1997, 102, 104). Bennett's reference to "occasion and place as signals for art" (1997, 99) is both global and local in conceptual intent and is derived from one of cultural studies' foundational thinkers, Raymond Williams.

The phrase "importance of occasion" is a correlate of the concept of event. In turn, the idea of place blends the everyday worlds of both artistic production site and audience perception. It is through these conjunctures — between and within occasion and place — that everyday meanings get made, that pleasures are experienced, and that global and local intersect. Thus, the *occasion* may be signaled as such by its cost. "The high price of a seat at a hit Broadway show is perhaps part of the attraction of attending that kind of theatrical event. . . . This suggests the power of economics to alter the production-reception contract" (Bennett 1997, 118–19).

But other constituents making this an occasion will probably be present too (e.g., this high-priced seat may be a special anniversary present or a chance to bring the family together in one leisure-event activity, etc.). Thus, the theatrical event also becomes part of everyday negotiation in the quite varied and multiple lives of audience members. "Multiple horizons of expectations [in the audience drawn to an event] are bound to exist within any culture and these are, always, open to re-negotiation before, during, and after the theatrical performance. The relationship then between culture and the idea of the theatrical event is one that is necessarily flexible and inevitably rewritten on a daily basis" (Bennett 1997, 106).

There is an important methodological cue here in Bennett's recourse to the theatrical event as everyday *process*. The event is processual not only in the sequence of production, performance, circulation, and reception but also *as* reception. It is an *audience* event insofar as multiple horizons of expectations are renegotiated "before, during, and after the theatrical performance." Thus, any "flat" methodology, such as the familiar quantitative theatre audience surveys that Bennett derides, is likely to miss important aspects of the "live" relationship of negotiation between occasion and place. An audience participates in a performance processually, across a changing temporality before, during, and (sometimes long) after the performance.

> Theatre audiences . . . tend to consist of small groups of friends, family, and so on. Reception can be prolonged by group discussion of all aspects from general appreciation to specific questions to other group members about small details of the production. Beyond the ability to talk about the production . . . audiences may follow up by reading the text (if available), by reading reviews, or (at a later time) seeing another production or even a subsequent movie adaptation. All these acts have the potential to reshape initial decoding of the production. All these elements of post-production are potentially significant in the audience's experience of theatre and all promote, if not ensure, the continuance of the culture industry's attracting audiences to the theatrical

event. It is the reciprocal nature of production and reception which characterizes the formation and reformation of cultural markers for theatre. (Bennett 1997, 164–65)

By examining Bennett's passing references to the theatrical event, we can see how use of the concept encourages a particular methodological focus in her book. The two elements of production and reception should be central to a study of theatre not only because they are inseparable. Both these elements also need to be studied in *local* theatre sites among the "*small* groups of friends, family, and so on" (my emphasis) that constitute the typical theatre audience. Further, this analysis of theatre reception needs to be sensitive to the *interactive changes* in "reading" the performance that viewing live theatre as a small-group communal occasion (with pre- or postshow dinner, interval chat over drinks, etc.) encourages. Clearly, the methodological tendency here is toward some kind of very localized, interactive, qualitative approach.

But this is not to say that Bennett eschews global analysis or generalizable statements when talking about the theatrical event. In her analysis two features in particular mark out the theatrical event from other conjunctures of occasion and place within the broader leisure industry. First, there is the issue of "liveness" in the context of communication and culture. "Television, above all, lacks the sense of public event that attaches to both theatre and cinema. It denies the audience the sense of contact with the performers that is integral to any theatrical performance and, moreover, it denies the spectator-to-spectator communication (in both its positive and negative aspects) within the larger framework of audience as community. . . . [T]heatre is an obviously social phenomenon. It is an event which relies on the physical presence of an audience to confirm its cultural status" (Bennett 1997, 84, 86).

Second, Bennett draws on Victor Turner (who has been as foundational an influence on theatre-performance studies as Raymond Williams has been within cultural and television studies) to widen the implications of theatrical event to the macrosocial. "Anthropologists such as Victor Turner argue for the indispensability of the theatrical event. . . . Theatrical performances are, according to Turner, deliberately structured experiences 'which probe a community's weaknesses, call its leaders to account, desacralize its most cherished values and beliefs, portray its characteristic conflicts and suggest remedies for them' (Turner 1982, 11). . . . Thus audiences have become aware of the event of theatre as in some way important in socio-cultural processes" (Bennett 1997, 104–5).

Important issues are raised here that I will develop later. Suffice it to say at this point that the concepts of liveness in a "mediatized" society (Auslander 2000) and of audiences themselves performing amid the "theatricalization of everyday life" (Abercrombie and Longhurst 1998) are current and ongoing themes in both theatre and cultural studies, which in this book will have a more central place in discussing globalized aspects of the theatrical event than Turner's more functionalist formulation.

Bennett's emphasis on the power of the theatrical event to "desacralize . . . cherished values and beliefs" places her firmly in the cultural studies resistance tradition; and, as in the work of many of the leading scholars in this field (see, e.g., Ien Ang's critique of Janice Radway's work on romance novels [1996, 98–108]), there is a tendency here to a "vanguardist" approach to everyday resistance. In *Theatre Audiences* Bennett tends to dismiss both mainstream theatre and popular television for operating within hegemonic frames rather than providing the liminal spaces (Turner) of alternative theatre. Thus, decentering of occasion and place becomes the guiding theme of Bennett's book, with her revised edition taking this further into non-Western alternative theatre events.

Bennett's reference to the interactive small-group audience process within both local and global contexts is extremely valuable, but it is limited by two things: the need for situated qualitative and ethnographic analysis of both production and reception of the theatrical event and the assumption, especially evident in her book *Performing Nostalgia: Shifting Shakespeare and the Contemporary Past*, that we need "an alternative methodology to the one that is usually called upon to 'do' Shakespeare" (1996, 156). Even though she quotes Andrew Sinfield to say that "[w]e need a stronger sense of how texts are negotiated in reception, for it is what you do with a book or record that counts" (Sinfield 1989, 302, in Bennett 1996, 158), Bennett eschews this need for actual audience research in both her theatre audience and her Shakespeare books, though her citing of brief audience responses from Brian Cox's book on performing *King Lear* at Broadmore is a tempting foray in this direction. Ethnographies of mainstream productions are also missing, which means that her contention about the "nostalgic impulse to produce seminal texts" (Bennett 1996, 155), whether by right- or left-minded theatre workers, has to be taken on (this academic critic's) trust. "Shifting Shakespeare," for Bennett, is primarily a matter of shifting our attention to *alternative* productions, often performed to relatively small or specialized audiences.

But I would like to know more about production/audience negotiations to decenter texts at the heart of mainstream theatre, as in Shakespeare and Chekhov. For the very reason that these negotiations of the first and second most popular dramatists on the high-cultural stage do appear before very large numbers of people, they become interesting — alongside, not instead of, the alternative decentering that Bennett describes. Just as she dismisses the methodology of quantitative survey, Bennett also tends to ignore or consign to insignificance the idea of popular audiences that has greatly interested cultural and media studies. Moreover, there are many local decenterings within mainstream itself, and it is not always helpful to locate "shifting Shakespeare" or Chekhov only across the binary of mainstream and alternative methodology.

As we will see in later chapters, Trevor Griffiths's engagement with Chekhov, Janet Suzman's with Chekhov, Mary-Anne Gifford's with Shakespeare are all local but mainstream examples taken up as case studies here to illustrate a much broader and ongoing thesis: that the mainstream authors of theatre are open to decentering too by way of new popular and intercultural forms, often in the context of Auslander's mediatization. And, as the Q Theatre production of *Much Ado* illustrates, this decentering can open out to very considerable pleasures in all age groups of audiences.

By way of his own empirical audience research, Dutch scholar Peter Eversmann, in the forthcoming *Theatrical Events*, has also emphasized theatre audiences' processual negotiation (before, during, and after a performance) with the theatrical event. As a psychologist, Eversmann is interested in relating a number of dimensions of audience interaction with the *specificity* of theatre production. He takes the particular features of a theatrical event to be the *transitive* nature of theatre, whereby "in the theatre the stimulus . . . develops up to a certain point in time after which the stimulus ceases to exist altogether and hence is no longer available for direct reference or for a renewed encounter"; the *collectivity* of production and reception, where communication between audience members and between audiences and artists is especially important; the *multimediality* of theatre, or the practice of differentiating between the "different sign systems that can play a part in performances and identifying their relevant codes and techniques"; and *ostension*, the fact that "the story on the stage is not told but shown and the audience looks directly at the action." Eversmann argues that theatre audiences relate to each of these across perceptual, cognitive, emotional, and communicative dimensions, and he suggests a "flow" form to the theatrical experience as these four dimensions interact. One may or may not be instantly hooked by a theatrical performance — sometimes pleasure resides in a slow buildup of understanding and/or immersion in the emotions of the piece. However, in "the process of watching a show the perceptual and the emotional dimension clearly take precedence over cognition. And what cognitive activity there is seems more concerned with following the story line and with storing the performance in memory than that it is analytical in nature." The moment just "after the performance . . . is mainly described [by his audience respondents] as an emotional one." Eversmann emphasizes here *embodied* emotion: "feeling it in one's stomach, shaking, being breathless, being immobilized, shock-experience, cold-sweat, laughing and crying. So, obviously, the emotions in the theatre can have a very strong physical component that most of the time seems to be absent in the accounts of aesthetic experiences in other art forms."

After this emotional reaction, Eversmann suggests, "the communicative dimension also comes into play. Quite a lot of respondents want to discuss the performance with colleagues or friends." Further, "the theatrical experience doesn't stop after the performance but in the later reactions (that sometimes last for years) the cognitive, analytic approach becomes dominant." In Eversmann's view, whereas "the emotional and perceptual dimensions are experienced individually, the cognitive analysis of a production is to a large extent a collective phenomenon." Audience members also often feel a strong sense of communication with a certain director, comparing her or his ideas for directing the play with their own. But playwrights are "seldom mentioned as a partner in theatrical communication" because a performance is always contemporary, here and now, within our own culture. This aspect of theatre means that "every performance is, in a way, an act of politics" (*Theatrical Events*, forthcoming).

Eversmann's reference to "politics" is underdeveloped, and his primarily psychological emphasis of theatrical event is clear in his focus on the interplay of the cognitive, perceptual, and emotional "dimensions" of individual theatre experiences. In this respect his definition of theatrical event is the opposite of Bennett's, since she suggests that individual-level analysis of audience responses is not important and is even misleading. Nevertheless, there are also continuities between Bennett's and Eversmann's definitions of the theatrical event, most particularly, their emphasis on the live performer–to–audience and audience-to-audience interaction. Also, they both insist upon the importance of the sociopolitical dimension of the theatrical event. Bennett and Eversmann seek the particular sets of relationships between a theatrical occasion and an audience place, and Eversmann (for all his psychologist's tendency to weaken the cultural implications of this) does have the considerable advantage of putting his focus on audience *affect*. His respondents' emphasis on embodied emotion accords with my own experience interviewing theatre audiences, and I will take this up within a risk perspective at the end of this chapter.

In *The Theatrical Event* Willmar Sauter argues that what is different from current theatre studies debate about using the concept of theatrical event is that it "attempts to present a model of the complexities of theatrical processes. At the same time, it avoids a push for certain methodologies. The concept of the theatrical event describes an approach to theatre studies, open to traditional as well as post-structural ways of thinking."

As well as being methodologically more open than either Bennett or Eversmann, Sauter also argues for a paradigm shift with his concept of theatrical event, shifting "from the idea of theatre as a 'work of stage art'... toward an understanding of theatre as a 'communicative event'" (2000, 20). And his notion of theatre as communication rejects the traditional sender-message-receiver model as well, arguing for a mutual, ostended relationship of play between actor and spectator. But like that of both Bennett and Eversmann, Sauter's major emphasis is *processual*. He constructs four segments of the theatrical event process. Thus, culture, context, theatricality, and play become stable ingredients of the composite event, but only because each of them in turn is decentered, interrogated, or inflected by their contiguous adjectives: playing, cultural, contextual, theatrical. The first two segments, for example ("playing culture" and "cultural contexts"), immediately bridge the gap between Eversmann's more individualized performance/spectator (emotional/cognitive) pleasure and Bennett's cultural "horizons of expectations."

Playing Culture

The importance of skills and style in a performer/spectator's pleasurable play is what distinguishes this behavior from what Sauter sees as the functionalism of religion, on the one hand, and "the trivial experiences of everyday life," on the other. Playing culture is at the very heart of Sauter's communicative model of theatre research, as in his definition of theatrical event as "the communicative mutuality of performer and spectator, the elements of play, and their dependence on the surrounding contexts" (2000, 14).

Cultural Contexts

The recognition here is that the "theatrical event must be understood as a process as much as it is a happening. . . . Every theatrical event has a *socio-political* aspect, both in relation to its content and in the way it is presented" (Sauter 2000, 121, my emphasis). An example Sauter elaborates is that of the actress Sarah Bernhardt, whose career was aided by the late-nineteenth-century movement on behalf of women's emancipation in political, legal, and cultural spheres: "In the theatre, the actress had conquered the stage some hundred years earlier, but many young women were now exploited in the commercial theatres of the late nineteenth century. Sarah Bernhardt, the successful and significant woman, was perceived as a necessary counter-image to these insignificant chorus girls. She was used as a symbol of independence by American women's liberation movements, an involvement to which the actress willingly contributed" (2000, 121).

Contextual Theatricality

This covers the interplay of artistic conventions (e.g., Sauter gives as an example Brecht's "alienation effect"), organizational conventions (e.g., the "long perspective" of the Berliner Ensemble, where Brecht wrote or chose the entire theatre program), and structural conventions (e.g., the GDR's political/economic relationship with Brecht's theatre). Elsewhere, Sauter blends together organizational and structural conventions and refers to the conceptual context as "showing the attitudes and appreciation which theatre receives in a certain society — the position theatre enjoys within the value hierarchy of other art forms and cultural events, but also in relation to other obligations for which a society is supposed to take responsibility" (2000, 138). Thus, cultural theatricality engages with the local-global dimension of theatre. "In Germany . . . every state of the federal republic has its state opera and its state theatre. By contrast, the long-lasting problems in establishing an English National Theatre . . . and the rebuilding of the Globe through a private foundation [are] an indication of how difficult it is to gain support from the 'public hand' in that country. . . . In most African countries cultural politics ends with signing far-reaching documents, since there is no public money to support such plans" (Sauter 2000, 110).

Theatrical Playing

Sauter argues that the "intersection between the performer's actions and the spectator's reactions — which I see as the core of theatricality — is characterized by three interactive levels, called the sensory, artistic and symbolic levels of theatrical communication. These levels can only be activated during the process of a theatrical event. It is the very 'event-ness' of all theatre, the interaction between performer and spectator, which facilitates theatricality" (2000, 63). Sarah Bernhardt's remarkable sensory rapport with her international public included her very conscious use of her voice, the form and size of her body, and her "way of displaying her costumes — as a way of staging her personality and creating a fictional character" (Sauter 2000, 125). Bernhardt adopted the classical French nineteenth-century artistic convention of the gesture preceding the word. But when "she added the mimic expression of her face to anticipate the gestures, which, in turn, were to precede vocal delivery, this certainly constituted a break with accepted codes.... [T]he face did not necessarily have to express the same mood as the gestures, which allowed for contradictory comments to the spoken lines" (Sauter 2000, 129). Finally, in Sauter's theatrical playing schema, there was Bernhardt's symbolic construction of her roles, and he quotes Cornelia Otis Skinner, who regarded Bernhardt's interpretation of *Phèdre* as a turning point in theatre history. "Racine's women had hitherto been deprived of their sex by two centuries of falsely noble interpretation, but Bernhardt's Phèdre was all sex, a female devoured by insatiable lust and abject guilt" (Skinner, 106, cited in Sauter 2000, 135).

It is possible and productive, says Sauter, to begin by entering analytically any one segment of the theatrical event process for research purposes. Nevertheless, "all of these segments are present every time a theatrical event takes place, whether we are aware of them as participants or if we are concerned with them as researchers." So although "the interaction between performer and spectator — or rather between stage and auditorium — represent the nucleus of the theatrical event, the event itself is defined by its position in the theatrical, cultural and social world at large" (Sauter, 2000, 27).

Fundamental to Sauter's position is the observation that "theatre — and hereby we mean all kinds of theatrical performances — always and everywhere takes place in the form of events.... When we speak about a

Theatrical Event, we think of someone doing something, ostentatively enough to be distinguished from everyday life. . . . The distinction is twofold: on the one hand there is someone who does something in a different way than in regular life; on the other hand, there is also someone who sees and acknowledges this difference. . . . Theatre becomes theatre by being an event in which two partners engage in a playful relationship" (2000, 27).

Like Eversmann, Sauter insists on the particularity of the theatrical event, wherever it is played, as an ostentative performance. This, combined with the play, mutually acknowledged by actor and audience, on the *difference* between the event and everyday life is what establishes the playful relationship. Importantly, too, Sauter insists on the weakness of audience research that "does not follow the spectator into the theatre" (2000, 27).

But useful though Sauter's processual segments are in insisting on a map for theatrical event studies, he does not explore the relationship between a theatrical event's distinction from other kinds of doings and those daily doings themselves. How does the theatrical event work among different cultures, genders, ethnicities, ages, and so on in relation to the other social events through which we perform our everyday lives? Among other things, this has been a focus of media audience research.

Third-Generation Audience Studies

Theoretically and methodologically, as part of the ongoing project of cultural studies, this book positions itself within current third-generation audience analysis (Alasuutari 2000). This recent theoretical trend is an attempt to recombine notions of encoded texts (and their interpellated spectators) with ethnographically oriented active audience theory and methodology. It starts from a focus on what Alasuutari calls "audiencing," a concept that sees audiences not as a facticity "out there" but rather as discursive constructs located within multiple interpretative frames. On the one hand, coming from active audience theory and the ethnography of daily life, Alasuutari asks questions about the frames through which we *constitute ourselves* as audiences among our other daily practices. On the other hand, beginning with the notion of the encoded production text and with theories of spectatorship, the audiencing concept examines the moral frames or discourses about audiences that are inscribed in the performances themselves.

My own notion of audiencing in this book will, in fact, draw on four theoretical traditions.

A Processual Semiotics of Production

I understand this within the considerable tradition of theatre semiotics (Elam 1980; Carlson 1990; Fischer-Lichte 1992; Marinis 1993), in particular, Elam's emphasis on the pragmatic character of performance as works or productions and focus on strategies and professional values of practice in transforming and transcoding the written text into a semiotically thick audiovisual performance for a viewing audience. Elam deals with Eversmann's multimediality aspect of the theatrical event, and my audience research indeed reveals that audiences very often refer, with detailed discrimination, to many of these different semiotic communicators when assessing a performance (see chapter 4).

Reading Formation

I define this concept in Tony Bennett's sense as a *semiotic institution*: "a set of discursive and inter-textual determinations that organize and animate the practice of reading, connecting texts and readers in specific relations to one another by constituting readers as reading subjects of particular types and texts as objects-to-be-read in particular ways" (Bennett and Woollacott 1987, 60–69). Reading formation analysis has been particularly useful in examining the surveillant intertextual relations of reading constituted in both popular and high culture in terms of fandom and in terms of the elite discourses of university criticism. It is the latter context of reading formation that is a subject of this book. I have looked at popular cultural fandom elsewhere (e.g., Tulloch and Jenkins 1995). My focus in chapters 3 and 4 on university academics and students as audiences of Chekhov draws on the comparative institutional focus of reading formation theory. Elsewhere (Tulloch 1999b:97–99) I have suggested how the notion of reading formation can be important in understanding the process of rewriting the canonical text for performance, as in the case of Trevor Griffiths's *The Cherry Orchard* and his transforming and transcoding of Raymond Williams's work on Chekhov. Here I extend the comparative approach of reading formations to performances and audiences of canonical theatre, concentrating on this occasion on a professional television production of *The Cherry Orchard* and student audiences.

Active Audiences

I understand this familiar media studies concept in terms of the subject positions and horizons of expectations that different audience members bring to the reading of the text according to gender, class, ethnicity, age, regional, and other affiliations (Morley 1981; Radway 1991; Press 1991; Ang 1996; for a detailed survey of this field, see Tulloch 2000). This tradition within media studies helps account for the strongly methodological focus of the book. Theatre studies has tended, as Susan Bennett emphasizes, either to ignore active audiences or to reduce them to the passivity of demographics. Neither of these perspectives reveals the attributes of the theatrical event. Instead, what we need is a multifaceted analysis of active theatre audiences. Quantitative analysis of audiences will not be eschewed here, but we also need to be reflexive about how we claim to know theatre audiences, whether we approach them quantitatively or qualitatively. The concept of active audiences also needs to be related to theories of spectatorship.

Spectatorship

Here the emphasis is on an audience's selfconstitution and textual constitution as audience in the process of representation. The distinction between audience and spectator is not so much one between a general group and unique individual viewers as between socially and textually constituted ones. Annette Kuhn, for example, has argued that the "*spectator . . .* is a subject constituted in signification, interpellated by the film or TV text. . . . Whereas in classic cinema the concentration and involvement proposed by structures of the look and point-of-view tend to be paramount, television spectatorship is more likely to be characterised by distraction and diversion" (1984, 343). If, as Kuhn argues, cinema constitutes spectatorship "through the look and spectacle" and television via "the textual operations of different programmes into the rhythms and routines of domestic activities" (1984, 345–46), then what is live theatre's characteristic construction of spectatorship? How does this relate to its social audiences? I will develop later the notion of theatre's "intimate gaze," which draws together both encoded spectatorship and the everyday preoccupations and rhythms of social audiences. Particularly in chapter 4, I will try to bring together notions of (audiencing) spectatorship and (audiencing) social audiences, which, as Kuhn notes, tend to have been kept separate in film and television studies. I will also draw on Kuhn's sensible response to her own question: "Is there a way in which spectator/subjects of film and television texts can be thought about in an historically specific manner, or indeed a way for the social audience to be rescued from social/historical determinism?" (1987, 347).

> Both spectators and social audience may accordingly be regarded as discursive constructs. Representations, contexts, audiences and spectators would then be seen as a series of interconnected social discourses, certain discourses possessing greater constitutive authority at specific moments than others. Such a model permits relative autonomy for the operation of texts, readings and contexts, and also allows for contradictions, oppositional readings and varying degrees of discursive authority. Since the state of a discursive formation is not constant, it can be apprehended only by means of inquiry into specific instances or conjunctures. (Kuhn 1987, 347)

Put another way, psychoanalytically driven feminist film theories of spectatorship have tended to ignore "discursive formations of the social, cultural and textual" worlds that exist outside the spectacle of cinema text, while sociologically inclined active audience television theories have tended to focus on the minutiae of everyday routines and rituals, leading in the extreme case, as Meaghan Morris once complained, to a "banality of cultural studies," where endless local cases of gender (and genre) resistance to the TV text were exposed. If the former problem leads to an overgeneralized universalism, the latter has the fault, as Kuhn says, of "limited analytical scope of studies of specific instances and conjunctures" (1987, 346).

We need to get beyond this impasse. Tony Bennett's notion of reading formation certainly helps us locate film and television texts within broader formations of social, cultural, and intertextual contexts while still focusing on textual interpellations of the reader. Alasuutari's emphasis on audiencing also takes us further into theories of discourse, insofar as the production, circulation, and reception of media texts are seen as a series of interacting discursive moral frames.

Three problems remain. First, reading formation theory in relation to theatre studies needs greater specification in terms of some of the most popular of canonical texts. I approach this issue here via a substantive focus on the continuing history of Shakespeare and Chekhov. Second, there still seems to be a failure to separate individual spectators from the idea of a formation or general process of audiencing. Indeed, Susan Bennett overtly eschews a focus on individual audience members. The relationship between individual subjectivities and social formation in terms of audience analysis will underpin my emphasis in this book on the use of both qualitative and quantitative methodology. It will also be developed in terms of the concept of individualized life projects within risk modernity (Beck 1992). Third, film theory's emphasis on spectatorship and spectacle and television theory's focus on the audience's everyday experience often pose foundational differences of position, and potentially even of epistemology, between a postmodernist emphasis on society as spectacle and event and a reflexive-modernist focus on the nonexpert's "real" everyday. I will discuss this issue in the final section of this chapter.

The Continuing History of Shakespeare and Chekhov

Over the last three decades the humanities and social sciences have gone through a succession of rapid and disconcerting changes. As Norman Denzin and Yvonna Lincoln (1998) have said, scholars in all fields, including theatre studies, have been faced with both a "blurring" of academic genres (following the "linguistic turn" of the 1970s and the "ethnographic turn" of the 1980s) and with the current poststructuralist moment. Today as a result, in theatre analysis as elsewhere, "the search for grand narratives will be replaced by more local, small-scale theories fitted to specific problems and specific situations" (Denzin and Lincoln 1998, 22).

Local, contextualized, and situated knowledge (of the kind Susan Bennett advocates for the analysis of differently positioned theatrical events) is the current academic condition of our postmodern experience. The "situated, constitutive self can no longer hide behind the imperialism of unifying conceptual schemes embodied in 'master' narratives; rather, each one of us has to engage with the fluid ambiguities and uncertainties of tentative, 'local' stories or accounts" (Adam and Allan 1995, xv). And it is this emphasis on local and situated (rather than on archivist or globally comprehensive) histories of Shakespeare's and Chekhov's theatre that is the substantive focus of this book.

Still, if the author's master narrative is dead (post-Barthes) in many academic circles, Shakespeare and Chekhov certainly live on as theatrical events with enormous international followings and sponsorships. Similarly, though the objective metalanguage of science is supposedly dead (post-Lyotard), and the power of its articulation and legitimacy is being deeply challenged in the risk society (Beck), still, its instrumentalist focus within media studies continues to propel the "hope that . . . the final scientific account of 'the audience' can eventually be achieved" (Ang 1996, 43). And despite the new emphasis upon local history or microhistory, many scholars take a traditional cultural studies approach to theatre, so that grand theories about class, gender, postcolonialism, and so on still apply, often in tension with the idea of situated knowledge.

Theatre studies is itself in a complex, fascinating, and inevitably fragmentary condition after postmodernism. Symbolic interactionism, constructionism, phenomenology, critical (Marxist) theory, semiotics, structuralism, poststructuralism, feminism, performance theory, and various ethnic paradigms have all been part of the process of academic genre dispersion. In their varying, overlapping, sometimes contradictory approaches to the relationship of text, performance, and reception, they have variously engaged with the crises of representation (how do we show?) and legitimation (how do we know?) that Denzin and Lincoln (1998) document throughout their study. Theatre, with its major emphasis on ostension, is deeply involved in this process of showing and knowing.

Yet there have been fascinating differences according to the local, contextualized, and situated knowledges within this broader field of theatre studies. For example, since the early 1980s we have witnessed an explosion of theoretical debate in Shakespeare studies. Postmodernist, new historicist, cultural materialist, feminist, and other interpretative communities have swept into the gap exposed by the supposed death of the author and the critique of the canonical text. The debate of power versus subversion (post-Foucault) in various of these interpretative communities has marked them, in their different ways, as promoting voices of the ordinary other (including the audience) into negotiation with the canonical author, even though Shakespeare scholars have been surprisingly shy of devising methodologies and concepts to approach the actual audience or, indeed, approach actual theatre production (Tulloch 1999a, 1999b).

In contrast, Chekhov scholarship has hardly begun the path traveled thus far by Shakespeare studies. Research on Chekhov criticism in the 1980s and 1990s (Tulloch and Burvill 1996) revealed that an empiricist positioning of the author and the canon within the history of modernism still reigns supreme. Chekhov scholarship continued to be deeply embedded in old historicism, which assumes a hierarchical relationship between the literary text (as the object of value) and its (undertheorized) historical background or context. A comparatively tiny proportion of significant pieces of work have been written within structuralist, poststructuralist, and new poetic approaches. And the view of most Chekhov academics that Tulloch and Burvill interviewed internationally is that these (with the possible exception of Raymond Williams's work) have by and large been marginal to mainstream Chekhov scholarship. This was also confirmed by Tulloch and Burvill's quantitative study of university student readings of Chekhov in the United States, Britain, and Australia. In particular, approaches from within the international growth areas of cultural studies, cultural materialism, new historicism, and feminism had hardly touched Chekhov at all.

Nevertheless, although frequently not articulated as theoretical debate, paradigm assumptions about Chekhov, modernism, and modernity do create a powerful subtextual convention in Chekhov criticism. The persistent effort to rescue Chekhov's canonicity from his historical moment (of a perceived mundane naturalism) has led to readings of Chekhov that position him in terms of many of the key tropes of modernism: internal irony, paradox, subjectivism, reflexivity, energies of spirit beyond the representation of appearances, absurdism, and so on. *Modernism*, then, as an aesthetic device rather than the *modernity* (or postmodernity) in which his audiences are now positioned has been a key academic excuse for Chekhov's authorship, as we will see via a brief excursion into Chekhov criticism in chapter 4.

So Shakespeare and Chekhov, as read by the international academic community, still represent interestingly polarized cases within the fragmented condition of theatre studies (each, though, with its local contextual conditions, like the perceived influence of Russian émigré scholars in U.S. university Russian departments). But there is also a continuity between them, especially so when we consider what Denzin and Lincoln refer to as the current theoretical moment of radical contextualism and ethnography. Neither Shakespeare nor Chekhov studies have traveled far down the track of Denzin and Lincoln's "tales from the field," that is, an understanding of theatre as the production of situated narratives among the daily horizons of expectations of current audiences. Nor has the ethnographic turn had a significant influence on scholars approaching the theatre of Shakespeare or Chekhov productions.

There are several useful directions that can be taken here. First, we should make a virtue out of a blurring of genres as we put together theories of performance and theatrical event from theatre studies, theories of spectatorship from film studies, and theories of audience and reading formation from media/cultural studies. Second, we should give attention to the "dual crises of representation and legitimation" (Denzin and Lincoln) as we examine locally, in specific theatrical contexts of occasion and place, how Shakespeare and Chekhov are "shown" within risk or postmodernity and by what means we "know" (as audiences or researchers) how they are shown. The issues here are about interpretative communities, reading formations, and our own performance accounts as audiences or researchers. Third, we should place emphasis on empirical (local and contextualized) ethnographies of theatre. For example, in this book there is some focus on the production of situated knowledges of Shakespeare or Chekhov as performed in a heritage theatre in Bath, England, compared with a regional touring theatre in Penrith, New South Wales, or as produced in a stridently "non-State" inner-city Sydney theatre compared with the Royal Shakespeare Theatre in Stratford-upon-Avon.

Modernity, Postmodernity, Risk Modernity

If we want to shift between local, contextualized tales from the theatre field to more global concerns, we are currently faced by two influential competitors in theorizing this relationship between the global and the local/everyday: theories of postmodernism and of risk modernity. These in some ways replicate the theoretical differences between spectatorship and social audience that Kuhn describes.

Postmodernism has become a familiar if not hegemonic academic/ epistemological approach to our global contemporary condition (certainly within cultural studies and in many of the humanities disciplines). It also has a wide public currency. So, for example, one audience member at a recent production of Trevor Griffiths's *Comedians* (Tulloch, forthcoming) wondered whether Griffiths's emphasis on social conflict was now out of date. "Having the real audience as the stage audience did work — but the message was lost because our postmodern, ironic stance on racist/sexual jokes creates a different mood to what must have been the original impact of the play. . . . The problem resides in the difference between a year 2001 audience and a 1970s audience: is conflict too strong a word for us now?"

But other scholars of the contemporary information age, while not altogether leaving behind the society of spectacle and its promiscuity of information, have begun to put forward a broader *risk* agenda. Leslie Dick, for example, argues against the fact that the "priority of basic social needs such as health, housing, education, labour standards and community issues [has] been relegated to a secondary status" behind conventionalized chatter about "an information society in the same breath as globalisation, international competitiveness, foreign direct investment, scientific and technological innovation, life long learning[,] ... information and communication technologies and other staples of a neo-liberal outlook" (2000, 7).

Mary-Anne Gifford, one of the theatre directors considered in this book (chapters 2 and 9), puts forward the same agenda as Dick but in the different language of an artistic director who struggled to keep her theatre open within a neoliberal economy. As she wrote in a desperate "final-season" appeal to audiences at the Q Theatre in Penrith, New South Wales, the risks of living at the beginning of the twenty-first century and the economic costs of leisure and pleasure are at one and the same time intimate and systemically connected. Her performative audiencing appeal in that final season's brochure (which was entitled "Better Than the Movies" and imaged a film noir–style hero and heroine) was overtly about the need for political agency and change and the role of theatrical events in that process. Sauter would call her emphasis here on "the position theatre enjoys within the value hierarchy of other art forms and cultural events, but also in relation to other obligations for which a society is supposed to take responsibility" (2000, 138), a focus on the conceptual level of contextual theatricality.

Better than the movies, huh? ... All right, it's a blatantly cheap attempt to get you to spend your hard-earned money. .... It's getting increasingly harder to make the money go around — for theatre and for people who want to see theatre. That's what this is all about. There is serious doubt as to whether the Q will be open this time next year. I love this theatre. I optimistically plan another subscription season for the second half of next year but I can't promise it's coming. More than ever theatre is in competition for your money — we're competing with sport, with the flicks, with nights at the pub, with paying the rent. ... Once upon a time most Australians could have done all those things if they wanted — had a night a week at the movies, gone to the footy at the weekend, had drinks with their friends, gone to see the occasional show at the local theatre, educated their kids, had enough food in the larder *and* paid the rent. Those times have gone for most Australians. We've watched them go pretty rapidly over the last 25 years and we haven't made a lot of noise about it. Sad that. So, what am I complaining about? Compared to food, rent and education, what's the big deal

"Better Than the Movies: First Feature" Q Theatre poster.

about not being able to see a few shows? I don't know ... it's something about voices not being heard, stories not being told, talent not being fostered. Something about people not coming together, about not seeing their lives given artistic expression, about not being able to have fun. Are we going to let the bastards take even that away from us? (Gifford 2000, 2)

I want to argue here that risk modernity has at least as wide a public currency as postmodernity and enters the horizons of expectations of all of us. As I began to write this opening chapter, Britain was faced daily by newspaper headlines that constructed a society considerably at risk, often the direct or indirect result of the same kind of neoliberal government policies that Gifford despaired about. Day after day the public read about, faced directly, or was threatened or inconvenienced by floods that endangered property and seriously delayed travel. This was said to be the result of global warming and thus a sign of the world's regularity and future rather than isolated and, as once thought, increasingly controllable occurrences. At the same time, travel was also catastrophically affected by cracked rails, derailments, and (in two serious incidents in less than two years) horrendous deaths in train accidents. And with media concern about the risks of genetically modified food still visible (after some years of controversy), the debate about the risk of mad cow disease again breaking out in both Britain and France, and the British rural catastrophe of foot-and-mouth disease rampant in the media, regular (daily) reports on risk in all of these areas were then interspersed intermittently with stories of racist killings, systematic sexual abuse of children, teenage suicide, drug- or alcohol-induced carnage, a record level of fear of crime, and the incarceration of asylum seekers as Britain's response to ethnic cleansing elsewhere in Europe. I choose these particular daily news events to mention because they had all been a feature of extensive media coverage during the two weeks before I began writing this chapter. While each risk had its own long history, clearly they were both endemic and about to expand generically into public risks of terrorism, as events subsequent to September 11, 2001, indicated dramatically.

The audiences who attended the local theatrical events described in this book faced these other media events every day also. Sometimes they faced one or another of them personally. And more than occasionally the theatrical event they attend draws on other current local or global risks to add a particular time-space resonance to an otherwise classic play, as, for example, the Belvoir Street Theatre did in relation to rural teenage suicide (then much publicized in the Australian media) in its production of *The Seagull* in Sydney (chapter 5), or Janet Suzman did in commenting on ("Stephen Lawrence–style") systemic racism in her "South African" version of *The Cherry Orchard* (chapter 7), or Trevor Griffiths did in revealing sexual exploitation within the home (at both master and servant levels) in his *The Cherry Orchard* (chapter 3).

Speaking with audience members who went to the Suzman play *The Free State*, I was aware of how they could be enormously affected (a case of Eversmann's embodied emotion) as they watched the old black servant abandoned at the end of act 4 in the chiaroscuro of a vast room that was slowly decaying to the savagely loud sound of chain saws outside.

I was almost *paralyzed* by the sadness of it.

Oh, I thought it was shattering, shattering. I mean I, you know, people start applauding and everything at the end of a play, but I just felt that I just wanted to sit there quietly for a little while.

Comments like these indicate that what some audience members distinguish as a theatrical event has also a more global context in terms of embodied emotionality. A long-term worker with underprivileged youths in London recognized in the somewhat guilty laughs of herself and other audience members at the racist gaffs of the postapartheid white landowner in *The Free State* their own unconscious complicity with racism. And another audience member remembered with embarrassment her own experience of "house boys" in Zambia through the performance style of the black actors who played the servants in Suzman's play. The risks embedded in a changing (new world order) scheme of things are what both Gifford and Suzman are referring to in their statements about theatre, and these risks appear in their play performances.

The originator of the term *risk society*, Ulrich Beck, like Baudrillard, has identified a trend away from an old industrial modernist social order based on class labor and the production of goods. But whereas Baudrillard understood the new order in terms of the communication and circulation of signs, Beck sees risk modernity in terms of science and technology's replacement of "goods" with "bads," which he identifies as the scientific/technological uncertainty of ecological/environmental catastrophe and the risky underemployment that has grown with a microelectronic world order.

Both environmental and underemployment risks are, of course, important features of classic plays like *The Cherry Orchard*, while scientific/technological uncertainty can become key themes in the play's interpretation, as occurred in the Adrian Noble production at the RSC in the late 1990s (Tulloch, Burvill, and Hood 1998). But risk (just as much as the postmodernists' "image") is much more ubiquitous and multiple than this (Tulloch and Lupton 2001, 2003). Most people, including the audiences of theatrical events, are continuously perceptive of risks at the level of intimacy and personal relationships, sexuality, gender, ethnicity, employment, health, crime, work, and finances.

To make my emphasis in this book on risk modernity clearer, it may be useful to compare and contrast current thinking about postmodernism and risk modernity. There are, of course, many postmodernisms in current cultural theory. In consequence, there tends to be some blurring of philosophical, sociocultural, and aesthetic approaches among them. (For an excellent overview, on which I draw extensively here, see Bain 2001.) But most tend to emphasize some or all of the following positions:

The development of moving image technology has led to the public ubiquity of visual images to the extent that the real has been replaced by signification and the referent by the sign, so that spectacle and visual events are everywhere. In this postmodern context, everyday reality becomes no more than a simulacrum, a fragmented tissue of memories, intertexts, and other stories, none of which offer access to "authentic" experience. "Simulation" (Baudrillard) replaces truth, surface replaces deep structure, performance replaces authentic reality as the focus of analysis, and, as the modernist project of ever-increasing rationality, progress, and equity is lost in relativism, the (human) subject is fragmented as spectator among a plethora of signs. Not surprisingly, some observers today have called this the *performative society*.

At the same time as the "grand narratives" (Lyotard) of scientific reason (including Marxism) lose their legitimacy, so too art loses its privileged status and becomes indistinguishable from any other cultural commodity in everyday life. The philosophical loss of belief in progress through reason in the social sphere is matched by a new aesthetic relativism, which has lost confidence in the value or progressiveness embedded in modernist art. In consequence, the boundaries of high and popular culture become permeable in the free-flowing world of undifferentiated image, simulation, and spectacle. Cultural products (in both the aesthetic and anthropological senses of culture) become simply nonhierarchical commodities on offer (for performance and consumption) as in a supermarket. This tendency is enforced by the collapsing of international borders because of the globalization of the industries of shopping, service, and leisure. Cultural perspectives become mixed and pluralized.

Direct, "authentic," face-to-face experience is replaced globally by mediated experience, and the resulting acceleration of transfer of images and information has deterritorialized culture and helped construct identities that are much less embedded in place than before.

Moreover, some postmodernists argue, democratic processes are enhanced (despite the collapse of the "Enlightenment project"), since the proliferation of images "guarantee[s] . . . the freedom of the subject to choose, to position one's *self* within the culture, while the constant flow of images, sounds and narratives seemingly demonstrates a cultural abundance and promise" (Bukatman 1997, 75). At the same time, it is argued, the plenitude of images, the "promiscuity of information" (Baudrillard), and the "surplus of texts" (Collins 1997, 193) offer space for discourse to marginal groups no longer under the surveillance of grand narratives and benefiting from new media technologies.

Instrumentalist concerns (e.g., the TV sex and violence debate) are replaced in research agendas by an emphasis on pleasure and affect, and worries about a dark reality are displaced by release and exploration of fantasy. Thus, the focus is on the transient and playful landscape of postmodernism rather than the serious and interrogating social-engineering vision of modernism.

All these features of the postmodern condition confirm the fragmentation, differentiation, and pluralization of subjective identity, social control, and aesthetic value. Michael Pickering is right to argue that postmodernism's "radical critique of the great meta-narratives of modernity, its attention to universalizing market 'logics,' its debunking of the radical pretensions and values of High Modernism, and its de-centering of the 'sovereign subject,' have been useful and provocative" (1997, 82). But Pickering is also right when he says that postmodernism's collapsing of opposed positions into each other "in the name of stylistic eclecticism, irony, and pastiche, a self-conscious delight in mass-produced art, kitsch and the play of surfaces, and anti-realism and anti-historicism . . . is no solution to the problems they pose" (1997, 82). Such problems include, for example, what Bert Olivier calls the "awesome power" (1996, 163) of new media technologies (including the ubiquitous surveillance camera) in our lives. The problem of power indicated in just this one example (and yet the increasing ubiquity of new technology surveillance's legitimating alibi of risk in public places) is not readily addressed within conventional postmodernist paradigms.

Though there are similarities between theories of risk modernity and postmodernity, particularly in their perception of a breakdown in trust of metanarratives, risk theory also has a different focus.

> It is *risk*, rather than the image itself, that is ubiquitous, and this is associated especially with technologies of the image. In Beck's version of risk theory, the ubiquity of risk images brings to the public a condensed sense of commonality in the face of potential environmental catastrophe.
>
> Whereas postmodern theory tends to a notion of spectatorship in which the spectator "becomes a pure screen, a pure absorption and reception surface of the influent networks" (Baudrillard 1988, 27), an important part of risk theory emphasizes the potential for the social subject's agency in the "lay knowledge" of our individualized everyday lives (in contrast to the "expert knowledge" of professional information systems). Risk theory shares with postmodernism a critique of the grand narratives of science, technology, and class but locates risk images more sociologically within the broader shift from industrial to risk modernity and, in an important variant of risk theory, within the performativity of lay social groups (Wynne 1996). Against postmodernism's dystopic vision of the schizophrenic subject, whose identity is splintered in passive response to the profusion of discontinuous signs without referents, in Beck's risk theory there is the more optimistic agency of new subpolitical interest groups (e.g., around environmental issues) and in Wynne's risk theory the agency of everyday lay knowledge.
>
> Postmodernism's blurring of boundaries between high and popular culture is replaced by risk theory's permeability between the authenticity of expert and lay accounts, and this will apply as readily to artistic as to scientific knowledgeability.

While, as in postmodernism, risk is globally mediated, this — for Beck at least — becomes potentially a positive and democratizing experience, since people become aware of the contradictions between various "expert" accounts and so trust all of them less and the images of technological dystopia make people of all classes, genders, and cultures citizens in the face of potential catastrophe.

Fear about and negotiation with various orders of risk are the basis for individualized life projects. Like postmodernism, risk theory emphasizes the breakdown of private and public spheres. As a result of the decline of industrial modernity and with it of class, familial, and workplace securities, the "resultant individualization . . . opens up a situation where individuals reflect upon and flexibly restructure the rules and resources of the workplace and their leisure time" (Lash and Wynne 1992, 3).

The detailed, daily negotiation of work and leisure, risk and pleasure thus becomes a biographical and individualized project for individuals within risk modernity, as the following account by a single mother of her pleasure in *Much Ado about Nothing* at the Q Theatre indicates: "You need time out from taking the children here, there, to school, soccer, and sports training. The children accept that now — that I go to the theatre every couple of months or so if I've got the money. There's no money around — my daughter's just had braces on her teeth. . . . My friends and I love going to the Q because the productions are always excellent. The city [i.e., Sydney] is too far away and costs too much, and it's too hard to safely leave the children" (Susan, personal interview).

To understand Susan's account of her theatre visits, we need — rather than postmodernism's notion of a society communicating via the inward spiral of simulation, or performance theorist Victor Turner's notion of a "society talking to itself" — theories of our time and our experiences that are both much more fine-grained and systemic. Beck speaks of the "project of individualization" and, like the postmodernists, focuses on the viewer of media as potentially lost in a world of "transitory finalities" (1992, 137). But Beck's vision is sociological: the spectator is also a social subject. Individual biography, says Beck, "is the sum of subsystem rationalities," insofar as expert knowledges in each of these subsystems (of law, education, media, medicine, politics, and economics) so often contradict each other.

[P]edagogy and medicine, social law and traffic planning presume active "thinking individuals" ... who are supposed to find their way in this jungle of transitory finalities with the help of their own clear vision. All these and all the other experts dump their contradictions and conflicts at the feet of the individual and leave him or her with the well intentioned invitation to judge all of this critically on the basis of his or her own notions. With detraditionalization and the creation of global media networks, the biography is increasingly removed from its direct spheres of contact and opened up across the boundaries of countries and experts for a *long-distance morality* which puts the individual in the position of continually having to make a stand. (1992, 137)

Like postmodernists, then, risk theorists observe a current deterritorialization of identity as "direct spheres of contact" are lost. But, crucially, globalization's crossing of territorial borders is linked to issues of expert knowledge, among and against which individual citizens are "continually having to make a stand." For Beck, "world society becomes a *part* of biography" (1992, 137), and though he is often as guilty as leading postmodernists in contemplating his media audience as "blind citoyens" who are lost in the confused "reaction of not listening, simplifying, and apathy" (1992, 137), there are also aspects of Beck's theory of the media that articulate a more optimistic relationship between the social subsystems of law, the media, and individual biography (Tulloch and Lupton 2001, 23). Further, some risk theorists follow Wynne's emphasis on lay knowledge in exploring methodologically Beck's sense of individualization as a series of long-distance and morally framed border crossings (of countries and experts) via the notion of "risk biographies" in relation to the media (Tulloch and Lupton 2001, 2003). For example, we need to find methods to allow us to explore the way in which the single mother mentioned above, Susan, experiences her "walking on air" feeling after seeing *Much Ado about Nothing* at Penrith in the context of her everyday risk routines of child minding and being quite poor. Lay accounts of performance meaning and pleasure will be an important part of this book's focus. So, too, will be a notion of the intimate gaze of theatre, where, in the direct communicative (actor/audience) interaction of the theatrical event, many people find pleasure as their biographies are restored to "direct spheres of contact."

Within any one risk biography, we need to be able to see how theatrical events, media events (including risk events), and other social events interact. They are all part of an audience's everyday life, and their different forms, discourses, conventions, overlaps, and distinctions have hardly begun to be charted. Nor will I be able to go far with this at the empirical level: it is a much bigger project than the (already large) one I have embarked on.

But there are theoretical pointers to further theatre and media research in one area of current risk theory, and these can connect usefully with aspects of the theatrical-event concepts that I have explored so far. For example, we may be helped in understanding the audience responses mentioned above to Suzman's *The Free State* by Scott Lash's analysis of aesthetic reflexivity and the sublime within risk culture. The risks that *The Free State* audiences were contemplating were those associated with the past and current politics of race in South Africa, and for some of that audience this included a residual connivance in British racism. The risk (HIV/AIDS) that Lash uses as an example is different, but it is a useful analogy nevertheless.

> [In risk culture] we assign meanings to "bads." But these are not just, and not even primarily, logical meanings or determinate judgements. There are more than just bads or *dommages*, coming under the calculation of ... some sort of [risk] insurance principle. Consider, for example, the famous Robert Mapplethorpe photography exhibition that toured the world's art museums between 1990 and 1995 and featured violent homoerotic photos, especially of black men. A number of viewers of the exhibition no doubt thought of Mapplethorpe's death from AIDS, and about AIDS more generally as they looked through the exhibition. Surely this is a vastly different way of judging the bad, the event, the risk of AIDS than subsuming it under a set of statistics, under probabilistic logic. It takes the particular, i.e. the photographs which can potentially open up a space of existential meaning. To consider AIDS through probabilities and statistics is a way of looking at risks via determinate judgments. The more aesthetic consideration of AIDS through the existential meanings of Mapplethorpe's images instead involves reflexive judgment. (2000, 53–54)

This is to take Eversmann's interest in the emotional, cognitive, perceptual, and communicative aspects of art into new *risk*-theoretical dimensions of spectatorship and social audiences. Lash refers to this aesthetic and existential dimension in art, where risks are almost experienced physically as the "terrible sublime."

In fact, Lash's notion of a reflexive risk culture is an important critique, from within risk theory, of Beck's risk society. He criticizes Beck for being too trapped by the "legislation of cognitive reason" (Lash 2000, 54).

I want to argue that the notion of risk . . . *society* presumes a determinate, institutional, normative, rule bound and necessarily hierarchical ordering of individual members in regard to their utilitarian interests. Risk *cultures*, in contrast, presume not a determinate ordering, but a reflexive or indeterminate disordering. Risk cultures lie in non-institutional and anti-institutional sociations. Their media are not procedural norms but substantive values. Their governing figurations are not rules but symbols: they are a less hierarchical ordering than a horizontal disordering. Their fluid quasi-membership is as likely to be collective as individual, and their concern is less with utilitarian interests than the fostering of the good life. . . . Risk cultures . . . are based less in cognitive than in aesthetic reflexivity. (Lash 2000, 47)

Aesthetic reflexivity itself is of two kinds in Lash's formulation. First, there is "judgement of the beautiful":

Stable memory-grounding institutions . . . are the "house" of collective memory, of narratives of cultural artefacts and rituals. Institutions are nothing without the permanence of the latter. These cultural artefacts are the configurations, the forms through which we judge aesthetically, judge reflexively the risk events, the objects that we encounter and from which we produce other cultural artefacts, other forms, other meanings. Gadamer (1986) says that this is the basis of the continuing relevance of the beautiful. . . . In judgements of the beautiful we come across objects or events, including the possible future "bads" which are risks. We do not subsume these under the logical concepts of the understanding, but, instead, these judgements are a sort of "feeling" as we intuit them through *imagination* . . . through, not logical categories, but the "forms of time and space." . . . But most importantly, what the imagination synthesizes or produces through the schemata are "representations" or "presentations." (Lash 2000, 56)

We can readily think here of the conventionalized aesthetics of high culture, for example, the "housing" of theatrical (and audience) nostalgia for an authentic Shakespeare, which Susan Bennett has described as "in its praxis, conservative (in at least two senses — its political alignment and its motive to keep things intact and unchanged); it leans on an imagined and imaginary past which is more and better than the present and for which the carrier of the nostalgia, in a defective and diminished present, longs" (1996, 5). We can also think of the appropriation of the risks in Chekhov by the Bloomsbury group, where Chekhov's talent for exploring the pain of social loss and change was elevated to an aesthetic plane (chapter 4).

But then there is Lash's other aesthetic of risk, the "terrible sublime":

> In "sublime" judgements, the event or object is so powerful that the imagination cannot make a presentation. We experience such events and objects not through the imagination, but through *sensation*, through pure perception. Sensation is raw. The body takes in the world through sensation. As such it is unable to make a presentation. It is unable to effect a productive (or constructive) synthesis. The body is open and receptive. The body . . . lives with its lack. The judgements of the sublime bridge, on the one hand, sensation and, on the other, indeterminate or existential meaning. They connect sensation or subjectivity as singular and as exposed beings. Aesthetic judgements of the sublime expose bodies with lack, expose open bodies to the ravages of contingency, to darkness to "fear and trembling." . . . Risks and threats, thus re-experienced and subsumed under neither determinate judgement of the understanding nor the judgements and syntheses of the imagination therefore bring us in touch with our finitude. Kant called this the "terrible sublime" in which dangers were actually physical. This is a very important means by which we ascribe meaning not only to risks but also to the sensibilities of risk culture. (2000, 57)

This may suggest an alternative, risk approach to the conjuncture of text and context, spectator and social audiences. But unlike some psychoanalytical approaches to spectatorship in film theory that explore a textual (or performative) world of fear, anxiety, horror, and dread, it also situates this among social audiences.

In particular, for Lash (as for postmodernists) these social audiences are positioned in a technologized world where the "predominance of material and industrial goods is displaced by a new prevalence of information and communications" (2000, 58). But Lash moves to a different conclusion from postmodernists. On the one hand, "the flows of information and communications, replacing the heteronomy of social structures, introduces an overwhelming flow of determinate judgements as images, sounds and narratives are brought twice under the logic of determinate judgment: as they are digitized first as information and yet again for transmission as communication" (Lash 2000, 58). On the other hand, there are three other "disorganizing" principles. First, the expert systems that order these determinate judgments are extremely complex, and this complexity will build "more risk, more uncertainty into the system" (Lash 2000, 58). Second, there is the uncertainty that the markets within which the global information system operates will require innovation and rule-finding behavior. Third, all this is possible only through risk cultures, which are themselves "effective disorganizations."

Lash's description of the *audiences* of disorganization within postindustrial communities provides a powerful new-historical context for Sauter's observation that distinguishes the theatrical event from religious ceremony. As Lash argues:

> Positioning risk in technological futures must take account of the growth of hierarchies, from Murdoch's media empire to supra-national bodies. This may be an expansion of the reaction of the centre against the borders and can be expressed in enhanced nationalism, racism or "occidentalism" (Venn, 1997). Alternatively, there is the challenge from what Douglas and Wildavsky call the "sectarians" from the borders, from the margins. Unlike institutions which are characterized by closure, sects are open, vulnerable, lacking collective bodies. Sects are in the first instance non-institutions; indeed they are anti-institutions. Typically they are without hierarchy; they bond through intense affective charge; they are based in friendships in affinity groups. They are rooted in common practices, with ideas of the good life, with notions of internal goods. Sects are not means to ends like institutions, like the church.... Sects tend not to distinguish the private from the public.... They are "disorganizations." They form reflexive and flexible communities, enduring only a short while and then forming once again. ... As members of churches and other institutions, we are self-identical, self-enclosed and self-interested subjects. As sect members, in contrast, we form communities, not in our self-identity, but only in our self-difference: that is, with that part of ourselves that is not subsumed under narratives of self-identity; with that part of ourselves in which we are incomplete and unfinished subjectivities, unfinished, lacking bodies. If in churches trust is in institutions or in expert systems, in sects trust lies in the face-to-face or the mediated face-to-face of the affinity group. (2000, 59)

I will come back to theatre audiences as "reflexive and flexible communities, enduring only a short while and then forming once again," at the end of the book. Meanwhile, we can observe in relation to my opening anecdotes of this chapter that there can be something very particular about the relationship between "sectarianism from the borders" in theatre and the kind of "liveness" in audience/actor communication that (to follow Lash's point) engages with risk in emotive and affective as well as cognitive ways.

As we saw, the young audience (and pretty much everybody else) had fun at Mary-Anne Gifford's *Much Ado*, which was about "boys back from war," about a patriarchal Catholic society, about male to female violence, about the fun and utopian dream of popular culture, about multiple roles and subjectivities, about liveness, about commoditization and modernity, and not least about the language of Shakespeare. This particular production indicated very clearly the local-global relationship between theatrical event, audience, mediatization, risk, and the continuing history of Shakespeare as a series of stories currently and locally told.

I have covered a lot of ground in this chapter, which discusses a theoretical matrix that will be drawn on with different emphases throughout the book. It is meant to suggest the broader problematic in which the book is placed rather than provide a step-by-step account of what will be done here. Because it does cover so much ground, the following chapter is designed as a practical application, introducing ways of bringing together some of the key parts of the matrix — notions of theatrical event, spectators and social audiences, the continuing history of Shakespeare, postmodernism and risk modernity — in relation to one case study. The following sections of the book then rework the concepts in two different ways via a variety of case studies. Why are there separate parts in this book? They indicate two quite different traditions, one that has seen active research in media studies for two decades and one that is very new in theatre studies. Both of them will help us approach theatrical events and audiences but with different emphases.

Part 2 draws strongly on central traditions in media and cultural studies. It is based on a large research project conducted by Tom Burvill and myself in the late 1990s and funded by the Australian Research Council. Entitled "Chekhov: In Criticism, Performance, and Reading," it draws on processual models from media and cultural studies that brought together ethnographies of production, textual analysis of circulation (e.g., newspaper reviewing and academic literary criticism), and qualitative and quantitative audience analysis to examine the meanings established around productions of Chekhov among different reading formations and in different media forms. Unfortunately, there is space in this book only to examine part of the sequential focus of this research project, which covered in a series of linked case studies authored text, rehearsals, production, newspaper reviews, academic criticism, and audience readings. So the focus in part 2 will be on production/audience relationships, with an emphasis on theories and methods of how we "know" what others "show" coming from media studies. There will be enough here to indicate the ethnographies of production and audiences approach, which has been productive in media studies and which has had too little application in theatre and performance analysis.

If part 2 is, in principle, based on a sequential and synchronic plan from media studies, in part 3 I adopt a more paradigmatic approach current in theatre studies. I take seriously here Sauter's emphasis that in theatrical event research it is legitimate to choose any segment of the process as an analytical starting point. His own artificially constructed segments — contextual theatricality, cultural contexts, playing culture, theatrical playing — are paradigmatic sets through which we view the same events from different perspectives. In part 3 I take each of these sets separately, relating them to a different empirical case study, with a brief attempt at the end to bring them all together again.

Mention of case studies indicates an important ordering principle of the book. It is based on a commitment to empirical work in both production and audience areas. Theory is important here but, as I said, as a matrix. Unlike major sections of postmodernist (and before that structuralist) film studies, I am not only interested in representation and texts, mainly because of the theoretical commitments I reveal here to concepts of production and theatrical event as social action, agency, and structure within risk culture. The matter of how we access these empirical activities (of production, event, audience action, and agency) becomes crucial. And so issues and debates about methodology become the most central running theme of the book.

2

SPECTATORSHIP, SOCIAL AUDIENCES, AND RISK

SHAKESPEARE AT THE Q

Under what conditions is the past re-presented for spectators in both global and local viewing economies. And what do we make of that past when we "see" it? —*Susan Bennett,* Performing Nostalgia

In early March 2001 I was standing on the railway station platform right opposite the Q Theatre in Penrith, New South Wales, twenty-five miles from the center of Sydney. I had just seen an evening performance of *Much Ado about Nothing* by the Railway Street Theatre Company. Near me on the platform waiting for the midnight train and carrying on an animated conversation were some girls from Springwood High School who had also seen the production. At the end of the performance these teenagers had jumped to their feet next to me, clapping, whistling, and cheering. And now several minutes later, as they waited for the train, they were still fired up, talking excitedly about the young actor Don Hany, who had played the role of Claudio. The girls would certainly have subscribed to most or all of the sensory abilities that Willmar Sauter describes in the theatrical playing between Sarah Bernhardt and her audiences, where "the body contributes physical charm, the most melodious voice, an aroma, attraction, even sex" (2000, 127). As the teenagers talked excitedly about how close Hany had been to some of them as he played his guitar, they were playing between the sensory (sexual), artistic (the quiet and cool guitar player who also rocked like Elvis), and symbolic (the gentle lover who destroys his girl) levels of theatrical communication that Sauter emphasizes.

How can we understand this level and intensity of audience response among young people who have had little exposure to Shakespeare? How and why did this kind of engagement with Shakespearean performance occur? To what extent was it to do with Shakespeare being presented to these students by way of a recognizable history through the popular cultural references immediately available to them? Was this production successful because it included within its artistic codes some of the popular pleasures that the girls sitting near me at the Barbican's *The Tempest* only gained "externally" via their Walkman radios? What did the very intimate space of the Q Theatre have to do with it, given the close-to-touching distance between the students and the very young actors whom they clearly identified with (or fancied) on the stage? And what of the physical context of the theatre itself, in the city of Penrith, where "footy" (rugby league) was a much more likely interest for teenagers, both male and female, than Shakespeare?

The Railway Street Company, under the direction of Mary-Anne Gifford, was clearly doing something right. After all, I had seen a similar response from students and older audiences to the same director's earlier *A Midsummer Night's Dream* at the Q Theatre, which also situated Shakespeare within a popular cultural history. So what was the secret?

Let's take a look at these two productions, *A Midsummer Night's Dream* (1998) and *Much Ado about Nothing* (2001). This will be a preliminary case study that takes up many of the theoretical themes of my opening chapter. I will look at the live theatrical event as a matter of occasion and place in the "now here," "inescapably local," and fragmentary yet also contextual and "interconnected" (Adam and Allan 1995, xvi) performance. Drawing upon Eversmann's interest in the affect of the event and upon Sauter's concern for a processual analysis, which links the playful actor-audience interaction to the "social world at large," I will focus on continuing histories of Shakespeare and Chekhov as local and situated performative events. This case study will tell tales from the field, understanding theatre production and histories as situated narratives among the daily horizons of expectations of current audiences. It will begin to examine both encoded spectatorship and the everyday preoccupations and rhythms of social audiences. It will ask questions about postmodernist emphases on society as spectacle and event in comparison with a reflexive (risk) modernist focus on the audiences' "real" everyday. In their everyday relationships, the teenagers on the station platform at Penrith were continuously perceptive about risks at the level of intimacy, personal relationships, sexuality, and gender, and their close-up interaction with the actors of *A Midsummer Night's Dream* and *Much Ado about Nothing* were linked to this. These teenagers, like others within risk modernity, engaged in the detailed, daily negotiation of their work and leisure, hazards and pleasures via biographical projects that built and drew upon extensive experiential lay knowledge, and they brought this to the permeable boundaries between high and popular culture that Gifford's Q Theatre offered.

In this introductory case study I will bring together analysis of Gifford's productions with textual approaches to spectatorship, but the focus will be on the way, as Bennett says, that "the past [is] re-presented for spectators" in a very specific local theatrical economy. The social audience will also be considered within the context of gender and risk. This chapter on Gifford's productions examines her Shakespearean texts, performances, and spectators in terms of their local occasion and place. When we return to these productions in chapter 8, my frame will be methodological, about how we gain access to the social audience.

The Theatrical Event: Inescapably Local and Interconnected

On a very hot summer's day in 1998 I attended a Sunday matinee performance of *A Midsummer Night's Dream* in Penrith. The audience sat around the intimate thrust stage of the small Q Theatre. Surrounding us outside was the city of Penrith, inland from and thus hotter than Sydney. Penrith is at the outer edge of Sydney's Western Suburbs, a suburban sprawl that contains 30 percent of Australia's population. It is known in popular caricature for its "crass Westies" culture: of cars, footy, Hills Hoist (rotary clothes drier) in the backyard, and wall-to-wall television (or video, or computer games, or country-and-western music, depending on the generation that is being caricatured). Perhaps the city's main claim to fame is the Penrith Panthers Rugby League Club. Not so long ago they were the Australian Grand Finals champions in a country that consistently wins the Rugby League World Cup. By now they had fallen on uncertain times.

But the Panthers Rugby League Club remained a leisure Mecca for Penrith's population of mainly working-class, migrant, and unemployed people. With its "pokies" (gaming machines), its restaurants, and its bars, sitting amidst the familiar MacDonald's, KFC, and Pizza Hut complex and across the road from the rugby league stadium itself, this was a significant focus for Penrith's day, night, and weekend life.

Most of the weekend leisure activity in this city did not take place at the Q Theatre but at the Panthers Rugby League Club, or in the vastly expanded shopping mall and cinemas near Penrith railway station, or at the endless car sales yards that are such a feature of Sydney's Western Suburbs generally. Just two years after my theatre visit to *A Midsummer Night's Dream*, Penrith's river and lakes would be hosting the rowing and kayaking events of the 2000 Summer Olympics held in Sydney. But for the moment, at the time of the production of the play in the summer of 1998, Penrith sat hot and, in terms of tourism, liminal to both Sydney's worldwide profile for cosmopolitanism, theatre, opera, and multicultural fine eating and the world heritage site that rose up just on the west of Penrith's Nepean River, the top bushwalking territory of the Blue Mountains.

Actors who play at the Q Theatre are aware of this sense of the liminal Penrith. They speak of the more familiar Sydney audience that may visit the play on opening night as composed of "theatre-ati." In contrast, they thought of the nearby Blue Mountains audience as typical middle-class suburban subscribers, comparable with those in Sydney suburbs. But between the Sydney and Blue Mountains audiences geographically there was the Penrith audience, which was often, the actors said, "fresh" (to theatre) and "a challenge." Indeed, the actors later tried out one performance of *A Midsummer Night's Dream* at the Penrith Rugby League Club itself with considerable success.

This theatre company drew on a traveling middle-class clientele as a key part of its audience. Indeed, it had begun to perform its productions "up the Mountains" for short runs, as a local extension of the Railway Street Company's on-the-road strategy. As well as its audience traveling, this theatre company also traveled. At this point of time of diminishing state subsidies, it was the only wide-ranging professional touring theatre company left in New South Wales, taking its productions to such remote rural towns as Nyngan, Taree, and Gunnedah after finishing its run in Penrith.

By the time of the Q Theatre's production of *Much Ado about Nothing*, the economic risks of this touring policy were threatening the theatre's very survival, according to newspaper reviewers.

All actors and crew are paid professional rates, as well as living-away allowances, while on tour. Each regional arts council accepts the risk of a show, paying a flat fee of about $2,200 for each performance. But

Railway Street Theatre's *Much Ado about Nothing* touring van.

as a company travelling to play "one-night stands," Railway Street can usually perform only four shows each week, earning less than $10,000 for a week's touring, its artistic director, Mary-Anne Gifford, says. The company is left short about $10,000 each week, a deficit not covered by government grants. . . . Although audience numbers are growing, touring costs are increasing each year, Gifford says, and arts councils in areas such as Warwick, in Queensland's Darling Downs, are also losing money . . . "but they just think it's important, even if there's only 50 people there," Gifford says. . . . "People do tend to come from vast distances to see a show. . . . There's a real sense of occasion — often it's the only theatre they will see all year." (Hallett and Gotting 2001, 14)

Whether at home in Penrith or touring, the Q was a stridently local theatre. Sitting unpretentiously next to the main Lithgow–Sydney railway line, it had recently been part of a merger, renaming itself the Railway Street Theatre Company in a determined effort to break with the "North Shore" (professional middle-class) image of many Sydney theatre companies.

This strategy was not, however, easy to implement in an increasingly deregulated economy. As the *Sydney Morning Herald* described it, "Penrith-based Railway Street is well-accustomed to playing schools and town halls in regional centres and remote towns throughout NSW and South-East Queensland. . . . But touring is by no means cheap and is a large factor contributing to the company's dire financial state. Railway

Street says it will be forced to close in August unless it receives further government support of about $200,000 this year. It has appealed to Penrith City Council for an additional $180,000" (Hallett and Gotting 2001, 14).

The newspaper article was actually written just prior to March 7, 2001, when, "in Nyngan, Railway Street Theatre introduces western NSW to its critically acclaimed production of Shakespeare's *Much Ado About Nothing*" (Hallett and Gotting 2001, 14). But the same economic conditions, of a largely unsubsidized local touring theatre company, existed three years earlier when they played *A Midsummer Night's Dream*. Both of these Shakespeare plays were Higher School Certificate (HSC, the New South Wales school-leaving exam) set texts, and the Railway Street Company, like theatres in Britain in an economic rationalist climate, was seeking a particular niche market to put "bums on seats." Peter Thomson describes how, in "the age of accountability . . . [e]ven Shakespeare, and even Shakespeare at Stratford, is subject increasingly to the archly expressed 'bums-on-seats' test. . . . Run-of-the-mill productions of Shakespeare, spuriously decorated school texts, are products of an industry under threat" (2001).

Plenty of theatres globally aim at this market, but none have achieved it in my experience with the conspicuous audience pleasure among young people that I watched at the Q Theatre. A significant reason for this success was the appointment a few months before *A Midsummer Night's Dream* of Mary-Anne Gifford, the new artistic director as a result of the merger with the New England Theatre Company.

Directing the Classics: Shakespeare and Chekhov

Prior to her move to Penrith, Gifford had been artistic director at the New Theatre in Sydney. This theatre was originally subsidized by the trade union movement and still had a semiprofessional "Leftie" image. Gifford herself came from an old Left family (her parents were in the Communist Party). But the Railway Street Theatre Company was in no overt sense political or polemical theatre. Mary-Anne Gifford knew it could not work like that, and in any case she didn't want it to.

This is not to say that her productions didn't have a strong social and historical reference. For example, when she played Chekhov's *The Cherry Orchard* at the New Theatre in December 1997, the "warehouse-style" walls of the threatened gentry's home were designed, she said, the "color of blood" to represent the social exploitation that went on there. She dressed and directed her servants in a range of vaudeville styles, deriving from early-twentieth-century theatre, music hall, and silent film. This postmodern, popular cultural approach to her servant class, in contrast to the more naturalistic style of performance and dress of the main characters, was meant to signify that these servants represented social and historical disorder itself. "Servants in the new [social] structure . . . would never have been able to behave the way they did twenty years previously, wanting change, but with nowhere to go, and with nothing solid to hold on to" (Gifford, personal interview, 1997).

But Gifford emphasized also the contemporary relevance of her *The Cherry Orchard* at the New Theatre, since, for people on the Left under a new, neoliberal government, "there is also nothing solid to hold on to, things have been taken away we thought were solid." She was very aware of risk modernity, where the "goods" of the welfare state (which the Left had thought were enshrined as entitlements) have been broken down by the "bads" of globalization, uncertainty, and neoliberal economic rationalism (Beck 1992). Indeed, this contemporary aspect of risk modernity became a kind of offstage global context against which she performed many of her plays, including *The Cherry Orchard, A Midsummer Night's Dream*, and *Much Ado about Nothing*. The link between history and contemporaneity was a continuing signature of Gifford, who wove together, through her seasonal programs, risk in its most personal sense and risk in its local-global "contextual theatricality" (Sauter 2000). Thus, in her late 2001 subscription season brochure, Gifford wrote:

> *Hey, we're back!* Railway Street has had a reprieve, at least until the end of the year. The support we have had has been incredible and we want to thank Penrith City Council, the NSW Ministry, the local press, the regional presenters and our audience for all the moral and practical help you have given us over the last few months. . . . Coincidentally (there's no such thing as coincidence?) the two plays we are producing in this second session are both about survival. Different places, different times, very different scenarios, but basically they ask the same question: How do you survive the cruel times without abandoning the things that matter . . . things such as personal honesty and integrity and a respect and consideration for each other's humanity? These are cruel times for all of us. Not just for the company but for the country. How we survive them seems an appropriate and essential question. (Gifford 2001, 2)

As well as referring to a globalized free-market scenario, Gifford's words were also acknowledging a very local survival threat, both for the company and for its audience. In her 2001 Q Theatre subscription brochure, Gifford railed at the same Australian conservative government policy responsible for the loss of the welfare state and the goods of risk modernity as she had at the time of her 1997 *The Cherry Orchard* in a different theatre in Sydney. Whether in Sydney in 1997 or in Penrith in 1998 and 2001, many of her subscribers were facing these risks as a constraint on their choices, as governmental services and support diminished. But despite her leftist politics and anticonservative government polemic, Gifford's *The Cherry Orchard* did not present a Socialist message, as had Trevor Griffiths's version (chapter 3), which she admired.

Gifford's leftist and gender politics were certainly there in various aspects of the multimediality of her production. But a broader variety of Gifford's personal/political performance identities also played across this series of histories of Chekhov then (the color-of-blood set walls signifying Russian class exploitation at the turn of the twentieth century) and Australia now (the neoliberal risk society). When asked why she used David Mamet's adaptation of *The Cherry Orchard* rather than Trevor Griffiths's recent version, Gifford said that although the Mamet translation was already chosen when she took the play on, she rejected and worked against his purely individualist, sexual-risk obsession. Nevertheless, even if she had been faced with a free choice of script, she would have had problems with Griffiths's, especially because of his emphasis on Trofimov.

Trofimov reminded her, she said, of the early seventies Lefties she had spent so much time with who claimed to put revolutionary change above interpersonal relations. According to Gifford, "You can't change the world if you can't love." Her production of *The Cherry Orchard* was primarily a tale of love and romance played out (with the whole cast always onstage watching) through a postmodern mélange of vaudevillian and early cinema styles and performances.

Gifford foregrounded a similar emphasis on love in her program notes for the 2001 production of *Much Ado about Nothing*.

It's strange to think . . . that we might forget how powerful, how beautiful Shakespeare's words are. . . . Words have this strange momentum of their own once they are dropped or hurled or whispered into space. They blossom or fester depending on their nature or when or how

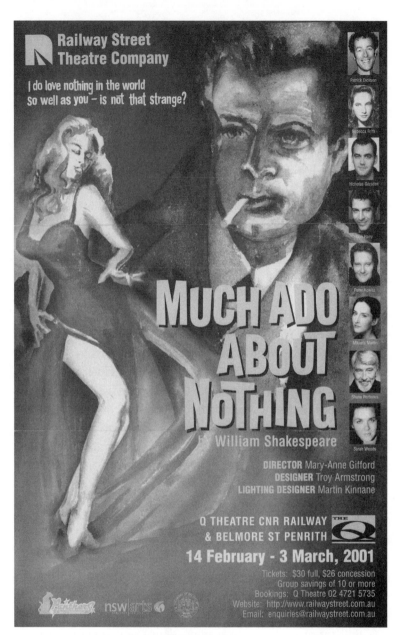

Q Theatre poster for *Much Ado about Nothing*.

they're spoken. . . . My favourite word thing is . . . the care we take with the word love. We even call it "the L word," so frightened are we of its power. Everyone knows how that word can stay in your head and your heart forever with no real power, but once it's spoken . . . there's a contract there. And a freedom. And both things are pretty bloody scary. . . . That word, love, changes the air around us and the world we live in and the people we are. You can say it over and over to as many people as you love, scrawl the word a million times . . . write it all over the world and, every time, it hits you like a bomb in your guts. Why? Because people don't want to be alone in the world. Alone is cold and lonely. People want to belong. And love promises belonging. Everything Shakespeare writes is about that need. . . . That's our sadness, our hope and our salvation. (Gifford 2001, 2)

Spectatorship and Risk: *A Midsummer Night's Dream*

Love was also in the air as the audience first engaged with Gifford's *A Midsummer Night's Dream* at Penrith on that hot summer afternoon of 1998. Prior to the lights going up on the thrust stage (which the audience surrounded intimately on three sides), Mario Lanza was singing his hit from *The Student Prince*, "Serenade."

Overhead the moon is beaming
White as blossoms on the bough
Nothing is heard but the song of a bird
Filling all the air with dreaming.
Could I hear this song forever
Calling to my heart anew
"My darling" —
While I drift along forever
Lost in a dream of you.

The lights came up, and Hippolyta, the conquered Amazon queen soon to be forced to the bed of Theseus, walked slowly to the front of the stage as Lanza's words were also lifted audibly: "Could this beauty last forever / I would ask for nothing more." Hippolyta (Sarah Woods) was dressed in the silver lamé of a 1920s Hollywood vamp star. Thus, this first scene, which Gifford played with the undertones of male militarism and the overtones of patriarchal violence (as Egeus threatened his daughter

Hippolyta (Sarah Woods) as 1920s Hollywood vamp in
A Midsummer Night's Dream. Photograph by Geoff Beatty.

Gifford's *A Midsummer Night's Dream* as a "long 1920s cocktail party."
Sarah Aubrey, Kathryn Hartman, Trent Baker. Photograph by Geoff Beatty.

Hermia with death or the nunnery if she did not marry the man he chose),
was established melodramatically by means of acting style and costumes
for the "long 1920s cocktail party" (Gifford, program notes). Director
Gifford's historical intertext here was Scott Fitzgerald and his partying
1920s. She said in the program notes, "Germany, like the Amazon nation,
is defeated in the war and forced to repay impossible debts. The allies of
the western world try to forget the bloodiest war in our history, and the
roar of the ten-year party of the 1920s deafens them to the sound of
Germany remembering."

But this was not another overtly situated "Shakespeare and Fascism"
production set in the 1920 and 1930s (e.g., Ian McKellan's *Richard III* film).
History in Gifford's production was deliberately used to cue audiences'
more media-saturated and fragmented memories. This, the actors said,
was an audiencing appeal different from the one made to the Sydney
theatre-ati, who might compare the production with the currently running light and frothy comedic *A Midsummer Night's Dream* "in the park,"
where we hardly ever notice the awful violence of that first scene. Gifford's
program notes, her costumes (including First World War soldiers and
nurses), her simple set (an arch of trees that crashed down to spill out
rifles, masks, and other First World War impedimenta), and Bottom's ass
head as gas mask were there to cue quite different memories, primarily,

film and television image recollections of the twentieth century's most media-remembered contrast of war and partying, the Roaring Twenties. This was also a proto-Fascist twenties, but the politics were conveyed in this production by the mood of *absence* of political concern rather than by directly setting the play in, say, Mussolini's Italy.

Gifford's use of Mario Lanza to introduce this first scene of act 1 derived, in fact, from a different, later time-space context than the 1920s and a different set of cultural memories. It connected with her own biographical memories of childhood in a Marxist, working-class family where she sang along with all the musicals. In those days, Gifford remembered, Lanza's hit love songs resonated for her parents with an "optimism of the will" embedded in popular cultural pleasure. So for her, Mario Lanza's voice represented both some sense of utopian togetherness deriving from her old leftist family beliefs and a "slightly camp" over-the-top sentimentality relating to her own recent career as a rock singer. It was a tension between identity and fragmentation that would soon be embodied on her stage.

While watching the opening of this performance I was reminded that, like Lanza's "Overhead the moon is beaming," Arthur's "Prairie Moon" in Dennis Potter's television drama series *Pennies from Heaven* had also injected popular cultural performance (in each case, of a particular gendered male kind) into the heart of the "high art" text. Unlike the Barbican production of *The Tempest*, in the Q Theatre's *Dream* popular music was *included* by Gifford (as in Potter's *Pennies from Heaven*) in the performed text itself. This "culture of physicality, tacitly transferred from generation to generation and often used for subversive purposes" (Sauter 2000, 81), was Gifford "playing culture"; and, as "resistance" to the canonical Shakespearean text, it added an explosive energy to the set HSC text that the school students whom I interviewed enjoyed enormously. In this way, for Gifford a range of historical cultural forms become active in her productions, thereby loosening the constraints of familiar canonical texts. In her *A Midsummer Night's Dream* popular cultural songs from the 1920s and 1930s ("When the red, red robin" done to Busby Berkeley routines) could generate a working-class energy as the rude mechanicals matched the romance of the aristocratic lovers with the collective energy of their own dreams. And yet there was personal uncertainty here, too, as actors and characters entered spaces they were unused to.

Gifford also emphasized that in contrast to all this popular cultural energy, the romance of Pyramus and Thisbe is a tragedy. In her production this micronarrative offered an alternative ending to the dominant

Multiple roles: Nick Garsden (right) playing Bottom as part of the rude mechanicals' collective energy in *A Midsummer Night's Dream*. Photograph by Geoff Beatty.

theme of consummated aristocratic love. And in this alternative trajectory, Lanza's "Let this night live forever," which might be expected to predict the familiar fairy-guarded narrative closure to the play (with three aristocratic weddings), was, in fact, made ambiguous by Puck's "Now it is the time of night that the graves all gaping wide, every one lets forth his sprite."

Gifford's Puck (Sean O'Shea) was not the fairy Puck that Sydney's theatre-ati were so used to. He was dressed and propped after medieval woodcuts of the Pucka, the Devil, presaging that alternative ending where Hippolyta finally left the stage in Gifford's *Dream* to the popular Billie Holiday 1930s Depression-era musical number "There may be troubles ahead . . . / Let's face the music and dance." So this production's encoded meaning and potentially lasting memories were of personal, sexual, and economic risks, not of fairy dells. But these risks were also challenged by the sensory, artistic, and symbolic (utopic) energies of the rude mechanicals' singing and dancing, as Scott Fitzgerald's 1920s social world was replaced by a new 1990s class energy, even though, still, "there is nothing solid to hold on to" (Gifford). So Gifford's continuing history of Shakespeare offered three senses of an ending: the "classical" conclusion, when, as one female teenage audience member said, "the men get their

Multiple roles: Nick Garsden as Pyramus (with Sarah Aubrey) in
A Midsummer Night's Dream. Photograph by Geoff Beatty.

Gifford's Puck (Sean O'Shea), the helpful devil, in
A Midsummer Night's Dream. Photograph by Geoff Beatty.

women — all of them!"; the "troubles ahead" Billie Holiday / Pucka 1920s/1930s/1990s analogy to partying in the face of worldwide risk; and the working-class utopia of musical energy.

Faced with the budget restrictions of a small, minimally subsidized, fully professional theatre company, Gifford used a small cast to play multiple roles. Many productions of the play have actors doubling as Theseus and Oberon and as Hippolyta and Titania (as Peter Thomson notes, for at least a decade after the 1970 Peter Brook production at Stratford, this doubling "became almost conventional" [2001, 172]). But Gifford trebled and quadrupled her actors' parts: Theseus, Oberon, *and* Bottom and Pyramus (Nick Garsden); Hippolyta, Titania, *and* Peter Quince (Sarah Woods). Consequently, when all the characters crowded together onstage for the finale, the director had a logistical problem. She resolved it in part by a reflexive emphasis on performance (the dying Pyramus removed his First World War soldier's helmet, rolled over, and became a relaxed Theseus watching the mechanicals' play). But Gifford also edited Shakespeare's text, cutting some of the characters (and lines) where courtiers deride the working-class performers. In Shakespeare's play, much of the energy of that last scene is in the bantering language play between courtiers as intellectuals. Their superiority is "natural," taken for granted. But Gifford argued it would have a different effect on audiences then and now, since in Shakespeare's time the tacit, taken-for-granted superiority of aristocratic wordplay could be countered by witticisms from the pit.

In place of this high art energy of sophisticated language play, Gifford's editing and direction established an intertextual plenitude of popular culture: the 1920s/1930s/1950s songs, the (stage-limited) choreography that evoked Busby Berkeley routines. Even some of my school-age audience respondents recognized the Berkeley references, and all audiences in the three performances of the *Dream* that I saw stomped, clapped, and laughed to them. One of the songs, "Red, Red Robin," had originally been sung by Al Jolson in blackface, but Gifford attempted to efface that racist memory and instead used the song to evoke working-class dreams and energy. From the deliberate Hollywood melodrama of the opening scene to the popular musical of the last, from the opening shadow of militarism, sexism, and risk to the closing, guilelessly innocent "Red, Red Robin" knees-up, Shakespeare was here being made to perform again in a new historical context.

Susan Bennett has warned against a Left no less than a Right Shakespearean "nostalgia" in production (1996, 32), and, arguably, Gifford's positioning of a working-class energy within the 1930s musical might be seen as an example of Bennett's concern with Shakespeare "citation," where ideological "containment [is] an inevitable effect of re-articulating the past" (1996, 12). Thus, says Bennett, in "new" versions of Shakespeare, "collective nostalgia can promote a feeling of community which works to downplay or ... disregard divisive positionalities (class, race, gender and so on); when nostalgia is produced and experienced collectively ... it can promote a false and likely dangerous sense of 'we' " (1996, 5). Nevertheless, Bennett is optimistic enough to say (this time following Certeau) that "interminable (and it might be argued, often dissonant) recitations can produce effects that escape the discipline implied in the recitation. If 'we' are bound to cite and recite, then 'we' might as well explore this as a generative practice" (1996, 25).

It is this kind of recitation of "Shakespeare" and "history as a generative practice" that I saw as spectator to Gifford's *Dream*. For me, as in the case of Potter's *Pennies from Heaven*, Gifford's rude mechanicals were not 1930s nostalgic in any "authentic community" sense but, rather, were seen only through the traces of popular cultural memories and fragments. Even if, Bennett says, "the contemporary sign is doomed to dream of signs of the past, its signification need not be bound to the narratives of a single History" (1996, 160). Gifford's Shakespeares were never bound to single histories ("then" *or* "now"). They were "recitations" that depended on the interaction of different (popular) cultural histories as well as different theatrical contexts. Thus, for example, soon after the performances I saw at the Q Theatre, Gifford took her *Dream* for one day to the huge theatre at the Penrith Panthers Rugby League Club, where the working-class audience enjoyed the working-class mechanicals as much as any audiences had at the Q Theatre.

The use of music in Gifford's *A Midsummer Night's Dream* was playful, postmodern, historically fragmented, and energetic. It was also parodic in terms of both gender and race. If it was a slightly pompous white-male voice (Lanza) that opened out the romantic-pastoral "dream" ("Overhead the moon is beaming / White as blossoms on the bough"), it was a black female voice (Billie Holiday) that concluded with "There may be troubles ahead" as the dusky-skinned Hippolyta left the stage. And these differences were deeply embedded both in the histories of the musical genres that Lanza and Holiday represented and in the performances and alternative narratives within the play itself.

Gifford was performing gender consciously and in ways with which she knew her young audiences could identify. No familiar *Dream* romp in the woods followed the "Hollywood melodrama" opening. Rather, the young actors' performances developed deeply into romance *and* risk. Gender positions were worked for, taken, taken away, and assaulted. Scenes of young female and male love and lust, female bodily offerings and male rejections, and male-female violence and jealousy were all played out as the young men and women (Sarah Aubrey as Hermia, Trent Baker as Lysander, Christopher Johnson as Demetrius, Kathryn Hartman as Helena) moved from the court to the woods.

Gifford's *Dream* began, in its first scene, with a heightened and stylized emphasis on a woman's enforced performance of gender and race. Hippolyta is a woman, and she is dusky, the Amazon queen. Hermia is also female, but she is white. And, in a long, silent moment at one side of the stage in act 1, scene 1, the darker Hippolyta and the white Hermia stood breast to breast, as the older woman slowly transferred her silver lamé shawl to the younger one. Then there was a brief pause as the shawl covered both their heads, screening them from the audience and also from the eyes of the raging, *speaking* males onstage.

A number of young audience members, when interviewed about this moment, saw it as a type of "mother-daughter solidarity thing," and we can perhaps dip into theories of a film genre that strongly influences Gifford's productions, women's melodrama, to understand the kind of spectatorship that was being offered here. Linda Williams, analyzing spectatorship in *Stella Dallas,* contrasts the mother-daughter relationship in the film with the masochistic relationship that Laura Mulvey argued exists for female spectators within the fetishistic, male-controlled narratives of the classical Hollywood film. Williams argues that though the female spectator of this film "has seen Stella lose herself as a woman and a mother . . . at the same time she *believes* that women exist outside this phallic economy, because she has glimpsed moments of resistance in which two women have been able to represent themselves to themselves through the mediation of their own gazes . . . free of the mastery and control of the male look" (1987, 318–19). The violently (militaristically) patriarchal language of Gifford's *Dream* was unusually strongly articulated in the opening scene, where the "phallic economy" of Shakespeare's play (i.e., Hippolyta forced to Theseus's bed) dominated. In this scene Hermia speaks far less than the men, and Hippolyta hardly speaks at all. But Gifford had given Hippolyta the opening stage-visual *presence* in her own vamplike iconicity. It offered a strong, silent, slightly older female sexuality in the face of Lanza's verbose "dreaming."

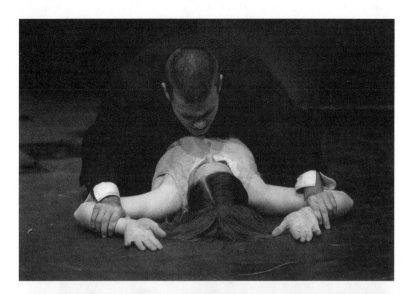

Romance and risk, offering the female body as love, jealousy, and lust.
Kathryn Hartman (Helena) with Trent Baker (Lysander) and Christopher
Johnson (Demetrius) in *A Midsummer Night's Dream*.
Photographs by Geoff Beatty.

A long, silent moment: Hippolyta (Sarah Woods) and Hermia (Sarah Aubrey) in *A Midsummer Night's Dream*. Photograph by Geoff Beatty.

A postmodernist might argue that the "real" (of the Shakespearean Thebes) had been replaced at the very opening of Gifford's production by signification and spectacle, its language by 1950s music, its visuals by 1920s film, and the high-cultural referent by the signs of popular culture. Simulations, then, replaced the "truth" of Shakespeare's history; surfaces (of slightly camp pop songs and Hollywood signifiers of the "bad girl") displaced deep structure, and the "performance" of Shakespearean gender relations replaced the original author's "authentic reality."

But we know what Gifford thought about theatre language and love (and many members of the audience knew her views too, since the whole season containing the *Dream* was on that theme). So when we heard the Shakespearean language begin (as the men burst out onto the stage in act 1, scene 1 to surround the Hollywood vamplike Hippolyta), it was probably obvious to many spectators not only that the boundaries of high and popular culture had become permeable but that this historically fragmented tableau was clearly signifying powerfully between its spoken and visual modes. Far from this being part of a free-flowing postmodern world of undifferentiated image, simulacra, and spectacle, these performed act 1, scene 1 significations — of music and song, embodiment and icon, gender and language, sensory, artistic, and symbolic physicalities — were clearly positioned spectatorially. They were *embodied* in Hippolyta's and Hermia's mutual gaze by way of the active agency of a female director and two female actors. Where there was a moment of "undifferentiated" space (Williams 1987, 319), as in the scene where Hippolyta's and Hermia's heads were hidden from the male protagonists (and the spectators), this was *worked for* in production and performance. Hippolyta used her main signifier of the 1920s Hollywood "bad girl," the silver lamé stole, at a key moment of this scene to share a "space between women free of the mastery and control of the male look" (Williams 1987, 319). Though this women's scene was wordless, even while the rampant males still held the stage with their talk, audience survey responses indicated that almost 100 percent of the school student audiences focused on this intimate interaction of the two women.

This detail of audience data may suggest that the gaze of theatre is different from the gazes both of film and of television (Kuhn 1987, chap. 1). It is, as we will see empirically in chapter 8, much to do with a sense of "liveness," of shared physical, cognitive, and emotional intimacy (within the communicative mode of theatrical playing) between the young women on- and offstage who were "almost in touching distance" of each other. This cognitive and emotional "belief" in and between women deprived, in Williams's words, of hegemonic language is close to Lash's notion of the "terrible sublime" (chapter 1) and part of Gifford's thematic focus of "love . . . [that] hits you like a bomb in your guts," and, arguably, it was a key motivation for the sexualized agency of the two young women in the scenes in the woods that followed the opening scene of Gifford's *Dream*.

The point is that to understand textual, performance, and audience meanings in this production of Gifford's *Dream*, we need to relocate analysis of this scene between Hippolyta and Hermia in terms of theatrically communicated negotiations (Sauter 2000) between sexual risk experience (both on and off the stage). This was a negotiation between the spectatorial positions established by actors' embodied interactions (and established also by the director's intertextual use of popular film genre conventions) and the actual social audiences' direction of gaze at the stage. If spectatorship in that silent moment of act 1, scene 1 was established by an interaction between actors Sarah Woods (Hippolyta) and Sarah Aubrey (Hermia) wordlessly embodying together a new, female-empowering use of Hollywood's 1920s vamp shawl, to what extent was this offer (or interpellation) of spectatorship embraced by the school students as social audience?

Teenage girls from the Q Theatre audience spoke of their own particular focus on this opening scene and also of how, as Gifford's ambiguous risk narratives continued into the woods, these later scenes engaged with their own personal experiences. There was shared emotional empathy, cognitive experience, and memory among these girls as Helena, desperately in love, offered herself bodily and without words to Demetrius in the woods. Karen, one eighteen-year-old audience member, said she found this scene with Helena and Demetrius very disturbing, while at the same time it introduced her own personal dating memories into the performance. As she put it, "Although Helena is giving herself up to Demetrius like that, it also shows a character strength in a way, because if she's got the mindset just to do that, for me it *was* a decision . . . that she has thought the process through and . . . therefore she has a certain amount of power and strength."

The other young women in Karen's focus group discussed the ending of the play, where the men, they complain, get what they want — "all of them!" But these young women were also able personally to negotiate this male-gendered finale via detailed and experientially based interactions of their own biographies and those of Shakespeare's women, who, they said, drive the narrative actions in the play via Hippolyta's shawl scene and via the young, sexualized women in the woods.

Eversmann rightly emphasizes the importance of perceived similarities between audience members and characters onstage. But I disagree with him that social characteristics such as age and gender or race "only play minor parts here . . . triggering . . . the sense of (partial) similarity between oneself and the character" (2004, forthcoming). Clearly, Karen and her friends were aware that the similarities were only partial. But the triggering of spectatorship among social audiences in an intimate theatre space can be powerful and in this case certainly had to do with gender, age, generation, and audience-to-actor proximity and interaction. My interviews with one hundred young audience members for *A Midsummer Night's Dream* were limited in number, but more extensive audience analysis of Gifford's next major Shakespeare production, *Much Ado about Nothing*, enabled further exploration of the social audience.

Social Audiences and Risk: *Much Ado about Nothing*

For her production of *Much Ado about Nothing* in 2001 Gifford set the play in 1950s Italy. In an interview she described the frustration of watching other productions as well as the Kenneth Branagh film of *Much Ado*, because though they showed the return from war at the beginning, they missed the point of that particular arrival: "The starting point is . . . a bunch of guys coming back from war. . . . My real starting point [in interpreting this] was Claudio's change. How can Claudio believe what Don John tells him? Particularly a man that he has learnt not to trust and, just like that, believes him about Hero. So I thought, 'Okay, let's look at the world they're in.' And the world these guys come into is a particularly gracious world. The people are well mannered, warm, welcoming. They obviously know them. There's obviously love and affection for them. And they're a world of good people." In her early preparation for the production, Gifford puzzled over this paradox of Claudio believing a soldier he actually didn't like rather than the "good people" he met in Messina about the character of Hero. Gifford had picked up from her first reading "a very strong image of the place — a small seaside place in Sicily called Messina . . . [during] the late fifties." But she had no idea why this particular image kept recurring to her until . . . I came up with all these questions about Claudio. . . . And then it clicked with me why I was seeing it at that time. . . . It's about post-war, and particularly post–Second World War. I don't want historical exactitude going on [in the production], but I do want to allude strongly to that time. Because there's a sense, particularly in the late fifties, that the war is far enough behind everybody, it's being forgotten. There's the sense of getting on with your life, repopulating, those things. And when these boys rock into Messina, Claudio tells us straight away what they want, why they're there. Claudio sees Hero straight away, goes, "I want to be in love with her. I want to marry her." He wants to embrace everything that this town has to offer. "I want goodness, purity, beauty, youth, wealth, happiness." So he starts the party rolling. (Gifford, personal interview, January 2001)

For Gifford, there was a tension between Claudio wanting this dream so much and his past experience as a soldier. When Claudio is told by Don John, "All that's a sham. She's not what she appears to be," Gifford said he can believe it so quickly "because he's been in a war. And in a war what . . . you learn to believe . . . is that evil [is all that] exists, that nothing is certain, that you can't trust anybody, that you have to keep looking over your shoulder or someone's going to kill you, that people are worthless, that you're just sent into battle, and if you get killed, you're just a number."

So Gifford, in fact, situated both her *Dream* and her *Much Ado* immediately after a world war. She acknowledged that these choices had a lot to do with her own understanding of war ushering in "a certain extreme form of masculinity": "To me that [masculinity] is at the heart of both of those plays. . . . You would think at my age the war that has left the most impression . . . would be the Vietnam War. And that's probably true on a personal level. But at an imaginative level, it's actually the two world wars that haunt me, because they are still the biggest, the most horrific things that have happened in the twentieth century on a world scale. So they are my . . . cultural references when I start. . . . I think that they still mean most to most people living in Australia who would come and see . . . and . . . make sense of the plays" (Gifford, personal interview, January 2001). Gifford argued that when the soldiers come into Messina, they all want to believe in the happiness and beauty they seem to see before them. "But it's a long journey to believe in those things, and I think the play ends just at the *beginning* of that journey to maybe . . . regaining . . . trust that goodness is possible, happiness *is* possible."

The first fifteen minutes of the production were when the huge enthusiasm for the production among the school students I encountered at Penrith railway station was set off. These few minutes were dominated by two tableau moments featuring Don Pedro, Benedick, and Claudio. First (with Don John), these three soldiers walked beneath the towering image of a crucified Christ on the backcloth and through the central archway of the 1950s-situated Italian town. The walls of the archway facing the audience were plastered with 1950s consumer advertisements for Vespa motor scooters, hot rod V8 cars, cappuccino, and movies starring Gina Lollobrigida and Frank Sinatra. This was the world of *La Dolce Vita*, also featured by Gifford in the show's advertisements, a particular moment of global (yet also local Italian) consumption that was instantly recognizable (even, it seems by sixteen-year-old school students) as "1950s." This historical moment of postwar growth and consumerism was signified by way of the Italian American stars plastered on the wall, the music (Dean Martin, Frank Sinatra, Mario Lanza again), the coffee bar with its red awning. The figure of *La Dolce Vita* herself, Beatrice (Rebecca Frith), was also lounging against the coffee bar wall in fifties clothes and big red sunglasses. This was the "soft life" town where Leonato (Shane Porteous) is mayor, his daughter, Hero (Mikaela Martin), is pertly virginal (within a dominating, patriarchal Catholicism), and his niece, Beatrice, is a feisty, cool, and apparently confident young woman.

The soldier-men walked wearily into this frothy world in act 1, scene 1, still introspective over their masculinist wartime conflict, their recent physical risk, and their possibly ill-gained survival. Confronted by *La Dolce Vita*, they stood silent for an interminable moment, like a waxwork tableau, staring as if for the first time at a world that suddenly included women, potentially, as equals. These soldiers were experienced with the world and its evils. They were male killing machines, which is why Gifford saw this wartime background as foundational to her approach to the play. Thus, the moment of the first male tableau of the Gifford production of *Much Ado*, as the soldiers stood both in their wartime past and their idealized future at the town gate, was one of extended tension, exhaustion, new risks, and new desires.

That was the perspective of the soldiers, as Gifford saw it. But from the women's point of view, as Hero and Beatrice watched the men come in, this was also a moment that marked the town gates framing the men as a liminal space, a window between the world of *La Dolce Vita*, popular culture, fun, happiness and trust, and an "other" world. Describing

Consumer advertisements: Rebecca Frith as Beatrice in
Much Ado about Nothing. Photograph by Geoff Beatty.

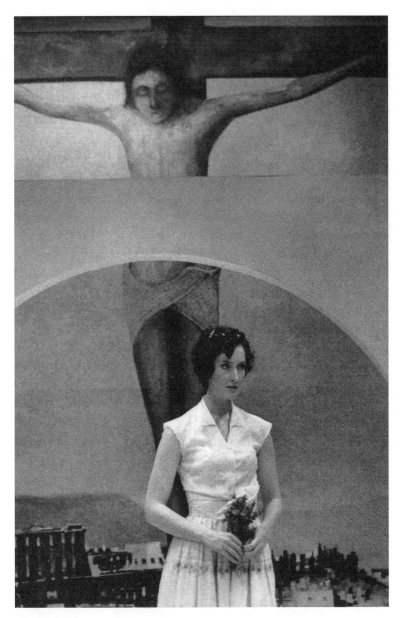

Hero (Mikaela Martin), pertly virginal within patriarchal Catholicism, in *Much Ado about Nothing*. Photograph by Geoff Beatty.

Tableau 1, the soldiers at the gates in *Much Ado about Nothing*.
Photograph by Geoff Beatty.

spectatorship within women's films, Mary-Anne Doane speaks of how "the window has special import in terms of the social and symbolic positioning of women — the window is the interface between inside and outside, the feminine space of the family and the masculine space of production" (1987, 288). The women who sought marriage and family in Gifford's *Much Ado* (Hero in particular, but also, despite herself, Beatrice) looked through the gates and saw the men return. And it would be the *men's* "space of production" (the kind of warfare that, in *A Midsummer Night's Dream*, brought the Amazon queen to Theseus's bed) that would soon penetrate this domestic world of *Much Ado about Nothing*, sour it, and smash Hero to the floor at her wedding altar. That harsh male-dominated altar was predicted at this early moment of the production as the women stared through the gate at the men, because beyond that gate there was a huge, patriarchal image of the crucified Christ. It would be the institutionalized Catholic religion established around that looming and patriarchal image that would later cite, via Hero's father, her own sexual "sin."

The second male tableau occurred just a few minutes later, when Don Pedro (Patrick Dickson), Benedick (Nicholas Garsden), and Claudio (Don Hany) again entered together through the arch from backstage. But this time the frozen war weariness and muted violence were replaced by the eruption of Elvis Presley impersonators singing "Such a Night, It

Tableau 2, rocking into Messina. Nicholas Garsden (Benedick), Don Hany (Claudio), and Patrick Dickson (Don Pedro) in *Much Ado about Nothing*.

Really Was, Such a Night." Here the soldiers really did "rock into Messina" (Gifford). Again, though, this group-soldier performance was strongly gendered as male, with Elvis swagger, gyrating hips, posture, and identical black wigs. The school matinee audience (quiet until now) exploded with applause at this moment when the three "kings" appeared. This was the first sound this audience had made, and, as with that same evening's audience, it was easily the loudest. So, as in Gifford's *A Midsummer Night's Dream* (and her New Theatre *The Cherry Orchard*), the energy of popular culture again burst physically into Shakespeare.

One high school student commented on this juxtaposition of the two (soldiers and Presley) tableaux this way: "I thought the . . . Elvis bit was very stylized and was very sort of light, bubbly comedy, and it wasn't trying to say anything too deep or make any huge statements. It was just entertaining, like with the running and dancing around and the sort of slapstick comedy. But in contrast you had the earlier aspect, which was the soldiers coming back from war, the potential violence, and Christ on the cross looking over it all in a patriarchal society. I think those two elements . . . are strongly in conflict, they sort of tried to bring them out equally. . . . I thought they compromised each other." As this student suggested, the Presley scene was deeply ambivalent. On the one hand, it continued the dangerous performance of the leading (lordly) men, the men who have killed and will "kill" (Hero) again. Each soldier then performed as Elvis Presley, their outstretched arms signified as a dangerous male posture, since it linked them, via the stretched arms of the huge crucified Christ image behind the gate, to both death and the moralistic Christian patriarchy of that other "king." It would be in his name, and according to his naming of sin, that one of these men would later beat Hero to the ground at the wedding altar, set up on the very same spot where they were performing now.

Audience members tended to recognize this Presley performance as either pastiche (in Fredric Jameson's sense of recycling scenes, styles, and elements of plot from other popular cultural narratives as a neutral form of pure mimicry) or as parody, which, while similarly emphasizing simulation and intertextuality, has a subverting and critical project, as the student's comment "Christ on the cross looking over it all in a patriarchal society" suggested. Mary-Anne Gifford's signature, as a theatre director, was (as postmodernists would say) to "flatten out" a range of histories (Shakespeare, 1950s Italy and the United States, Lanza and Presley, the First and Second World Wars, early-twentieth-century vaudeville, 1920s

Hollywood, early sound cinema, etc.). But this playing with different histories was equally part of her critical project to subvert old meanings by repositioning powerful high-cultural discourses.

Whether the spectator positions that her production offered were read as pastiche, parody, or whatever would depend significantly on the cultural competences of actual audiences. For the student quoted above, there was a lack of coherence between the "bubbly slapstick" of the Presley pastiche and the "potential violence" of the soldiers under Christ superintending a patriarchal society. But for a young female theatre teacher I interviewed (see chapter 8) who knew the Shakespeare text well, there was no destruction or "compromise" of narrative perspective within this scene, since, she pointed out, the Presley imitation scene was justified in the Shakespeare text by his mask scene with these same characters, and she could relate this narratively to 1950s patriarchy.

But even for those who did not know the text as this English teacher did, there were also clues toward narrative coherence in the performance of Benedick. In the Presley scene he was part of Gifford's parody of godlike maleness. But the actor Nick Garsden's performance allowed this surface bravado in Benedick to develop as an ambivalence, because the *performed* narrative increasingly embedded his posturing, swaggering repartee in intense, decent, human-male fragility by way of the love that, Gifford said, "changes the air around us and the world we live in and the people we are."

Fooled in act 2 by Hero, Leonato, and Don Pedro into revealing his love for Beatrice, Benedick postured and gyrated his pleasure again, this time to Mario Lanza's "There's a Song in My Heart." But his act 3 exchange with Beatrice — "Come into dinner, there's a double meaning indeed" — was marked performatively as inadequate, because his posturing wink to the audience was undercut by her dismissive scowl. Love him she did, and "cum" she would, when the play had ended. But in this scene it was now the woman, Beatrice, who sought to kill, saying her love for Benedick would depend on him killing Claudio (in revenge for him "killing" Hero). In her powerful presence, this man's wartime mateship quickly gave way to his agreement to challenge Claudio to a duel. Then Beatrice's dance of self-recognizing love, arms outstretched like the crucifixion she scampered around (and to the music of "I'm in Love with You"), was more powerful than his dance.

In Gifford's production the motif of ambivalence and mistaken or unrecognized identity (Hero/Margaret, Claudio/Borachio) moved beyond the plot to become a symbolic theme in the theatrical play between performers and audience. As such, it offered a spectator perspective on male identity itself. The performed relationship of Beatrice and Benedick carried this as a powerful but ultimately liberating and utopian device. In their mutual play, mistaken and multiple identity was theatricalized reflexively (or, as Eversmann would say, was ostended via theatre's multimediality), for example, in the scene where Benedick was "hidden" in full view from Claudio and Don Pedro behind his newspaper, *Arbur*, as he heard of Beatrice's love for him. There were all kinds of ambivalences recognized by audience members in this theatrical playing with identity, varying from Benedick's performative intertextuality, via his Groucho Marx cigar-and-moustache disguise in this scene, to a reference by one theatre teacher in the audience to the arbitrariness of signs and therefore of identity, since in this specialized semiotic reading "arbur/tree" is one of the words that Saussure draws on for his analysis of "reality." Different cognitive-symbolic readings of Benedick drew here on different competences among members of the social audience, but each also drew on the production of Benedick as doubtful and hybrid performer: both the brash soldier and the new age "soft-center" male that many of the female students who were interviewed recognized and liked. By way of this theatrical playing, Benedick was a "soft" shadow of Claudio's violent vulnerability, which some of the female students enjoyed.

The theatrical playing of hybrid, dual (and multiple) identities and the ambiguity of roles within the framework of men returned from killing to the loving world of women's homes connected this play at a number of levels: its economy (since minimal subsidy for the theatre led to eight actors playing eighteen parts, thus playfully multiplying their performative roles), its theatricality (the "hidden" Benedick/Beatrice scenes), its gender politics (Claudio loving/ "killing" Hero), and its mixing of high and popular culture. In this sense the Elvis impersonations were fundamental to the ambiguity of identity (between the energies of killing and love). Popular culture, via Elvis Presley impersonations, gave life to the solipsistic, war-dead/active men of the earlier tableau but was at the same time itself implicated in the patriarchal looks and language of the three "kings."

This was popular culture, after all, in Catholic, postwar Italy. To this extent Gifford did locate her history. But it was also a popular culture whose life was physical movement, dance, emotional fragility, uncertain symbolic identity, and (in the midst of it all) some generous and transparent emotions of mutual love. By means of these fragments, Gifford performed her own rhetorical question about these "cruel times for all of us": "How do you survive the cruel times without abandoning the things that matter . . . things such as personal integrity and a respect and consideration for each other's humanity?"

In this *Much Ado about Nothing*, the energy of "each other's humanity" (as also in Gifford's *A Midsummer Night's Dream*) was carried by popular culture. This was conveyed not only by its music fun (against the men's war-looking solipsistic gaze) and its dance movement (against their static tableau) but also because it offered symbolically divine promises in a world of class and gender power in the face of Christian patriarchy. These promises and hopes were presented as no less real than the more static male powers that they wove their movement and energy around. And this was just *because* they were the communicative vehicles of theatrical play, which expressed the pleasures of multiple, fragmented, and uncertain subjectivity. Hero — bashed to the floor by Claudio and then held, as in a Pietà, by Margaret and Beatrice while attended sympathetically by Benedick — offered the starkest example of the dystopian uncertainty of the woman blissfully in love one second and at risk from these soldier-killers the next.

But Gifford's fragmented *Much Ado* identity was never intended to be Baudrillard's spectatorial schizophrenia, where the endless play of simulacra inevitably prevents the viewer accepting any single perspective. Benedick, Beatrice, the "good male" friar played, as Gifford insisted, by a woman (Sarah Woods), and Margaret (Sarah Woods), who *played* with her sexuality in the scene where she dressed up as Hero for sex with "Claudio," were the utopic, life-affirming side of this world of multiple identity.

Finally, as in Gifford's *A Midsummer Night's Dream*, it was not only gender but also class that engaged in the joy and dignity of popular cultural energy. For example, Dogberry and Verges were represented, via Dick Tracy film noir voiceovers, music, and mise-en-scène, as achieving the kind of intelligence, singularly lacking in their "betters," required to ensure the comedy's happy ending.

Gender, class, risk, popular culture, and a hybridity of characterization worked together to establish very complex spectator positions in Mary-Anne Gifford's *Much Ado about Nothing*. Like her *A Midsummer*

Night's Dream, the production generated a complex process of interaction between stage, spectator positions, and actual social audiences that yoked the personal memories and experiences of young people in the audience to specific aspects of gender, risk, and generational identity represented by the young actors onstage.

Following the Spectator into the Theatre

After watching *Much Ado* I had the opportunity to interview some of the students at various high schools who had watched it. Fortuitously, some of the young people I encountered at Penrith railway station after the evening performance of the play were in one of the focus groups I spoke with at Springwood High School. How did the actual social audiences of young people respond to the complexity of risk positions, identities, and popular cultural intertextualities in the production? To "follow the spectator into the theatre" (Sauter 2000, 27) is, as Sauter emphasizes, to make a commitment to a theatrical communication model of research. But it is more than that. It is also to shift from a film theory notion of spectatorship, which tends to focus on unitary, "inscribed" subject positions, to a television studies approach, emphasizing the multiple subjectivities of "actual audiences."

The following extract with students from Springwood High School relates to the scene where Claudio, believing that Hero has cheated on him, smashes her to the ground at their wedding altar.

I thought that male and female roles were presented really well, it was so fifties you know.

That's why it fits into that era well. I think if you brought it forward much more it just wouldn't work.

It's not *that* distant.

I'd *like* it to be dated, but it's not.

It's still a bit like that where fathers can still be like Hero's.

The relationship between the characters are still the same.

It's nowhere near as severe, but there's still certain element like that you can feel.

A lot of these conservative ideas have been passed down.

Yes, and you still get angry if the person you are with cheats on you.

Our fathers *are* still controlling it all, but there are other factors as well, like . . .

The guy is the stronger in most circumstances because of his physical strength. In a relationship if I, say, cheated on my boyfriend, I could be scared he would hit me.

Because the men are the real dominating characters in it, and it still is [like that].

So then the games they play — like Beatrice and Benedick — those are the games us guys play.

Here the production's spectator position of avoiding historical exactitude while strongly alluding to the 1950s had been adopted quite closely by the students, since the focus group discussion generated a debate between then and now, clearly indicating that some of this audience at least recognized both continuing patriarchal control (through their fathers) and continuing physical risk in their everyday lives (in the context of their boyfriends and sexuality). In their theatrical play with Gifford's production, some teenagers identified with gender and sexual positions both in a directly sensory way (via body size and strength) and symbolically via characters like Hero. A teenage student at St. Mary's High School, Western Sydney, said she felt very close to Hero during the performance: "There's still a kind of taboo on sex. It's changed a lot, but there are still double standards, so you can relate to it because women are not supposed to be sexually promiscuous, and their reputation is stained or whatever, and in that way, especially in high school, there are rumors and all that stuff. So you can relate to it in that way, in that play, though it is still overboard that Hero has to die and all that."

Gender and sexual identification could also relate very directly to the theatrical playing of the performance itself, with the young audience sitting very close to the young, live actors. Teenage girls from St. Mary's High School said:

That guy playing Claudio — he is so hot!

He is gorgeous.

Tall, handsome, muscled.

Vulnerable.

It was like he was a sweet guy.

Theatrical play here is sensory (with the body of the actual actor), artistic (as Claudio plays between a high-cultural Shakespearean role and "Elvis"), and symbolic (since it is the same "vulnerable" Claudio who smashes Hero to the ground and reminds some girls of their boyfriends). It was also quite possible for the teenagers to adopt both a close-up sexual identification with characters and cast in the production and a distanced, reflexive view of this as performance. For example, at Springwood High School, as interviewer I probed students' responses to the Elvis impersonation scenes. Like all the other school students I interviewed, these said they enjoyed the production enormously. But unlike other focus groups I conducted, these particular students had "insider" knowledge of the theatre, since their school had links with the Q Theatre, and some of them had acted in its "alternative" space. So, while their earlier comments in the discussion showed a similar enjoyment of actor-audience live interaction as other interviewees (as at St. Marys), there was also a "professional" point of view as to how "you work an audience." These two parts of the interview immediately indicate the multiple identity aspect of social audiences.

Interviewer:
When I was there, what I noticed was that you guys were pretty quiet until the Elvis scene — and the actors noticed this too because they said so afterward — and then you exploded.

Interviewees:
[Lots of laughter] How to get a crowd warmed up! . . . It was done so well!

You got to the point where suddenly you knew what it was going to be. Like they were *really* going to focus on the period . . . where you thought, "Oh, well, this actually is a really funny show."

It was actually really curious because the whole costume ball — that is such a Shakespearean thing, like I saw it in *Romeo and Juliet* too. I was really interested in how they were going to make that, you know, "Italy, 1950s." And I didn't think *at all* of anything like that [Elvis scene]. It took me completely by surprise, and it was really, really entertaining.

Yes . . . that Elvis thing, like you just wouldn't have expected it in a million years, and you're going "Wow!"

You go to see Shakespeare and you think, "Oh yes Shakespeare, you are really going to have to concentrate and try and work out what they are saying," and then that [Elvis]scene was just so good.

That was what was so good about this one, that it was so easy to understand, and that really made it acceptable to any audience.

Here the insider competence of these theatre students accessed the 1950s theme in a slightly different way from other students interviewed, positioning it in a professional theatre as well as a contemporary risk discourse. In addition, they were displaying a "studying Higher School Certificate" discourse that was common among all the students interviewed.

You could have just *watched* it and not really even worried about the words because all the expression and movement said it all.

Yes, they physicalized the piece, so it wasn't so much the words but . . .

There were a lot of people that didn't go because they were worried that they couldn't follow it, that I talked to. But it was no trouble at all.

As in other theatre audience research conducted with students studying for final school exams (Tulloch 1999), the students made positive comparisons between the physicalization of the texts they were studying and the "dead" words on the page, which they said helped them understand the play much better. At Springwood High, I probed this common response, puzzling over the extra complexity of understanding the Shakespeare text via Elvis Presley!

Interviewer:
I'm interested in this — okay, you put in Elvis, you put in words that don't belong to Shakespeare, but you are saying that somehow that makes it easier to follow, not harder. So why is that then?

Interviewees:
The action.

Because you don't sort of translate quickly in your head when you're thinking "Shakespeare." When it has got sentences like *that long* that you have got to work out, "Are we still in that sentence?" sort of thing.

That's very often in your own mind — like you have got a bit of a hangup [about long speeches in Shakespeare]. But if it somehow relates to something you are familiar with, like Elvis, then it sort of lets you relax a bit, do you know what I mean? And then you get more the gist of it rather than having to concentrate on every word. And because Shakespeare uses examples a lot . . . and then he will have this big description, which is, like, a simile or metaphor for it, it is often very hard to get the general gist of where he is going. Whereas it is much easier to take it all in, like in this one — like putting a lot more contemporary ideas into it, that makes it a lot better for us young audiences.

This extract illustrates very well the value of Sauter's "paradigm shift" from "the historical model of written culture . . . to . . . playing culture" (2000, 79), from the studied Shakespeare of "simile or metaphor" and "*that long*" sentences to the physicalization of actor-audience communication ("the general gist of where he is going"). The playfulness of the Elvis impersonation scenes came as both a surprise and a moment of professional recognition among these theatre students.

Not everyone in the Springwood focus group agreed with this, one student arguing that "all the vaudeville and slapstick wore a bit thin" and seemed inappropriate. One of the advantages of using focus groups as a methodology is that they encourage debate and elaboration of arguments (including the opportunity to observe the interventions of the interviewer), and this happened in this case.

I can see where Lachlan is coming from because I have seen Shakespeare done in periods where it just didn't work . . . like the text just didn't feel right . . . and I know it did wear thin at some points, but I thought in this that overall it very much suited the period.

Yes, you didn't just go, "*Silly!*"

No, that's right, it felt natural, like that whole [Presley] illusion-type thing, and I thought it worked in the 1950s really well.

Interviewer:
What is interesting me, picking up your point about "contemporary," is that this is *not* contemporary for you guys, it is a long time back. It is *my* contemporary . . . I mean, I was just a bit younger than you at that period. This is when rock started for me. Elvis was *my* thing and

all that music then. But this for you is *old* stuff, isn't it, so why did you say it was contemporary?

Interviewees:
But we can relate to it.

It is contemporary to a point, contemporary compared to Shakespeare, anyway.

It's a few more hundred years, you know, onwards [general laughter].

Interviewer:
You know the music, presumably?

Interviewees:
[Multiple "Yes!"]

Interviewer:
But *why* do you know the music, where does it come from?

Interviewees:
Our parents — everybody knows it.

Also the world hasn't changed that much since then, like mass production and everything's come in. We can really relate to a world where there are microwaves and CD players — well, they weren't around then. But microwaves and push-of-a-button and that sort of thing.

Interviewer:
So you mean it's just part of modernity?

Interviewees:
[Multiple "Yes!"]

Interviewer:
And presumably there are radio channels with golden oldies all the time, are there?

Interviewees:
Yes, probably. We don't listen to those [laughter].

And as you grow up . . . that was what your parents were part of, they played the music . . . you are aware of that.

And *everyone* knows Elvis.

Elvis is king!

He's universal.

Interviewer:
There were other people too [in the play's music] like Frank Sinatra, "Love and Marriage."

Interviewees:
Oh yeah. That was everywhere. It's a TV show, Married... with Children — they're using that as its theme.

Interviewer:
Right, then there was Dean Martin, you probably wouldn't know Dean Martin so well, would you?

Interviewees:
No. Not as well.

But I loved all the Italian stuff.

We heard Lachlan speaking earlier about the conflict between the light and bubbly Presley scene and the ideas of the earlier tableau when the soldiers first appeared at the gates. Clearly, he liked the *ideas* ("the potential violence, and Christ on the cross looking over it all in a patriarchal society"), and he also liked the *comedy*, but he felt they didn't quite cohere. What the focus group discussion allowed us to see is how agreement and disagreement are negotiated in the audience as a social group and how interviewers engage in theatrical play. One girl felt strongly enough about Lachlan's point to cut off the point the interviewer was about to make about Elvis and "the contemporary" (which didn't stop him for long, however!). Yet she also agreed with Lachlan that there was some problem in the performance between these different modes of address. Lachlan in turn also adapted his position (he had been a bit hesitant about making his criticism in the first place), with his agreement that it suited the period. ("You didn't just go, '*Silly!*'")

On the one hand, the students' very local and timely need to understand Shakespeare for their HSC exams was a clear factor in their pleasure at recognizing the "gist" of Shakespeare's ("long") language through theatrical devices like the Elvis scene. On the other hand, through my question about "the contemporary," a strong globalizing sense appeared of various popular culture industries' own marketing reflexivity. So although the students were quick to reject my suggested channel of influence (golden oldie radio channels), they were closer to Frank Sinatra than to Dean Martin via recent television theme music. Some "kings" *are* universal, simply because they are constructed as ubiquitous, reappearing in one mediatized form after another.

Conclusion

As Susan Bennett has said, "The past, in the present, has become a powerful trading economy on a global scale," and in this international marketing economy of the past, Shakespeare's "face and voice are literally everywhere" (1996, 15, 36). In her own valuable book *Performing Nostalgia: Shifting Shakespeare and the Contemporary Past*, Bennett follows Jonathan Dollimore in seeking out the "creative vandalism" (1996, 1) that takes place around Shakespeare. That is, she focuses on the ways in which *new* texts that work off and challenge the canonical Shakespearean text may produce "transgressive knowledge" (Bennett 1996, 12). As Bennett says herself, though, we do need to go beyond the Left-critical academic institution to visit other places "to witness strategies of performing the past which demand of their actors as well as their reading/viewing publics an engagement which denies the inevitability of containment" (1996, 13). It is certainly not among Shakespeare academics alone that "the positionalities of gender, class, race, and sexuality have re-entered the arena in ways that traditional humanist interpretation and collective nostalgia would seek to inhibit" (Bennett 1996, 28).

Outside the Q Theatre, immediately after the performance of *A Midsummer Night's Dream*, some teenage girls spoke to me of the emotional closeness that the theatre space allowed them with the female performers, especially in the moment between Hippolyta and Hermia in act 1 and the love/violence scenes of the young male and female actors in the woods. The relationship of proxemic theatrical intimacy that yoked together play narrative and personal memory was very important here. Many of these students were the children of local Western Suburbs parents who watched little or no theatre. Their brothers, they said, tended to be into cars, and they themselves watched a lot of television. But these were not just the "fresh" and "challenging" Penrith audiences that the actors looked for, nor were they just the "inscribed" spectators crafted by Gifford's production. It was, in fact, the "freshness" *for them* of theatrical play with actors so close up on stage — live actors who dressed and undressed before them as they performed their different roles — that these teenage girls found so different from television and so pleasurable and that they negotiated in terms of both the risks and pleasures of their everyday lives. Then, too, these were school students studying Shakespeare (many of the students emphasized their pleasure in the language as spoken by *these* actors). And then again, several others, both in focus group discussion and on questionnaire forms, spoke of hearing Shakespeare's language "for the first time" through this process of actor-audience participation. The relationship for them here of school reading formation, gendered personal memories and emotions, domestic social contexts, cognitive gaps in relation to secondary school texts and intertexts, and the proxemics of audience-actor and audience-audience playful interaction were all part of the performance's local context and thus the necessary fabric of our theatre spectator and social audience analysis.

Part Two

Production /
Audience Studies

3

IMAGINING AUDIENCES
THE EYRE/GRIFFITHS
PRODUCTIONS OF
THE CHERRY ORCHARD

*It seems to me that the word "freedom" has now been
unleashed in this text [The Cherry Orchard], and it
resonates throughout the play. . . . The heart of [act 2]
for me is the arrival of the stranger. . . . Nobody from
that underclass has ever appeared . . . in Chekhov's
kind of drama. . . . Released by the French Revolution a
hundred years previously and still wandering, still
looking for social justice, equality, fraternity. And,
clearly, failing to find it here. —Trevor Griffiths,
lecture, University of Birmingham, 1989*

Following Annette Kuhn's understanding of both spectators
and social audiences as discursive constructs, with "certain discourses
possessing greater constitutive authority as specific moments than others" (1987, 347), an important advantage of a production analysis is that
it allows a focus on the multimedial "authorship" of theatre and television professionals as they attempt to situate spectators and to approach
social audiences. Further, because television and theatre spectatorship
tend to be constituted in different ways, comparison of the same play produced by the same professional team in these different media will give us
access to the "specific instances or conjunctures" of the "contradictions,
oppositional readings and varying degrees of discursive authority" (Kuhn
1987, 347) in these different discursive formations.

In 1977 Trevor Griffiths, with a new translation by Helen Rappaport,
wrote a "new version" of Chekhov's *The Cherry Orchard*. In the introduction to the play script, he focused critically on the spectator positions
that half a century of English-speaking productions of the play had prepared. He argued that dominant critical interpretations had stripped the
play of so much of its class content that "the play's specific historicity
and precise sociological imagination has been bleached of all meanings

beyond those required to convey the necessary 'natural' sense that the fine will always be undermined by the crude and that the 'human condition' can for all essential purposes be equated with the 'plight of the middle classes'" (1977, v). Griffiths worked closely with director Richard Eyre and his actors for the 1987 production of *The Cherry Orchard* at Nottingham Playhouse and then again with Eyre for the BBC1 television version of 1981.

With Tom Burvill I conducted long interviews with Griffiths, Eyre, actors, and other professional and technical staff from the two productions of *The Cherry Orchard* as well as audience interviews with students of Chekhov in Australia, Britain, and the United States. The purpose of this research was to examine the ways in which "audiencing" (i.e., the composite of positioning spectators and imagining social audiences) is conducted as an integral but sometimes contradictory aspect of production and how university students' reading formations operated as a key aspect of their role as social audiences.

If we examine the two productions of *The Cherry Orchard* by Eyre and Griffiths first in terms of Sauter's four theatrical event categories, it is clear that these productions were part of a career-long attempt by Griffiths to reconfigure theatre and television spectator positions.

Cultural Context

Griffiths's process of reflexive and generic engagement with major macroideological systems of twentieth-century politics was central in this "new version" of the play. His earlier television plays and series (*Occupations, All Good Men, Bill Brand,* and *Sons and Lovers*) had cut an historical swathe from Leninism via Italian Fascism (and Gramsci) through British parliamentary Left politics to the class embedding of "art television" (which was critiqued in his TV versions of *Sons and Lovers* and *The Cherry Orchard*). For Griffiths, throughout his television career and especially in his *The Cherry Orchard,* postindustrial risk was centrally defined in terms of twentieth-century modernity's grand narratives of capitalism, socialism, Fascism, and cultural materialism.

Contextual Theatricality

The television version of *The Cherry Orchard* reworked, in the cultural-political context of British Thatcherism, the Brechtian techniques that Griffiths and Eyre had employed in their earlier (1977) production of the play at Nottingham Playhouse. For the BBC production they had to engage with the dominant naturalism of peak-time British television. In particular, Griffiths argued that while the "country house" acts 2, 3, and 4 were appropriately naturalistic in the TV version, "the opening of the second act [should be] the least naturalistic of anything in Chekhov. . . . It's like expressionism, the interior being turned outside, the subtext bursting through the text and becoming the text and the text getting washed away." Griffiths's preference, achieved on the Nottingham stage, was to "frame the play as a naturalist play with act 1, but act 2 [should] burst out of that for two or three pages, and then when it seems to recover its naturalist impulse, I would keep elements of that first three pages going through it. The vagrant [for instance] is an *incredible* disjuncture" (Griffiths, personal interview, July 1993). But just how to achieve this "incredible disjuncture" within the organizational and formal constraints of BBC television became a problem, given the spectator positions established by television naturalism (Tulloch 1990, chap. 6).

Theatrical Playing

Symptomatically, Griffiths encouraged his actors to play between Chekhov's "time then" (1903) and Thatcher's "time now" (1983), establishing a strong class subtext working beneath what he saw as the generally vacuous (and middle-class-based) "symbolic" interpretation of the play in the West (including television). Even while Griffiths admired and drew intertextually from Raymond Williams's interpretation of *The Cherry Orchard* (especially Williams's pinpointing of act 2 as among Chekhov's most important theatrical writing), he also criticized Williams's analysis of Chekhov for its "inert symbolism." In Griffiths's reading the famous "breaking string," together with Firs's act 2 talk about declining "the Freedom," were *specifically historical and class-based* symbols, both of opportunity and of "radical disjuncture." As such, they were irredeemably linked to the arrival immediately afterward of the vagrant and also to Trofimov's words at the end of the act (as written in Griffiths's new version) about serfs hanging from the cherry trees.

For Griffiths, Firs's words about "the Freedom" in act 2 had "unleashed" that term, and it was carried as a powerful, explosive subtext throughout the act. With the arrival of the vagrant, "released by the French Revolution a hundred years previously and still wandering, still looking for social justice, equality, fraternity" but dressed as a First World War soldier and potent harbinger of the coming Russian Revolution, Griffiths felt he had opened up a "black hole" (as he believes Chekhov did also) for his audiences:

In an odd way, by putting [the vagrant] into the set and presenting that person with such extraordinary menace . . . [Chekhov] menaces and metamorphises at one and the same time the property loss [of the play]. . . . [He] destabilises any notion [Chekhov's contemporary Russian] audience might have had of a settled world, *their* settled world. Even if you see it satirically and critically and comically, as Chekhov invites us to do, I think this moment really says there is a great unavoidable black hole underneath our world, and very soon we will disappear into it and become a pellet of energy for a new world. (Griffiths, lecture, University of Birmingham, 1989)

We should notice in this comment from Griffiths the play between the Russian spectator in 1903 and the 1981 audience (a hole underneath our world). Time then / time now was also particularly crucial for Griffiths's understanding of the playing of Lopakhin as the major agent of change. The relationship between Madame Ranevskaya (Judi Dench) and Lopakhin (Bill Paterson), particularly in act 2, where Dench performed an extraordinarily distanced emotional seduction of Lopakhin and yet also expressed deeply the desperately reactive role of a woman of her class within a patriarchal society, is central to the theatrical interplaying of sensory, artistic, and symbolic actor-audience levels within the television version of the play.

Playing Culture

At Nottingham Playhouse Griffiths and Eyre forged a group of players who worked closely and sympathetically with them. Mick Ford, who played Trofimov at Nottingham, spoke about how the presence of Griffiths at rehearsals clarified the role for him as an actor.

The most important thing to me of the production . . . was that . . . the eternal student was an eternal student . . . because he was not *allowed* to go on; that is, he was being failed because of [political] activities or interests that he had. That to me made a big difference just in terms of how you come on and how you do it. . . . So in Trofimov's case, that idea that he was being held back and then being left behind slightly as the world was changing was important. He was someone who I felt would be, by the time of the Revolution, . . . sunk and no longer needed, like all of them in that place outside of Lopakhin. . . . Those are the moments that allow you as an actor to have a bit of weight. And that's what I remember of the production. . . . People knew what they were doing. (Personal interview, June 1994)

Skills and style in what Willmar Sauter calls a performer/audience's pleasurable play were honed in rehearsals through a very close interaction of writer and actors. Bill Paterson, who played Lopakhin in the 1981 television production, made a similar point to Mick Ford.

> Trevor bit the bullet here by translating it, "I'm still a student. If the authorities have their way I suspect I'll always be one." . . . That was the first time probably that it had been translated at all in that way. . . . The later scene between Lopakhin and Trofimov then becomes a great scene because they both *know* that. . . . They both feel they have the clue to the new society. Lopakhin's [clue] is the one of the entrepreneur, leading people forward by looking after themselves by earning money and making profit and moving on, and that would therefore be to the good of all in the end. And Trofimov's is having that Socialist view that you have to attend to the needs of the weakest. (Personal interview, June 1994)

From Griffiths, Paterson also understood the time then / time now context of his performance, not as the "brash real estate agent impervious to beauty" so typical in Western performances but, in part at least, the "new Tory" of the 1980s who, like Thatcher, was taking the broom to the rather effete "wets" of the landed Conservative Party.

But BBC Television was not the Nottingham Playhouse, and the "comradely" ensemble at Nottingham was broken up to introduce a bevy of leading stars thought to be required by television events like BBC's *Play of the Month*. Trevor Griffiths and to some extent Bill Paterson himself spoke of the "aura" associated with a star like Dame Judi Dench, who played Madame Ranevskaya in the television version. For Griffiths, this tended to refocus the play on the landowners rather than the "change agents" Trofimov and Lopakhin whom he had emphasized in his writing.

Within this framework of shifting between theatrical and television events, in a larger analysis one could examine the relationship between diverse but institutionalized discourses, intertexts, and spectator positions established within and between these two productions of *The Cherry Orchard*. In the space available here it is important to mention a few of the "discourses possessing greater constitutive authority as specific moments than others" (Kuhn 1987, 347) in the television production. These included Griffiths's "rediscovery" of Chekhov's more radical short stories as a narrative subtext for *The Cherry Orchard* in order to subvert Raymond Williams's own interpretation of a "rather static symbolism";

producer Richard Eyre's appropriation of John Berger's TV series *Ways of Seeing* for the mise-en-scène in act 2 of *The Cherry Orchard*, in particular, Berger's "landownership" reading of Gainsborough's *Mr. and Mrs. Andrews*, which was used as a visual intertext for the bench scene of Ranevskaya and Gayev listening to Lopakhin's scheme for selling the house and orchard; set designer Sue Spence's importation of a plethora of ferns and grasses in act 2 as an (unintended) naturalistic subversion of Griffiths's own "alienation" concept (i.e., replacing the stark, freestanding, two-dimensional single "Godot" tree of the Nottingham Playhouse production with "all that depth and space" of the TV version); the naturalistic intention of audio director Richard Partridge in spreading the stage with pebbles and shale for the "outdoors" act 2, which produced difficulties for audiences to hear actors' voices at times, not least Charlotta's Brechtian "Who am I? Where do I come from?" parting speech, which was muffled almost completely in the on-air broadcast of the play.

For Griffiths, the risks of modernity should have been visualized at the beginning of his "pivotal" act 2, with Charlotta and the servants spread out facing the audience. Griffiths's intended spectator position was to recognize a modernity in which Charlotta (among the other servants) is "a character edging towards Kafka, edging towards statelessness, edging towards 'Who am I? How can I define an identity, a self-identity, without a state, without values, without history?'" (Griffiths, lecture, University of Birmingham, 1990). Consequently, her parting lines in act 2 were important in Griffiths's subtext but went unheard by most audience members interviewed.

The BBC1 *The Cherry Orchard* was intended as part of a series of television events deeply concerned with Griffiths's "enlightenment project" of progress, egalitarianism, citizenship, and modernity that was "launched two hundred years before by the French Revolution" but truncated and reversed in the days of Thatcher. One week following the screening of *The Cherry Orchard*, BBC1 showed Griffiths's *Country* in the same *Play for Today* slot, originally conceived as the first of a six-part series of "Tory Stories" examining the political and economic scandals and achievements of a nouveau-riche brewing family as new technologies and economic rationalism developed from the 1940s to the 1980s of Thatcher. "Modernity" had also been prefigured by Griffiths's poster for the Nottingham Playhouse production of *The Cherry Orchard* (a cherry tree that is also "flowering" as a telegraph pole), and this had been embodied by Griffiths in the underclass characters of act 2, whom he "imaged" as "souls stretched out on a telephone wire" and with "four people lined up across a stage . . . not interacting, but simply talking straight out to the audience" (Griffiths, lectures, University of Birmingham, 1992, 1990). This imaging of the servant class was intended to reconfigure in a particular (formal-expressionist and technological) context Raymond Williams's notion of Chekhov's Russian characters, who are full of the need for social change but are unable to articulate it either to themselves or to the audience.

But the poster, the John Berger visual reference, and the servants "not interacting" were only the intended *ground* for this pivotal act 2. In the reality of television production, different discourses, intertexts, and spectator positions intervened. The 1981 Eyre/Griffiths *The Cherry Orchard* was notable not only for its "ideas" (from Griffiths). Among key production workers it was also seen as something of a technological breakthrough for TV drama under Eyre's guiding hand. Virtually every television professional interviewed who worked on *The Cherry Orchard* regarded it as one of the pinnacle productions of his or her career. Partly this was a matter of Eyre's meticulous preparation and control, which at the same time left space open for individual innovation. As cameraman Geoff Feld put it, "Richard . . . was determined to try and make it different. Also there were the very early meetings with the lighting man and [sound man] Richard Partridge about the . . . possibilities of shooting. Being at rehearsals much more than I'd ever been . . . I had a chance to make a real input — [with] all the things over the years that you feel as a cameraman but [for which previously] there is no method available" (personal interview, July 1993).

The space for technical innovation that Eyre provided was matched, in Feld's view, by the greater openness of the BBC at that time.

One of the great strengths of television in the sixties and seventies was that lots of writers . . . learned their craft because it wasn't a million, two million pounds every time you made something. . . . And so you had the chance to actually try things. . . . People could afford to fail because we had a cheap way of making programs. But no one takes chances anymore. . . . Now the international market is so important to the BBC. Everything has to have a potential sale value. So things which would have been made in the sixties and seventies would no longer be made. . . . The BBC says it still retains editorial control, but in a way it doesn't, because the things it selects are predetermined by their acceptability to coproducers. . . . When something comes in from a writer, the first question is, Will it attract coproduction money? So that immediately changes the potential of your production. . . . Studio drama is almost a thing of the past. (Personal interview, July 1993)

With this degree of both nostalgic memory and real investment in technological innovation (and in the four-wall sets made available by the new lightweight cameras), it is not surprising that Feld again and again emphasized that it was acts 1 and 4 (with their rostrum set) and not act 2 that were "at that time something quite different for studio drama." These were the most naturalistic of the four acts, and, as Feld explains, the technological and visual innovation of the new cameras allowed an ever more complete naturalism.

Inevitably, in multicamera your close-up shots are done on long lenses, telephoto lenses, so . . . you tend to crush perspective quite a lot. . . . But once you've got single camera, the camera can be exactly where you want it every time. And the lighting can be very particular. Do you remember the most marvelous moment in the first act when they open up the curtains? . . . The whole of acts 1 and 4 were shot single camera. So we did it shot by shot. . . . There is a visual unity in terms of the lens angles we used. This was unlike a normal multicamera thing . . . where getting the shot requires using different focal length lenses, which actually alters the visual texture. . . . This one was very particular. (Personal interview, July 1993)

The "wonderful moment" when they open the curtains in act 1 related directly to the "cube of light" signature of lighting director Howard King: "I knew the transition I wanted [from the immediately preceding scene]. I wanted the magic of when he puts the blinds up [in act 1] — that magic from one lighting state to another. And in order to get from one state to another, you actually had to have something rather subtle to go before it, so that when the sunlight came through there was this vast difference. . . . Before this you had this early dawn — dawn's a very tricky thing to do on television. . . . It's a very subtle thing. There's light, but there's no light. . . . There's no great direction to it at all" (personal interview, July 1993).

Looking for the appropriate indirect lighting concept, King drew on a Dutch painting by "van Gogh's teacher," Jozef Israëls (1824–1911), to establish what he called the unfocused "cube of light" effect of acts 1 and 4. This painting, which King had seen in Amsterdam, gave him the "sense of being in a cube of light — in other words, light all around you." What particularly impressed King about Israëls's style "was the fact that the floor . . .

was right. So often ... when you look at television lighting ... people do not pay attention to the horizontal surfaces. We are all obsessed with vertical surfaces, in other words, faces and things like that, but not with the horizontal surfaces, like tops of tables, tops of settees ... and [the] floor. ... [In *The Cherry Orchard*] we have light coming down ... and it all accumulates on the floor eventually, with a multiplicity of shadows" (personal interview, July 1993).

As designed by set designer Sue Spence and Eyre, the "clean, spare, and unfussy" sets for acts 1 and 4 were very light *and* showed a lot of empty horizontal surfaces. Therefore, Eyre's concept of set design, King's "bounced" lighting innovation, and a painting in Amsterdam came together to provide the cube of light in which, in the last scene of the play, Firs dies.

This servant's death is the last link in Griffiths's subtextual narrative, which, from its focal point in act 2, "unleashes freedom throughout the play." Here, at the very end of the play, Griffiths has Firs speak in a semi-consciously reflexive way about the wrong choices he has made. Yet an important question is the extent to which King's cube of light concept and Eyre's empty white set sentimentalized and individualized Firs for spectators rather than positioning him subtextually in class terms with the vagrant and Trofimov's peasants "hanging from the cherry trees." Certainly, the van Gogh drawing of an isolated old man, sitting in a chair, head in hands against a white background (of which King said the final scene as shot reminded him) is a sad, individualized portrait of age.

Jozef Israëls, as an important member of The Hague school, was part of the naturalist movement in European nineteenth-century painting, which specialized in genre subjects of peasant life, and therefore was not inappropriate to Griffiths's own interest in Chekhov's peasant short stories. But recent interpretations of Israëls's paintings of the rural poor — "realistic and compassionate" (*Encyclopaedia Britannica* 1973, 463), "subtle, low-keyed" studies of "loneliness, wretchedness and moments of private despair" (*New International Illustrated Encyclopedia of Art* 1981, 12:2368–69), "lyrical but faithful representation of . . . locality . . . advocating a patient acceptance of life's hardships" (*The Dictionary of Painting and Sculpture: Art and Artists* 1979, 92, 93), and the "principal actors ... bowed down under the cares of everyday life or . . . the humble rooms in which they are condemned to live" (Loos and Jansen 1995, 50) — also evoke for the viewer the canonical "fatalistic" Chekhov that Griffiths was challenging.

In both student audience surveys, which I will examine later, and in the focus group discussions I tried to examine to what extent this kind of lighting worked for or against Griffiths's spectator intention in the final "death" scene of Firs sitting alone on his chair. For Griffiths, Firs achieves some kind of reflexivity in this scene, seeing himself as "an erasure, a non-event" for the first time. But, as with the rest of Griffiths's interpretation of the play, it is supposedly a moment of recognition of the farce of life in a *defined* society, which is prepared for by the subtextual narrative connections of earlier acts, particularly act 2.

So to what extent did King's cube of light detract from the materialist context that Griffiths called for? In Griffiths's Chekhov the social definition of class exploitation was not simply in the contrast between a whimsically feckless, childlike gentry and their old dignified servant. It should also be recognized by the social audience, if not completely by Firs, as a political act that signals that oppression is not "dignified" but brutal and degrading. To what extent did the production encourage instead spectator positions adopting sad/melancholic and fatalistic readings of the text? Alternatively, would actual audiences read it in Raymond Williams's sense of a late-nineteenth-century Russian "structure of feeling"? In Williams's reading, "to get even the strength to see what is wrong, to sit up talking to try to get it clear," whether one is talking only to oneself or to others, is, in this context of a nonconnecting, inarticulate community, "heroism of a kind, of an ambivalent kind" (1968, 108, 8).

What can be said, prior to visiting the audience study (chapter 4), is that, at the production level, lighting, sound, and camera directors were in complete harmony as to the value of "greater realism" in acts 1 and 4. For example, sound director Richard Partridge saw acts 1 and 4 as innovative and special: "It sounded like a real room, with all the proper floors and all the walls around you; so it sounded much more like being on location in a real set" (personal interview, July 1993).

Greater naturalism, organic unity, consistent depth of field, historical accuracy in set design, the "real" sound of real floorboards: acts 1 and 4 (which were shot first) were the pinnacle of *The Cherry Orchard*'s achievement in the eyes of its technical producers. In contrast, act 2, shot last in some "panic" and "under tremendous time pressure" (Howard King, personal interview, 1993), with camera decisions like the use of nylon stockings over the lens decided "in a real hurry," was, in King's view, "criminal" in parts. Feld agreed: "I always felt Richard [Eyre] was least happy doing that one. I had the most problems shooting it. And it is somehow very different [from] the other three acts" (personal interview, July 1993).

Different from the other three acts was, of course, how Trevor Griffiths intended it to be. But, unlike acts 1 and 4, the technical professionals seemed to have had no confident concept for act 2, other than "it was very stylised . . . almost unreal. . . . It didn't look like an outside at all . . . dream-like" (Feld, personal interview, 1993). Sound director Richard Partridge called act 2 a "performance against the naturalism" (personal interview, July 1993), and set designer Sue Spence described it as "terribly difficult to do . . . dry, rather arid" (personal interview, July 1993).

If any concept did guide the professional transcoding of act 2 stylistically, it was Eyre's dislike of conventional television. As Feld described it, this was a major reason for the "soft" look of act 2: "One of the things about the electronic image is this sharpness and edge . . . and Richard had an abhorrence of that. And so [act 2] started off . . . as a way to lose that very gritty image. . . . When we got to the studio there was some experiment with how soft we wanted to make the image. . . . I remember discussions with Richard early on about the nature of the electronic image . . . and ways — filters, net, all sorts of things — to soften this edge" (personal interview, July 1993).

Other technical problems then exacerbated the problem, as Richard Partridge described: "Now Howard had lit the set almost entirely with bounced light . . . off the walls. And so with every new setup he'd be moving his lights around, bouncing off the wall that we were looking at a moment ago. The result was that the wall tended to be brighter than the faces. Because the camera was nice and sharp on all the bright bits and less sharp on all the darker bits due to a design feature in the camera, this meant that it always looked as if the cameraman had focused on the background instead of the faces" (personal interview, July 1993).

Add to these problems what Howard King called the "criminal" softening and diffusion of the image with stockings in act 2, and it is unsurprising that there was "a strong reaction against it . . . from the engineering side of the BBC" (Feld, personal interview, 1993). "They said that the image wasn't good enough. They said it's all right when you're in a good reception area. But you had to remember that so many millions of people don't have good reception of the BBC, so it was not the right sort of image." And it was not the "right" sort of image because, as Kuhn has noted, "television spectatorship is . . . likely to be characterised by distraction and diversion" (1987, 343) in the discourses and values of practice of television's technical producers.

The very soft quality of *The Cherry Orchard* image, particularly in act 2, did make our audience research among students more problematical than it might have been. Many said they were distracted by the poor quality of the videotape (taken directly off-air), and some of the negative reaction that I describe later (as among theatre students at Birmingham University) was partly attributable to this: "To be honest . . . it was hard to watch, hear etc. . . . From this production I couldn't pay enough attention to it to see any interpretative reasoning beyond the story. I am a fan of Chekhov, but I still couldn't pay attention. I'm sorry." But more to the point of this chapter, a whole range of aesthetic, technical, professional, and ideological values of practice were at work here, making act 2 indeed the most "alienated" of the play, though not in quite the way that Trevor Griffiths intended. Camera "impressionism" and set naturalism were likely to encourage very different (and perhaps more distracted) spectator positions than the performance that Eyre and Griffiths had produced at Nottingham Playhouse.

How audiences read this "impressionist" style may also depend in part on their interpretation of impressionism itself as social audiences. Impressionism, as feminist art historian Norma Broude (1991) points out, according to its dominant reading formations, has primarily been read in relation to positivism and male-dominated science (and hence as naturalistic in the sense rejected by Griffiths). Alternatively, impressionism has been regarded by innovators in business and industry (who began buying the paintings at the time Chekhov was writing) as fluid, unstable, and untraditional, thus reflecting their own male entrepreneurial "modernist initiative" and "originality" (Broude 1991, 171). This reading of impressionism equates with a dominant traditional reading of the "entrepreneurial" Lopakhin. Third, there is the feminist reading of impressionist landscape painters that "nature cannot be dominated or possessed" (Broude 1991, 177), which would support the Eyre/Griffiths "landscape as property" critique of *The Cherry Orchard* gentry. To go further with this, we need to turn to social audiences and actual readings.

How different audiences, in fact, did read either the act 4 conjuncture of audiovisual (gestural and lighting) signs that closed the television version of *The Cherry Orchard* in a cube of light or the "alienating" strategies of act 2 is for this and the following chapter to examine. To begin with, we need to examine the relationship between Williams's cultural materialist reading formation (to the extent that it is imaged and embodied in the Eyre/Griffiths text) and the variety of potential reading positions that the university students occupied, including the reading formations to which they had been exposed in school and university. The concluding discussion of this chapter begins to bring together "audiencing" in production with social audiences and their reading formations.

Student Audiences

The BBC television production of *The Cherry Orchard* represented a number of different modernities in terms of differently encoded values of various production practices. University students studying Chekhov in Britain, Australia, and the United States were showed the production, and their responses were analyzed, using qualitative and quantitative methods, to explore the extent to which Griffiths's (or others') modernity was also *their* modernity. Alternatively, to what extent did students follow their teachers (as a reading formation) in finding a different Chekhov of modernism? Elsewhere (Tulloch 2000b), brief qualitative case studies of a variety of university student responses in the United States, Britain, and Australia have been offered to examine liberal humanist, feminist, socialist, and other student readings of Griffiths's "alienating" act 2 of *The Cherry Orchard*. The emphasis of the remainder of this and the next chapter will be on combining qualitative with quantitative methods in approaching this audience more systematically and reflexively.

The postscreening survey and focus group questions that we asked our student respondents were never conceived as "neutral" but, rather, were directly related to *The Cherry Orchard* production team's somewhat contradictory notions of spectator positions. For example, Griffiths had spoken about particular differences between the Nottingham Playhouse and BBC productions as key determinants of his different levels of satisfaction between the two productions. In act 4 "Lopakhin begins to talk about the poppy fields in bloom. Now, there's two things going on here. He talks about the poppy field and he talks about how much it's worth. And in my version of that play both things have got to be very strong; both the natural, organic dimension of a poppy field and the accountancy. Dave Hill got that on the stage, though he leaned toward the natural dimension of the poppy field. Bill never got anywhere near that. He always had a calculator in his pocket. He was clicking up what it was worth" (Griffiths, personal interview, July 1993).

It is important to emphasize here that these differences between Hill's and Paterson's performances of Lopakhin were a matter of historical moment more than individual acting skills and style. In fact, Hill and Paterson both saw Lopakhin and Trofimov similarly, as the two "change agents" in the play. The *difference* between Hill's and Paterson's performances of the poppy field scene was fundamentally related to the specific decade of each production. For Paterson in the BBC production, Lopakhin represented a current intraconservative mobility in the Thatcherite Britain of the 1980s:

> We did it very much *of the time*: early 1980s . . . when the whole question of the upwardly mobile was the burning political question of the day. . . . The new nouveau riche were beginning to take over [during] the Thatcher period, where you had the entrepreneurial class rising above the landed aristocracy, the old Tory class. . . . We talked a lot about that in rehearsal . . . and I think it made it work very well, because you see Lopakhin *moving* from trying to say to them, "Look, you guys, unless you get your act together you're going to lose your cherry orchard" . . . to saying "It's guys like me who see the opportunities . . . you know, small holiday homes for the bourgeoisie, that's where I see the future. . . . The young or the striving individual like me will make the lot of life better for the others." . . . That was very much in the air, so it had very strong social connections here [at the time we made it], and . . . I think Lopakhin probably made more sense at that time [in the 1980s] than he'd done for a couple of decades. That was a great help in acting. (Personal interview, July 1993)

In contrast, Hill's Lopakhin was performed in 1977 in the dying years of what he described as a "selling out" Labour government, "when there was no suspicion in anybody's head that around the corner Thatcherism was about to descend upon us." Instead, Hill had three historical memories of his own for Lopakhin: that of certain enlightened Victorian mill owners who built a model village for their workers but still wanted to live in "the big house" themselves; his own father's belief that, as a worker in the cotton trade, "there would be a decent life for everybody"; and, finally, Gorky's *My Childhood*, which gave him references for the Russian background of the brutalizing and beating of the young Lopakhin.

These differences in discursive positioning of the part between Hill and Paterson helped determine the two actors' interpretations of the poppy field reference. For Paterson, though he saw (and played) the complexity of Lopakhin, the 1980s entrepreneur with a philosophy of enlightened individualism was definitely uppermost in that scene:

I played it with a sense of . . . him getting embarrassed . . . "That's something to behold, I can tell you, the poppy field in bloom." And it was as though it was a sign of weakness because maybe the cherry orchard would have been nice as well. But, "Well, anyway . . . I made the forty thousand, and you're welcome to some of it" — the fact that he does love that, that he has an attraction for beauty — but on the other hand, the beauty is the poppies he planted, which are making money. . . . Poppy seeds or opium . . . could have come from these. . . . So he may be thinking of it in the same way as a farmer looks at rape-seed oil in Britain today, these . . . yellow fields we have just now, which are all part of the EEC money. . . . They're dazzling, and they pop up everywhere. And you can see more money being poured into them. (Personal interview, July 1993)

Hill, in contrast, had recently been to Eastern Europe and seen its "very serious dream" of "getting away and being at one with yourself" by growing things "in small country dachas which were scarcely bigger than allotments." He felt, as a result, that he now understood better Lopakhin's plan of subdividing the cherry orchard estate:

Those [poppy field] lines were a wonderful combination of beauty, almost like it was a painting. But also that feeling of *getting your hands dirty* at the same time, which I think is some sort of key to unlocking the man — that he has the ability to actually get down and dig . . . and plant the field himself. He is somebody who has worked and respects the dignity of labour and comes absolutely from the tradition that you get it by doing it yourself and not by employing somebody else to do it for you. That the beauty of what you gain from life is enhanced by the fact that that's what *you've* done, and the fact that you are making money from it is not incidental, but there's more to it than making money. It's *all right* to take money because . . . money as a form of energy has got to be kept moving round. (Hill, personal interview, July 1993)

This was Hill's source for Lopakhin's "natural, organic" relationship with the poppy field that Griffiths liked, while Thatcher's new conservatives were the source of Paterson's entrepreneur "with a calculator in his pocket."

As researchers we thus approached the students already designing questions with a strong sense of differences in performance embedded in perceptions of the two formally different *The Cherry Orchard* events of theatre and television. The screening of the Eyre/Griffiths *The Cherry*

Orchard to students on three different continents was a further series of "events" under the rubric "research." So although, unusually in this book, the main audience focus of this chapter is quantitative, it is important to be reflexive: how to engage with both the important matter of generalizability (i.e., the issue of convincing the reader that this interpretation had wide acceptance) and at the same time be reflexive about the way in which, as researchers, we set up this event. Methodology (not separated from theory) needs to be a central focus.

Some Quantitative Approaches: Production Intentions

To leave behind for the moment a situated and/or ethnographic focus is not to abandon the thrust of the book in a processual or audiencing direction. The quantitative data will be related quite directly both to the television production team's somewhat varied intentions in constructing spectator positions and to a particular audience group (university students studying Chekhov) in terms of their earlier regimes of reading. There was, arguably, some symmetry in restoring to an academic audience community a television production that was, in the first instance, so influenced by the academic reading formation of Raymond Williams.

Survey Method

Over two hundred students of Russian and drama were surveyed at seventeen universities in Britain, Australia, and the United States. Theatre/drama (and theatre/English) courses were visited at the Australian National University, Canberra (Australia), Birmingham University (UK), Bristol University (UK), Cambridge University (UK), Charles Sturt University (Australia), Florida State University (USA), Hull University (UK), Loughborough University (UK), Macquarie University (Australia), Middlesex University (UK), and Royal Holloway College, University of London (UK). Russian studies / literature courses were visited at Columbia University (USA), Durham University (UK), Harvard University (USA), University of New Hampshire (USA), Sussex University (UK), and the University of Wales at Bangor (UK). In terms of numbers, 61.5 percent of the students were female, 38.5 percent were male, 69.5 percent were studying drama/theatre (and English), and 30.5 percent were studying Russian.

Students were given two questionnaires. A prescreening questionnaire examined students' familiarity with Chekhov's plays and short stories and their general idea of Chekhov prior to studying him. It included questions assessing their overall view of Chekhov on a seven-point semantic differential scale according to thirteen conventional binaries applied to Chekhov in the academic literature we had reviewed (tragic/comic; action/inaction; glad at social change / sad at social change; pessimistic/optimistic; melancholy mood / joyful mood; nonpolitical/political; apathy/hope; art for art's sake / art with a message; etc.). It asked which books and articles they had read on Chekhov (and which in particular they found most useful); whether they were familiar with *The Cherry Orchard*; whether they had seen the Eyre/Griffiths TV production; and whether they were impressed with a range of theoretical and other approaches to textual or performance study.

Students then attended a screening of the Eyre/Griffiths *The Cherry Orchard*, immediately followed by a postscreening questionnaire. This contained an open question that asked what the Eyre/Griffiths *The Cherry Orchard* was about; questions assessing whether they liked the way the various characters in the production were performed; multiple choice and open-ended questions about a character whom Griffiths saw as especially important (the vagrant); semantic differential questions (based on binaries indicated to us by the production team) and open-ended questions relating to writing and translation, staging, lighting, sound, acting; a semantic differential scale replicating the prescreening overall view of Chekhov but focusing this time on the Eyre/Griffiths readings; open-ended questions asking whether they liked this production (and why) and whether it was true to Chekhov (and why); semantic differential questions relating to two key scenes: Lopakhin's drunken dance in act 3 as new owner of the cherry orchard and the poppy field scene; a multiple choice question examining their reading of the final scene of Firs falling to the ground; and, finally, an open-ended question regarding which aspect of the performance, lighting, script, or whatever, led them to this interpretation of Firs at the end of the play. Then, subsequent to answering these questions, students at most universities were involved in a short (fifteen–twenty-five-minute) focus group discussion about the Eyre/Griffiths production.

The audience response process was the same at each university. Students were asked to complete the prescreening questionnaire, immediately followed by a screening of the Eyre/Griffiths *The Cherry Orchard*, which was again immediately followed by the postscreening questionnaire and focus groups in that order. This sequencing was designed to enable us to get students' individual responses (via questionnaires) prior to the group dynamics of the focus group interview and also to avoid intervening variables that might have influenced readings had the completion of pre- and postscreening questionnaires been separated in time.

Because this was a lengthy process (taking about two and a half hours each time), it was not possible to screen the whole of *The Cherry Orchard*. Instead, about seventy minutes were screened. The researchers' editing of it (consistent with the postscreening questionnaire focus on production goals) was determined by key features *as assessed by the various production personnel*. Given the significance of Griffiths's subtextual narrative in the "Brechtian" act 2, it was important to screen the whole of this act. Act 2's contrast with the more naturalistic acts 1 and 4 was also particularly important. Consequently, we screened the last section of act 1 (beginning with Lopakhin's reference to the summer cottage scheme and also containing the cube of light transition effect at the windows, Trofimov's "if the authorities have their way I will remain a student" lines, and Gayev's "wanton" lines about Ranevskaya, which "explained" the sensory/sensual aspects of Dench's performance); the first section of act 4 (including the "sensitive" scene between Trofimov and Lopakhin and Lopakhin's field of poppies speech); and the final section of act 4 (including the last Gayev/Ranevskaya scene and the death of Firs). Lopakhin's drunken "faither can ye hear me" speech in act 3 was an important extension of Griffiths's act 2 subtext (and was seen by Cambridge academic Peter Holland as "*the* crucial moment" in shifting "the center of the play" from Ranevskaya to Lopakhin). So the last section of act 3 (containing Lopakhin's return, his triumphant "dance" as he recounts his purchase of the orchard, and his sympathy for the defeated Ranevskaya) was screened.

Some Results

Students completed a series of semantic differential scales based on the readings of the production by its key personnel. For example, Eyre argued that Griffiths's writing of *The Cherry Orchard* was "clear, idiomatic, uncontrived," and neither traditionally "sentimental" nor especially "political," since it freed Chekhov of the "baggage" of the lyrical and elegiac rather than making him a "crypto-socialist." In addition, Griffiths spoke of the "fractured speech," particularly in act 2. The "writing and translation" semantic differential consequently had the following pairs of terms on a seven-point scale: clear/unclear; formal/idiomatic; uncontrived/contrived; unsentimental/sentimental; rewriting Chekhov / true to Chekhov; lyrical/political;

fractured speech / flowing speech. According to a similar set of principles (i.e., binaries established via interviews with the production personnel), students were asked to complete semantic differentials for staging, lighting, sound, and acting.

Writing and Translation

On a seven-point scale, where seven indicates the strongest agreement and four the middle point between the paired terms, students responded significantly to the writing only on the following scales: "clear," "sentimental," "true to Chekhov."[1] All other means ("idiomatic," "uncontrived," "political," "fractured speech") were very close to the midpoint. There were, however, significant differences according to *discipline* of respondent on the lyrical/political and formal/idiomatic scales.[2] Russian studies students read the Griffiths script as more lyrical, the theatre students as more political. This may seem surprising: one might expect Russian studies students to have a stronger "authentic Russian history" demand and thus to see Griffiths's characterization and altered words (e.g., the vagrant's "comrades!") as more political. In fact, though, the result seems to be a "shadow" effect of the students' general attitude to Chekhov. Asked in the prescreening questionnaire to respond to Chekhov on the nonpolitical/political scale, the theatre students were also significantly more inclined to read Chekhov himself as political than the Russian studies students. To this degree the theatre students were closer, of course, to the opinions of Eyre and Griffiths.

Staging Act 2

As we saw, Griffiths's emphasis here was on a Brechtian alienating effect and subtext, preferring (as at Nottingham Playhouse) a two-dimensional, schematic, "expressionist," and "threatening" (rather than lyrical) space in contrast to the "real depth" detail and naturalism that set designer Spence was aiming at for television. In addition, there were Eyre's interests in a set emphasizing "ownership," which was "dry, arid," and Spence's attempt to make it "dreamlike." The semantic differential contained the following pairs: detailed/schematic; expressionistic/naturalistic; dry, arid / green, opulent; indicating the future (e.g., telegraph poles) / indicating the past (e.g., shrine); emphasizing rootlessness / emphasizing ownership; natural/alienating; threatening atmosphere / lyrical atmosphere; historically specific / "any time or place"; two-dimensional / real depth; lifelike/dreamlike. Students responded significantly to the staging of act 2 as follows: "dry,

arid"; "dreamlike"; "alienating"; "expressionistic"; "emphasizing rootlessness"; "threatening atmosphere"; "any time or place."

Insofar as there were less neutral responses here, the set of act 2 struck
the students more forcefully than Griffiths's writing did. Some students
(in survey open-ended comments) undoubtedly responded to his attempt
to create a naturalistic/alienating tension between acts 1 and 2.

> Inside house — more naturalistic, less alienating (Sussex).

> Sterile environment [act 2] — not comforting (Sussex).

> Initially, it seemed painfully a "studio" set, but it gradually became less
> and less noticeable and well used with the gravely noise, the aridity and
> bleakness, and the underemphasized shrine mixed with the obvious
> telegraph poles. I never felt quite comfortable watching (Hull).

For other students, this staging tension in act 2 created problems, so
that whereas one student "liked the stillness of the camera coupled with
long shots. This overcame many of the problems in creating theatre on
television" (Middlesex), another student commented, "The atmosphere
was too large: . . . the bench was unnatural in such a vast space. It seemed
strange to have little clutches of actors in the vast, undefined spaces"
(Columbia). This reading responded directly to the real depth / two-
dimensional difference between Spence and Griffiths, since although
Spence seems to have achieved her dry and arid look with the students,
neither her "real depth" nor Griffiths's "two-dimensional" look was clearly
established for them, as the semantic differential data indicate. Rather,
these two spatial dimensions existed in some kind of tension.

Nor did students absorb Eyre's "John Berger / ownership" inflection
of act 2. Those who were made (negatively) uneasy by the contrasts and
tension in staging often reached for something more familiar and comforting, like the Columbia student (above), who added, "Also, the landscape of Act 2 should have been greener." Other students made similar
points.

> The lighting inside the house when the three windows are opened on
> to the orchard is quite good. It seems like natural sunlight and gives a
> real sense of the value of the orchard, in a sentimental sense
> (Columbia).

> Act 1: beautiful interior of house with the three windows shedding the
> spring light in (Royal Holloway).

Stark, tableau-like lightness, symbolic of orchard's bloom, ghost-like (Florida).

These responses (and another that praised the "hazy light through the windows" [Middlesex]) drew on Howard King's special lighting effects to underpin sentimental memories (among viewers as well as characters) of cherry orchard white while disliking the act 2 staging.

Other students, coming from a similar sense of attachment as King to the cherry orchard characters, felt that "in the first part of the play — before the estate is sold — the house doesn't feel lived in, so there wasn't so much of a sense of a house (or a life-style) being taken apart in the final scene — i.e., it felt cold all the way through — with, for example, the creaking floorboards" (Cambridge). Some felt that "the sparseness of the last act with all the boxes and suitcases was very chilling along with everyone wearing similar colours expressing bleakness" (Cambridge).

As regards the formal style of these internal scenes, some students admired Eyre's filmic approach: "All had the distinct portrait-like quality of Act 2. Almost too picturesque: scenic — with quite imposing settings" (Birmingham) and "They flowed like the brushstrokes of a painting" (Birmingham). But others strongly disliked the "theatricality" of a stage play on television.

> The scenes in the house were very unaffecting. I felt there was no sense of place, no atmosphere, just staleness (Birmingham).

> It was all pretty mundane, and any tension was lost by the alienation of watching a stage production on television (Birmingham).

> I found the use of "framing" quite alienating within a staged play for TV. I was constantly aware of a jarring between the two media, stage and screen: e.g., the specific placing of characters within a frame such as opening of act 1 with the grouping of the four characters, and the appearance of Anya in a doorway, and the arrangement of Ranevskaya, Gayev and Varya at the three windows (Bristol).

For some the staging was "lifelike, naturalistic, detailed, more towards the opulent" (Florida). For others it was "too naturalistic and logical — too logically connected to make many of the images the play contains meaningful" (Florida).

Students sometimes credited the "jarring transition" between acts 1 and 2 to the "symbolic" quality of act 2: "All of a sudden there's this very jarring transition to being out in that open space. And I didn't know why he did all that symbolism with the cross and all that. . . . I think there's a thing about the railroad coming through, isn't there, in that scene, and then you do have that side of modernity. There's the telegraph poles and there's the cross" (Columbia).

For Griffiths, too, the scene represented modernity in its characterization, acting, language, and staging. A textual analysis of this Columbia University interview with Russian studies students (Tulloch 2000b) indicated a traditional, "melancholic farewell to the past" reading that was evident in the academic Chekhov texts the students read and that influenced their evaluation of this scene. These Columbia students did read the scene formally in accordance with Griffiths's preference, that is, as a disjuncture in relation to act 1. But their reading was also aberrant in that they evaluated this "distraction" negatively (as a "jarring transition"). Rather than being jarred or alienated in Brecht's sense out of their common sense of naturalism so that they would be forced to reconsider the formal and ideological relations of the Chekhov text, they in fact found act 2 itself the "least successful set." This was because they were reading from a traditional position that identifies spectator positions with the gentry and its problems. Accordingly, the loss of a beautiful orchard "tugged" at their emotions and sympathies. It was clear from what was said here that Howard King's cube of light effect in act 1 interacted with this traditional reading formation to support audience identification with the gentry: "There was that bright sunlight. And it seemed so inviting. You could see why they were valuing the orchard."

Lighting

Eyre's camera emphasized filmic style via indirect lighting to provide "texture," atmosphere, and a visually unified feel rather than the standard "tennis court"–lit TV drama fare. Producer Anne Scott spoke of "there being very different temperatures" through the production, with a shift from cool to hot lighting between acts 1 and 2: "It's something to do with mirroring what's happening to characters; a kind of supporting what's happening emotionally. . . . It's lighting the subtext. . . . It's a . . . theatrical approach to lighting it rather than naturalistically" (personal interview, June 1994). Some students did in fact comment on the lighting being "quite theatrical for a TV studio" (Bristol). And some also took note of the "noticeable lighting effects," which "reflected mood changes" (Bristol).

Production problems had exacerbated a soft "impressionistic" camera style in act 2. The semantic differential scale for act 2's lighting contained filmic style / TV style; impressionistic/hard-edged; visually unified / visually fragmented; lighting creates mood / lighting reflects mood; hard light / indirect light; unrealistic/realistic; textured (light and shade) / flat (uniform brightness); noticeably different / standard TV lighting; cool/arid, hot; neutral style / atmospheric style.

Students responded significantly to the lighting of act 2 as follows: "atmospheric style," "unrealistic," "noticeably different," "impressionistic," "indirect light." It seems that whereas the students did see act 2's lighting as "noticeably different," this was less in relation to the "alienating" aspects of act 2's staging and more to do with the "atmospheric style," "impressionism," and "textured" aspect of "filmic" lighting and camera.

Some students also noted the specific lighting of act 2 in their open-ended comments:

The lighting in act 2 was ethereal and dreamlike, whereas act 3 was harsher and more "TV style" (Bangor).

I liked the lighting because it was not normal TV sitcom / chat show lighting (Royal Holloway).

Act 1 when the three characters opened the three windows seemed like a film — like there really was an orchard (Florida).

Some students also commented on act 2's impressionist style: "The lighting outside the house (act 2) was extremely impressionistic, whereas all of the lighting inside was more realistic" (Birmingham); "Act 2 was dreamlike, like a painting. More abstract, less real, impressionistic. Pastel/flowery colors" (Birmingham). This impressionistic camera style was liked by some: "The lighting in act 2 was better than 3 and 4 — more reflective of how and where the scene should be seen" (Columbia); "The cool and airy light inside the rooms contrasts well with the outside and also with the darker, more threatening lighting used for the ball" (Hull). But others disliked or were disturbed by it: "Act 2 was too static, but I suppose it was trying to be futuristic. Last act was too 'creamy' — not enough shade" (Middlesex); "Once they were outside the lighting stopped trying to be natural, which seemed to be inconsistent" (Royal Holloway); "The change from apparently normal lighting to almost surreal lighting in act 2 created an uneasy balance of styles — there seemed to be an uncertainty generally between a natural approach and a dramatic approach to the play" (Sussex). This "uneasy balance of styles" (between, e.g., Griffiths's "futuristic" act 2 and King's "'creamy' — not enough shade" cube of light effect) was to some extent deliberate. But it was not wholly so, and these students were exploring what was genuinely an "uneasy balance" in the production.

Sound

Sound director Richard Partridge had primarily naturalistic intentions for *The Cherry Orchard*. For example, he liked working on the raised set because of its "real" sound of actual floorboards. For some students this worked well, indicating the "hollow" world of the home, which was then put into relief by the "bench scene . . . [with its] separation of two viewpoints" (Birmingham). In contrast, a number of students both in focus group discussions and in questionnaires complained about the obtrusive sound of footsteps. For theatre students in particular the irritation over sound and music represented the problems of televising a stage play. "In act 2 I found the sound too intrusive, e.g., footsteps on gravel" (Middlesex); "[There were] too many sound effects in act 1. All scenes indoors had problems with echoing floors — it may have been deliberate, but it masked speech and was distracting" (Sussex); "Floorboards were too noisy — obvious attempt at realism. Why bother?" (Birmingham).

In fact, both Partridge and Griffiths had also acknowledged in interview the sound problems in act 2 (the shale underfoot) and act 3 (the audibility of voices beneath the music). Some students concurred: "I found the production technically lacking, particularly in sound, and I found this incredibly distracting, as I often could not understand what the characters were saying" (Birmingham); "The music in act 3 gets on one's nerves, as the characters are having a serious discussion, and it becomes more noticeable than the discussion due to the fact that the same inane bars are played over and over again" (Birmingham). Further, there was the "alienating" issue of act 2: did the sound, like the lighting, break with the naturalism of act 1? Was it more self-referential or self-reflexive than naturalistic? Some students thought so: "Yes: it makes one feel uncomfortable" (Durham); "At end of scene — act 2 — [the sound was] sinister and foreboding" (Hull); "I noticed the guitar in act 2 — [it] reinforced the dolefulness of Yepikhodov. Like him, [it] seemed out of place in the scene."

Others disliked the "out-of-place" music and sound in acts 2 and 3: "The 'breaking string' didn't really sound like anything, not even an omen (and certainly not a string). In act 2 Yepikhodov's guitar and singing were unsuccessful — a futile attempt to recall the 'leisure' days of the aristocracy (does Yepikhodov represent this class?)" (Bangor); "The ball scene — Russian dance music created a sense of Russia [that was then] lost by the Scottish accents!" (Bangor); "I thought 'Ah! Music!' When something is lacking in drama, add music. [It was] music for music's sake" (Bristol).

The semantic differential scale for sound (again based on production values and problems) contained music noticeable during performance / music not noticeable during performance; appropriate sound / obtrusive sound; always audible / not always audible; stands out on its own / backs up dialogue; sound or music reinforces picture / sound or music works against picture; naturalistic (e.g., breaking string is like snapping cable in a mine)/symbolic (e.g., breaking string is an omen).

Students significantly noted the following: "symbolic," "appropriate sound," "sound/music works to reinforce picture." Other than the symbolic reading there was no particular emphasis from students on reflexive uses of sound in the production. Primarily, they noticed the music of Yepikhodov in act 2 ("created a feeling of the past — peasants — old Russia" [Hull]) and the ballroom music, which most felt worked well because, as Anne Scott noted, it was "supporting what's happening emotionally."

In act 3 when Lopakhin demanded music it was crazed, causing an atmosphere of chaos, flux and was very loud, giving a sense of inability to think, tranquillity replaced by frenzy (Middlesex).

The music after Lopakhin buys the orchard is striking — like the scene, it matches the tense mood (Sussex).

I noticed the sound in act 3 where Lopakhin has bought the cherry orchard and demands music. For him this is a great personal achievement, so here celebratory musical background was appropriate (Bangor).

In act 3 at the ball music is used by Ranevskaya to cover her emotions . . . like a mask. It was then used by Lopakhin to try to show he was now the master, as he ordered the orchestra to play for him (Bangor).

I noticed the music particularly when Lopakhin purchases the estate. The music stops — [this] adds to the melancholic feel of the owners of the house, feeling that something is wrong. It is a long time before the music starts again, and then it is spasmodic (Bangor).

The music in act 3 enhanced the pettiness and triviality at the top and the somberness and inevitability of the end (Florida State).

The many varied hearings of the sound/music around the point of Lopakhin's drunken dance in act 3 is interesting, indicating how important to audience understanding the interaction is between multimediality and Eversmann's perceptual code. However, as Elam (1980) would predict, these different semiotic channels of theatrical communication wax and wane during a production. For example, only one student commented on the combined silence/sound/music effect at the end of the play. At this point the sudden silence of the axe as Firs collapses introduces the breaking string, which immediately is overlaid by a Russian folk song. This student remarked, "I thought the plonk music when Firs hits the floor a bit much" (Columbia).

No one at all commented on Griffiths's little Brechtian intervention with Charlotta's taped voice at the beginning of act 2, although one student did mention the "interrupting" and "ironic" effect of Yepikhodov's singing at that point: "[It had a] good interrupting and entertaining effect. It helped get across the mood, atmosphere in an appropriate ironic style" (Birmingham). Another student commented that the music was "particularly noticeable over the conversation between Dunyasha and the 'guitar playing servant,' emphasizing their lack of understanding and subsequent frustration with each other" (Cambridge).

As with those students who looked for comfortingly sentimental "cherry orchard" lighting and color, so too in the case of the music there could be considerable pleasure in (the conventionalized hearing of) the "sentimental" and the "haunting" refrains:

Yepikhodov's playing . . . was sentimental, which worked well with Lopakhin being about to warn them about the orchard (Middlesex).

The lone guitar music worked very well on an atmospheric level (Hull).

The haunting quality of the music after the play was very effective (Sussex).

[There was] a *lot* of music at the end credits — ominous and sad effect (Florida State).

Sad music at end. Guitar music — lilting, quite soothing but focused on apathy (Birmingham).

Acting

A major concern that Griffiths had with the television production of *The Cherry Orchard* was the star persona of Judi Dench, which he felt worked against the ensemble style of the original Nottingham Playhouse performance. He also worried that the "gravitas" of this star style suppressed the comedy of the text; and he was unsure whether the Scottish accents really worked. In addition, he wanted a Brechtian distancing of actors' performances in act 2 — a "hurting" stylization that might be seen as contrary to the familiar notion of Chekhovian "understatement." Our acting semantic differential scale included emphasis on ensemble / emphasis on individual stars; emphasis on the serious / emphasis on the comic; distancing/naturalistic; Scottish accents assist Chekhov's meaning / Scottish accents are inappropriate; heavily stylized / understated; emphasizing unconscious motivations / emphasizing conscious ideas.

The only significant student response to the acting on the semantic differential scale was "emphasis on ensemble." All other responses were close to the midpoint, though this disguises a very strong spread of differences of opinion in relation to the Scottish accents. Significant proportions of the student audience either very strongly liked or very strongly disliked the use of Scottish accents. For example, 63 percent of the Cambridge English/drama students strongly liked the used of accents, and 25 percent strongly disliked them. The "ensemble/star" responses were also relatively polarized, with only 16 percent of responses in the neutral column. There were also differences according to discipline on the distancing/naturalistic scale, with Russian studies students, expecting naturalism, finding the acting significantly more distancing. Acting students, in contrast, more familiar with Brecht, commented that they enjoyed the more alienated acting of Timothy Spall as Yepikhodov, particularly in act 2.

Clearly, a simple response on the "ensemble/star" scale does not tell us much about more fine-grained readings of the production. That will involve examining in the next chapter the relationship between Williams's cultural materialist reading formation (to the extent that it is imaged and embodied in the Eyre/Griffiths text) and the variety of reading formation positions that the students occupied.

Conclusion

The chapter began by examining the challenges that occur when presenting a canonical text like *The Cherry Orchard* on television. The problems described were aesthetic (e.g., how to interpret Chekhov in terms of previous productions, television naturalism and "impressionism," politics, popular culture, comedy, and tragedy), technical (e.g., types of camera, lighting, and sound problems), and institutional (e.g., funding problems, scheduling, professional conventions, prescribed spectator positions).

Different discourses and agencies were active in the production process, even in this case, where script writer and director broadly agreed on political concerns and aims. Yet while Griffiths gave priority to certain aesthetic matters (on promoting the "alienation" of act 2 as political statement) and to certain institutional challenges (the politics of using and subverting the BBC, the new Thatcher government, and a neoconservative climate of opinion), Eyre focused more strongly on technical challenges (how to design the set for the nursery, how to control and direct light). I have examined these different agencies in relation to a range of professional values of practice as citations and intertexts of the various players who produce the "semiotically thick" (Elam 1980) television text called *Play for Today's "The Cherry Orchard."*

Several discourses of modernism were at intertextual play here, as between, for instance, Griffiths's "Enlightenment project" and the various inflections of "modern" television naturalism via camera, sound, lighting, and set design. On the one hand, television naturalism can itself be seen as a discursive meeting point of intertexts, ranging from Raymond Williams's academic writing on Chekhov to production references to Gainsborough and Israëls. On the other hand, the particular shift from the Brechtian modernity of *The Cherry Orchard* as played at Nottingham Playhouse to the star-led version on television needs to be seen as a matter of institutional negotiation between production and other (social and visual) discourses, not least discourses speaking for spectator positions in relation to an assumed "mass" or "distracted" audience. So the historically located conjunctures of times (1903/1977/1981) and spaces (Chekhov's text as it moved from theatre to television) as well as the transformations and transcodifications in each of those times and spaces were an initial focus of the analysis of local production narratives in *The Cherry Orchard.*

Among a range of audience measures administered to university students of Russian and theatre studies in Australia, Britain, and the United States, this chapter has focused on semantic differential scale data relating to production-defined binary values to examine the extent to which the sometimes ambiguous and contradictory spectator positions offered by the television performance of *The Cherry Orchard* were taken up by these audience groups.

Data relating to the multimediality of the performance (writing, lighting, set design, acting) indicated that at the artistic level of communication Eyre/Griffiths's *The Cherry Orchard* was seen as "true to Chekhov." This level of theatrical play was seen to be conveyed by "clear" and "sentimental" writing; the "atmospheric style" of the sets; and "appropriate sound," which, with the music, worked "to reinforce the pictures." Above all, perhaps, and contrary to Griffiths's fears, Chekhov's well-known emphasis on ensemble was seen to dominate the acting. Nevertheless, act 2 was seen by many as symbolically in some tension with the other acts. This was especially communicated to the students via the staging of act 2 as "dry and arid," "dreamlike," "alienating," "expressionistic," "emphasizing rootlessness," and with a "threatening atmosphere." The lighting of act 2 was also seen as "noticeably different" from the other acts: "unrealistic," "impressionistic," and indirectly lit. At the sensory level, only the issue of the servants' Scottish accents was strongly noticed (according to the semantic differential measure), though we have seen a number of open-ended responses to the music and set design, which both emphasized the quality of Howard King's lighting in establishing emotional empathy with the threatened landed class and noted the sensory use of music in act 3 "to cover . . . like a mask" Ranevskaya's emotions at the ball, to celebrate Lopakhin's drunken emotions as the new master of the estate, and to "hauntingly" evoke the general "apathy" of all via Yepikhodov's guitar music. Still, this was seldom a consistent or one-dimensional reading of what is "true to Chekhov." The set design and lighting of act 2, in particular, "created an uneasy balance of styles," which students interpreted in a variety of ways, but overall with a sense of it being "unnatural" and "not comforting."

The audience studied in this chapter was of a very specific kind: students studying Chekhov. But the use of academic audiences established a symmetry, since Trevor Griffiths's first active engagement with the Chekhov text was via an academic, Raymond Williams. The epistemologies of that production-audience dialogue (between the different intertexts of Raymond Williams, Trevor Griffiths, Richard Eyre, Richard Partridge, Geoff Feld, Howard King, and the different academic texts and teachers of the student audience) need, then, to be seen as variable, unstable, even contradictory conditions of restraint underpinning the audience analysis that follows in the next chapter.

NOTES

1. All semantic differential terms reported were significantly different from the midpoint $p < .05$.

2. Reported differences between student groups were significant $p < .05$.

THE "READING CHEKHOV"
PROJECT SOCIAL AUDIENCES
AND READING FORMATIONS

4

*In 1977 Richard Eyre of the Nottingham Playhouse
commissioned Trevor Griffiths, an anti-establishment
playwright of vociferous socialism, to create his own
English* Cherry Orchard. *Steeped in Raymond Williams
and Gyorgy Lukács, Griffiths was a master of Marxist
dialectic. . . . In his eagerness to enlist Chekhov to the
cause, Griffiths produced a cartoon of the forces
leading to the Revolution. —Laurence Senelick,*
The Chekhov Theatre

Laurence Senelick's valuable book *The Chekhov Theatre: A
Century of Plays in Performance* is among the very few production-focused
studies of Chekhov. Senelick clearly did not like the Eyre/Griffiths production of *The Cherry Orchard.* To understand why, we need to go beyond
Senelick's concerns about "vociferous socialism" and "Marxist dialectic"
— though these are important — to his broader understanding of the
relationship between "sociology" and aesthetic value. In doing so, we may
begin to approach the kinds of interpretive communities of which the
student audiences that are the main subject of this chapter were part.

Our production analysis of Eyre/Griffiths's *The Cherry Orchard* was
part of a research project, "Chekhov: In Criticism, Production and Reading,"
funded by the Australian Research Council. This project had the aim of
using production studies conducted at Belvoir Street Theatre, Sydney, the
Royal Shakespeare Company, Stratford-upon-Avon, and the American
Repertory Theater, Boston, to examine production-determined spectator
positions for Chekhov performances in different cultures and at different
kinds of theatre. The project also explored Chekhov in criticism as well as
student audiences in each of these three countries, Australia, Britain, and
the United States. The Chekhov in criticism part of the project explored

paradigms in use in all major English-speaking books and academic journals over the prior twenty-five-year period, and leading Chekhov scholars (including Senelick) were also interviewed and their writing researched as part of this. Finally, audience analyses, drawing on a range of different audience research methodologies, were associated with these production studies (including the Eyre/Griffiths television production) to explore issues of social audience and reading formation. Eyre/Griffiths's television version of *The Cherry Orchard* was chosen to focus student audience discussion internationally for two reasons: as a television work, a videotape of the same production could be shown to different audiences worldwide; and, as a controversial production, it was likely to stimulate a range of responses and comment.

This cluster of "Chekhovs" (in different theatre and television productions, in academic criticism, and in audience interpretation) brought together "processual" forms of theatre analysis (Elam 1989), the notion of reading formation and interpretive community as intertextual sites for meaning production, and "active audience" research conducted from a variety of perspectives. There were advantages in using a combined cluster of ethnographic, textual, long interview, focus group, and survey methodologies. For example, the prescreening quantitative survey designed for university students included semantic differential questions relating to their interpretation of Chekhov in terms of tone, form, and meaning. These semantic differential binary choices (e.g., action/inaction, optimistic/pessimistic, "things will improve" / "nothing can be done," political/nonpolitical, joyful mood / melancholy mood, hope/apathy, art with a message / art for art's sake, etc.) were themselves based on English-language academic readings of Chekhov over the twenty-five-year period of analysis. The relationship of scholarly works on Chekhov to semantic differential responses could give a guide to students' reading formation, as could analysis of their university course guides, and further prescreening questions about which academic books and articles on Chekhov students had found particularly valuable. These prescreening data could then be compared with postscreening responses using the same semantic differential measures; with other quantitative measures (as we saw in the last chapter) relating to production intentions in writing, staging, light, sound, and acting; and with a range of open-ended, qualitative questions in the postscreening questionnaire.

The data for the "reaction to Chekhov's work" prescreening question indicated that Chekhov was read quite strongly by students internationally as a writer of melancholic inaction, pessimistic vision, and truth to life. Interestingly, in addition to this rather gloomy, inactive view of Chekhov's social world, his art was seen as providing a message. But what *kind* of message was this? What room was there, among students as social audiences, for a sense of critical agency as understood by Trevor Griffiths's notion of history as a site for social change? Students internationally tended also to place Chekhov at the social rather than individual end of the spectrum. But did the students' understandings of the sociology of Chekhov modify at all when they saw Eyre/Griffiths's *The Cherry Orchard*? A particular focus on Griffiths's "change agents" — Lopakhin, Trofimov, the vagrant — and their relationship with Firs was built into the audience research methodology to probe these questions.

Clearly, the quantitative methodology of semantic differential analysis used in the last chapter has its limitations. The seven-point binary scale central to that method can seem very limiting to scholars of Chekhov, especially when they are asked to position Chekhov on a scale between tragic and comic (students were, in fact, advised to gloss their responses discursively if they found this a problem). Yet the fact is that Chekhov *has* been positioned historically somewhere along that sliding scale from tragic to comic, as Chekhov's own complaint to Stanislavsky about the latter's productions of *The Cherry Orchard* as tragedies indicated only the earliest example. Senelick speaks of the *periodic* rediscovery that Chekhov was a comic dramatist as "a necessary antidote to the clichés of lyricism and melancholy" but adds that the "comic Chekhov" has itself become a cliché (1997, 3).

So semantic differential analysis does have its uses. For example, it can indicate short-term, generalized changes in students' reading of Chekhov. But it is also important to go well beyond this by way of other quantitative measures, qualitative research, and textual and discourse analysis (including the analysis of audience questionnaire responses as themselves texts) to begin to get access to people's cognitions and emotions around a particular production of *The Cherry Orchard*. By using long interviews with Chekhov scholars and university teachers, for example, one could begin to ask the question of what kind of "art with a message" Chekhov pedagogy has conveyed to university students. For example, Peter Christensen was a young, part-time lecturer in the United States who was well used to teaching mass introductory "great books" courses. He immediately recognized his own students in our findings: "What American students can connect to most easily [in Chekhov] . . .

is a doomed class. . . . Most Americans have a vision of the later part of the Russian empire as entirely stagnant and just sitting there waiting for a revolution that's inevitable, rather than as partially stagnant and a revolution that's not totally inevitable" (Peter Christensen, personal interview, May 1994). Christensen referred both to the ways in which he believed that Chekhov has been positioned sociologically by academic teachers and also to how he felt the overall American student body read Chekhov.

A further methodology in the research project was textual: what are the main academic paradigms in use among students? How do these dominant academic paradigms position textually the issues of social change in Chekhov? Which ones among these (according to a prescreening survey question) did students find most valuable?

In this audience chapter there is little space to cover the very large field of research in this project. I will, therefore, only very briefly visit the academic teachers of Chekhov surveyed, interviewed, and analyzed internationally before examining American, British, and Australian student responses to Eyre/Griffiths's *The Cherry Orchard*. In the short "Chekhov in Criticism" section of this chapter, I have chosen one well-known Shakespeare and Chekhov academic, Peter Holland, whose Cambridge University students feature significantly in the audience part of the chapter, and another internationally recognized Chekhov scholar, Laurence Senelick, who has not only produced one of the best books on Chekhov in production but has also critiqued both Holland's and Griffiths's interpretation of Chekhov; hence, his views were directly relevant both to the production study and to the audience study. In their different ways, I have found Holland's and Senelick's reading of Chekhov particularly subtle and provoking; hence, their "engaged" interpretations of each other and of the "sociological" in Chekhov was of considerable interest to me. This "Chekhov in Criticism" section, though representing minimally over one year of research, is offered also to indicate the mode of analysis employed in examining Chekhov's current interpretive communities.

Chekhov in Criticism: Two Academics and the "Sociological" Chekhov

One of the central themes of Senelick's *The Chekhov Theatre* is that "Chekhov's plays were written at a time when the stage director was becoming a paramount factor in the theatre. . . . The technical innovations of the modern stage, including electric lighting and *mises-en-scène* intent on reproducing 'real life,' required expert handling to blend and harmonize the various elements. Chekhov's development as a playwright from 1881 to 1904 coincided with this move from a stage governed by histrionic and spectacular display to one in which ensemble effect and the creation of 'mood' reigned supreme" (1997, 3). Consequently, a significant evaluative feature of Senelick's survey of American, English, European, and Russian productions of Chekhov is as "a chronicle less of great performers in starring roles than of the success and failure of directors and acting companies in realizing his plays and communicating them to a given audience at a particular moment of history" (1997, 4).

In the United States, for example, an "endemic" problem of producing between 1950 and 1995 was, Senelick argues, "the presence of a Hollywood celebrity" (1997, 286) who was guaranteed to sell out seats. This star factor — together with the commercialism and union rules of the U.S. stage, which circumscribed rehearsal periods and casts; the eminent but bland respectability, which elevated Chekhov to a pedestal that intimidated actors; the tendency of American critics to be ignorant of theatre history and literary criticism; the exposure of new productions to audiences who were "usually coming to Chekhov for the first time"; and the use of poor translations by non-Russian-speaking dramatists — had led to "the surface soap operatics of the usual American production" (Senelick 1997, 296, 304).

In the United Kingdom from 1950 to 1993 Senelick, following Kenneth Tynan (and also Trevor Griffiths), found an "ignorance of the social and historical context of Chekhov's works: the plight of his intelligentsia were identified with the decline of the English aristocracy; and their very specific crotchets equated with English eccentricity. His allergy to philosophical and political factions appealed to the British distaste for metaphysics and messages in the theatre, where productions of Chekhov well into the 1970s relied more on strong individual performances than on directorial concepts" (1997, 305–6). Thus, as in the United States but for different cultural reasons, the strong direction of ensemble playing of Chekhov was weakened, and Chekhov "was still chamber music played by a group of virtuosi, rather than an orchestral piece to be interpreted by a conductor" (Senelick 1997, 307). The British theatre, Senelick notes, "seemed to have an infinite capacity for neutralizing extraordinary or strong-minded reinterpretations, digesting their superficial traits, and converting the plays to showpieces for skilful acting" (1997, 321).

Russian theatre, postrevolution, had its own specific problems, and Senelick traces carefully the variety of Chekhovs "refitted . . . along the lines of Marxist sociology" (1997, 123). These included the early "revolutionary" changes of the Moscow Arts Theatre embedded in the revised, post-1917 perceptions of Stanislavsky, Nemirovich-Danchenko, Luzhsky, and Olga Knipper; the 1920s productions, in which "for the Reds, the gardeners were Trofimov and Lopakhin, regarded without irony as architects of utopia" and there was new recognition of the "common bond between comedy and communism" in Chekhov (Senelick 1997, 122, 123); Stalin's socialist realism of the 1930s and the "decreed positive qualities" of the war years; the "cruel" and "objective enquiry Chekhovs in the Khrushchev era of mild thaw" (1997, 203); the struggles of the 1970s for a Chekhov of artistic dissent eschewing "sociological explanations [that] showed us a departing gentry and an advancing merchantry" (1997, 219) and that divorced Ranevskaya and Lopakhin "from their usual sociological context" for theatre "audiences . . . alert to clandestine messages" (1997, 222); and, close to the end of the Soviet Union itself, Lyubimov's *The Three Sisters* of 1981, "flung out as an act of defiance" in "an attempt to make Chekhov reverberate with the problems of Soviet life" (1997, 229). Lyubimov's tactic included both using Olga's cruel and sarcastic final speech "as a class dictation for sophomores" of the "obligatory Marxist-Leninist optimism" and undercutting this by a "sarcastic subtext" of halting delivery (Senelick 1997, 229). A mere decade later, postglasnost, it was possible, in Senelick's view, to begin "to reach back to the sensitivity and refinement obliterated by eighty years of Communist lies, bloodshed and authoritarianism" (1997, 351), and he speaks of Shapiro's 1992 *The Cherry Orchard* produced for "a society in disarray," in which Lopakhin "was very much a businessman of the era of free markets and privatization, whose projects met with considerable sympathy from the audience" (1997, 352).

Two key evaluative positions are evident throughout Senelick's production history of Chekhov. The first is the importance of directors' control of actors in ensemble, thus potentially bringing a "purity and freshness" where the "spirit of the play was not betrayed" (Senelick 1997, 352, 357). Whether in the United States, Britain, or Russia, the best history of Chekhov production is a history of those directors who achieved this, at least in part, in the context of difficult Soviet-ideological, American-commercial, or British class-cultural constraints; and Senelick speaks with hope for the value in post-Soviet Russia of "the productions of Strehler, Brook and Stein" as "highly attractive models, because, for all their *distanciation* and abstraction, their fundamental humanism was untainted by decades of 'socialist realism' and academic tradition" (1997, 351). It is strong directorial models like these, Senelick argues, that can be valued by "a generation of Russians grappling with their cultural heritage in the face of an obscure future" (1997, 360).

Senelick finds some of his strongest pleasures in Chekhov productions by these particular European directors, and a brief look at his discussion of Strehler's *The Cherry Orchard* (1974) indicates the coherence of his evaluative position in his hostility to the merely sociological, which is a second major evaluative position of his book and a key to understanding his dislike of Griffiths's Chekhov works. Giorgio Strehler was, as cofounder of the Piccolo Teatro di Milano, Senelick notes, a leftist drawn to naturalism. Thus, when "he first turned to Chekhov, his concerns were sociological, but gradually his imagination unfolded to new aesthetic considerations" (Senelick 1997, 266). His 1974 *The Cherry Orchard* was "Strehler's greatest achievement to date, and certainly the most beautiful production of Chekhov of its era" (Senelick 1997, 272). For Strehler, Senelick argues, *The Cherry Orchard* existed outside any historic period" and thus needed to be "disengaged" from naturalistic, Stanislavskian, folkloric, and literary accretions to "favour a more universal, symbolic and fantastical perspective, but without falling into abstraction and a loss of reality" (1997, 267). To achieve this, Strehler

> offered his famous image of the play as a nest of Chinese boxes: the first is that of the "real," with its human interest narrative, *coups de théâtre*, events, atmosphere, characters and family background. The second, which encloses and amplifies it, is the history box: the dialectical relations of social classes, with objects, gestures, and costumes alienated as part of the historical discourse. And the third, all-encompassing, is the box of life, a timeless parable about mortality, played out in a metaphysical dimension. The House, its Rooms, the Generations, the Master-Servant relations take on capital letters, and the play becomes a poetic paraphrase of human destiny. (Senelick 1997, 267)

For Senelick, Strehler's successful "juggling" task was to avoid the "dangers" of reducing the play to any one of its "boxes": "The first [box] invited pedantic key-hole peeping and a taste for reconstruction, a la Visconti; the second might isolate the characters as historic symbols, drain them of common humanity and petrify them as thematic figures (the Marxist approach).... The risk of the third box was to place the characters outside time as neutral, universal ciphers" (1997, 267–68). Thus, whereas Strehler's earlier, "rushed," and "inexperienced" *The Cherry Orchard* (1955) was sociological, with an "end of society," naturalistic, "presentiment of cataclysm" focus, this "day-to-day lives of individuals tragically trapped in antagonistic social and historical circumstances" version was utterly transformed by his 1974 production, in which Chekhov reappeared as "a poet not of renunciation and relevance, but of the pain of living and doing what needs to be done, to the bitter end" (Senelick 1997, 266, 267).

Not surprisingly, Strehler's layered "theatrical, historical, existential, and true to life, all at the same time" achievement (Senelick 1997, 272) with *The Cherry Orchard* has structural similarities with Senelick's own analysis of the play. Senelick's engagement with Peter Holland's (and Trevor Griffiths's) interpretation of *The Cherry Orchard* indicates, in fact, issues that seem quite common among Chekhov's academic interpretive communities when speaking about the sociological — in the sense, for example, of Donald Rayfield, when he commented in a personal interview that "a very strong sociological . . . rising forces and decaying forces [interpretation of *The Cherry Orchard*] . . . is a betrayal [of Chekhov]. I think doubt should be left to the audience's mind" (personal interview, 1994).

In his own analysis of the play, Senelick certainly does not deny the sociological issues of servant-master relations in *The Cherry Orchard*, any more than Strehler did. In fact, he draws on the sociological notion of upward mobility (Senelick 1982, 249) in speaking about Lopakhin. But he locates these sociological issues within a layered and "all-encompassing" tension of aesthetic forms: the symbolist "concern for the passage of time, the sense of human beings trapped in the involuntary march of moments towards death" (1982, 248), and the New Comedy's emphasis on the social misfit's overstepping of rank, which is another way of engaging the sociological concept of upward mobility.

By way of these aesthetic forms, Senelick can then point to the complexity of layers of comedy in Chekhov. Noting the symbolist emphasis on time passing inevitably toward death, he points out that "those who respond least well to the passage of time, refusing to join it (like Gayev and Firs), or who rush to get ahead of it (like Trofimov) are among the most absurd" (Senelick 1982, 248). This positions them close to "the comic center of the play" (Senelick 1982, 249). Lopakhin, however, seems "most in step with time" and thus does "not appear immediately as comic until . . . seen in Chekhov's other context, that of displacement, of misfits not only out of step with time but also out of place" (Senelick 1982, 249). So by way of the abstractions of symbolism and the parodies of social reality in New Comedy, Chekhov's characters "exist both on the plane of reality and the plane of abstraction," simultaneously living in "vivid reality" and at the same time as a "schemata of reality" (Senelick 1982, 249). As in his comments on Strehler's achievement with his 1974 *The Cherry Orchard*, it would be reasonable for Senelick to claim of his analysis that it is theatrical, historical, existential, and true to life "all at the same time" (1997, 272).

Senelick's intertexts in this article are appropriate and authenticized. They have their historical foundation in the contributions and influences of the Russian critic Nevedomsky at the time of Chekhov's first production, the Russian symbolist Andrey Bely, and the "brilliant director" Meyerhold. All of these historical touchstones help in the "crystallisation" of Chekhovian "ambiguities" (Senelick 1982, 249).

It is the aesthetic play of forms with reality that is so important in canonical readings of Chekhov. So while Senelick's particular interpretation is both subtle and individual, it is also canonical in the precise sense described by a 1994 Australian Vice-Chancellors' Committee (AVCC) report on the university teaching of literature. The report emphasizes that it is terms like *play*, *duality*, *ambiguity*, and *complexity* that establish "the highest aesthetic value" that is essential to canonicity and that legitimize continuing academic exegesis. It is within this high-cultural framing of literary discourse that sociological issues in Chekhov have tended to be interpreted via a wide range of (often) modernist aesthetic forms. Thus, Donald Rayfield's rejection of "strong sociological . . . rising forces and decaying forces" interpretations of *The Cherry Orchard* may not necessarily agree with Senelick's particular interpretation. But he *is* agreeing with Senelick that doubt, ambiguity, and complexity are betrayed by reducing the work to the sociological.

I sense a similar view in Senelick's critique of Holland's and Griffiths's work on Chekhov as positivist. Senelick argues that "by endorsing Trevor Griffiths' . . . positivist viewpoint" Holland unwittingly echoes "an outdated Soviet interpretation no longer current even there" (1982, 246). Senelick's rhetorical move against Holland seeks to damage in two ways. First, in Western Chekhov scholarship, Soviet readings have been regarded as the epitome of ideological control and betrayal, the "refitt[ing] along the lines of Marxist ideology" (1997, 123) that Senelick traces through three quarters of a century of Chekhov productions. Second, Holland is accused of also being outdated, in other words, outside the exegetical flow of the current interpretive community and, worse still, outdated even by the standards of the Soviet Union.

Yet neither Griffiths nor Holland see themselves as positivist. Indeed, their central distinction (in Raymond Williams's cultural materialist sense) between a naturalism that draws on sense perceptions of the surface of appearances and a real world of dynamic cultural histories, social forces, and multiple identities directly challenges an empiricist position and provides as multilayered a Chekhov as does Strehler or Senelick (Allen 2000; Tulloch forthcoming). But, in denying this, there seems to be a slippage in Senelick's comment between positivist and Soviet-decreed positive qualities (see, for example, Senelick 1997, 191, 200, 216, 236), in which case it is easy to agree that Griffiths (and Holland) both emphasize the socially positive in Chekhov and that Senelick does not. It is symptomatic, for example, that Holland ends his "resistant symbol" article on Chekhov with the words "a cause for optimism," while Senelick ends his response to Holland with reference to Chekhov's "peculiar genius as a dramatist." One academic is claiming to emphasize Chekhov's "specific historicity and precise sociological imagination" (Holland, citing Griffiths 1982, 237); the other is reconstructing, via a new exegesis, the evaluation of Chekhov as author and genius.

Yet even while canonical literary-critical readings emphasize ambiguity in Chekhov, they very often elide *social* ambiguity, including the many subjectivities of class, culture, ethnicity, gender, and sexuality at any one time of writing, performing, and reading Chekhov's plays. And yet, as early as the mid-1990s the Australian Vice-Chancellor's Committee (AVCC) report was already emphasizing that it was important to interrogate aestheticist approaches by way of "issues of class, race or gender, and/or by exposing the relativity of the would-be discipline of 'English' *through the history of its assumptions, methods and subject matters*" (1994, 17, my emphasis). In this alternative approach of anticanonical literary studies, "assumptions about the inherent value of certain literary works have generally given way to an emphasis on understanding how and why value *gets attributed* to different types of text in different cultural circumstances" (AVCC Report 1994, 17, my emphasis).

As Annette Kuhn argues, "Representations, contexts, audiences and spectators" need to "be seen as a series of interconnected social discourses, certain discourses possessing greater constitutive authority at specific moments than others." The construction of sociology in relation to Chekhov interpretation is an example of the way in which literary critical communities attribute value differentially "to different types of text in different cultural circumstances." The attribution of the term *sociology* is part of aestheticized, high-cultural rhetoric of "certain discourses possessing greater constitutive authority at specific moments than others" (Kuhn 1987, 347). The elision of social ambiguity in Senelick's work is — for all his sensitivity to different national-cultural formations — only too evident in his reductionism in commenting on theatre audiences.

As Senelick admits, his approach to the reception of production as an historian "has to rely on the record of journalistic criticism, a dubious source at best; it is salutary to match one's own reactions against those of the press and to convey impressions obtained on the spot" (1997, 5). The latter is, of course, valuable, and I resort to it to open this book. But "one's own reactions" (and otherwise a reliance on theatre critics' accounts) can also lead to a reductive homogenization of the audience. Senelick does this quite regularly throughout his book: "What struck the younger spectators ..." (1997, 193); "The audience read into Chebutykin's dance its own awareness of the century's ghastliness" (1997, 216); "pity for the old retainer was the residual audience reaction" (1997, 225); "Most audience members took the message to be ... " (1997, 241); "more serious ... playgoers found it shallow" (1997, 296).

Sometimes Senelick's audience comments seem more precisely and locally situated, as when he speaks of a particular theatre audience — such as the one at the Taganka Theatre, which, "under Yury Lyubimov had been the hub of licensed artistic dissent" — as "alert to clandestine messages" (1997, 220, 222). And at other times, as when he speaks of the postglasnost portrayal of Lopakhin as a free-market businessman meeting "with considerable sympathy from the audience," it seems likely that this was an impression from Senelick's "own reactions" at the theatre. (Certainly, I had the same experience with Chekhov productions I saw in Russia in 1997.) But too often, Senelick's resort to *the* audience or to "most audience members" is based on no evidence at all; and — equally important as this empirical point — he eschews any possibility of there being just as many "layers" and "boxes" in individual and group audience subjectivities as there are in Chekhov's plays.

Further, there is a tendency in Senelick's all-encompassing layer of metaphysical and universal truth to the belief that the comedy in Chekhov revolves around those characters who do not accept the given passages of time and place as a hopeless struggle with illusions but instead act to change them. It is represented characters like these, as in Senelick's view of Nicholas Kent's 1988 *Trinidad Sisters*, who "sacrificed Chekhov's finer points to an activist message" (1997, 322). In *The Cherry Orchard* this refers specifically to the characters of Trofimov, Lopakhin, and Firs, who were so central to Trevor Griffiths's notion of the play.

Given Senelick's view of the reductionism of sociology, his especial dislike of Marxism, and his aestheticized (rather than sociological) understanding of complexity and ambiguity, it is not surprising that he viewed Griffiths's version of *The Cherry Orchard* as "a cartoon of the forces leading to the Revolution" and called Griffiths's Chekhovian play *Piano* "a series of didactic discourses" resembling a Chekhov "moulded into tendentious shape by Gorky" (1997, 313, 320). Also symptomatic is Senelick's resort to the literal Chekhov text rather than to significant sociological developments of Chekhov's time when he notes censoriously that the "passerby" is "significantly renamed a 'Vagrant'" in Griffiths's version, despite this designation of passersby at turn-of-the-century Russia being quite routinely accepted by current historians. For example, the program notes for Adrian Noble's far from Marxist 1995 *The Cherry Orchard* at the RSC, Stratford-upon-Avon, drew on historians Richard Wortman, David Floyd, and Hans Rogger to say of the emancipation of the serfs, "when emancipation left many peasants worse off than before the reaction was, as one provincial governor reported, 'heavy bewilderment and sorrowful disappointment.' Now free to travel, thousands left their estates to seek employment elsewhere; many moved into the towns to work in industry; most faced an uncertain future.... By the end of the century... the majority made up a discontented and potentially uncontrollable rural proletariat" (RSC, *The Cherry Orchard* program, 1995, pp. 3–4).

For Senelick, "the Griffiths approach is really a rape of Chekhov.... It's an attempt to place Chekhov in an ideological camp, and Chekhov, of all authors, spent his career avoiding that desperately. . . . Griffiths, by rewriting the part of Trofimov to make him an activist with no comic element whatsoever, with his rewriting of the language to make it much more squalid and much more brutal than it is in Chekhov, is actually rewriting Chekhov in his own image" (personal interview, May 1994). Interestingly, Senelick saw Griffiths's Chekhov as in continuity with the "star vehicle" productions that both he and Griffiths opposed.

> Chekhov has been largely a star vehicle in England. It was really for knighted ladies and gentlemen wearing gloves to show their stuff in a more or less modern piece. And that gentility needed to be scraped

off.... I remember vividly Mick Ford as Trofimov [in the Eyre/Griffiths Nottingham Playhouse production], because Mick Ford was an actor that I had seen a lot in the seventies, both on the London stage and on English television. He specialized in a line of very scruffy, malcontent Cockneys, and that was the element that he brought to Trofimov. And there was a class error there. By and large, I don't think the English get it when it comes to Chekhov. They keep rethinking him in terms of English class lines, and this becomes very clear in the accents that are chosen for the characters when they play it onstage. In most English productions of Chekhov the class biases are used for comic effect. Griffiths used them for violent effect, to set up, in fact, a class war. But that's not what the play is about. (Personal interview, May 1994)

Thus, Senelick believed, Griffiths reproduced the very English class representation that he was trying to destroy, with a different inflection. Chekhov's finer points tend to be, in Senelick's evaluation, aesthetic not sociological ones. Thus, as a critic who consistently lambasts writers like Griffiths for "his ignorance of Russian language and culture" (Senelick 1997, 313) — a somewhat unfair charge, since in other parts of his book he praises dramatists who work, as Griffiths did, with specially commissioned free translations of the Russian, including Senelick's own (e.g., 1997, 288, 293) — Senelick is surprisingly reticent of engaging with Russian language and culture himself when it comes to sociological and historical accounts of class, professional, and intellectual history of Chekhov's own time. Because Senelick almost entirely means "culture" in the aesthetic sense in his comments on Russian language and culture (and when he refers to playwrights like Michael Frayn "who had actually bothered to learn Russian"), an entire (and sociohistorical) range of layers in Chekhov's productions is simply lost to view. What then remains in this literary critic's notion of the sociological is a very reductive sociology indeed.

In this regard, it is curious that Senelick quotes with approval Vera Gottlieb's comment that "over the eighty years of Chekhov productions in Britain a strange anomaly has arisen: the plays are *always* staged within a period setting . . . but, with very few exceptions, the period itself or social context of the plays has been ignored" (cited in Senelick 1995, 306). Senelick certainly approves Gottlieb's criticism that "political, ontological or ecological questions [are] ignored" and that there has been an obsession with a Stanislavskian "exploring psychology rather than ideas" (1997, 306) in Chekhov interpretation. Uncited by Senelick, though, is Gottlieb's view that

Trevor Griffiths's *The Cherry Orchard* was a major marker in Chekhov production in this country.... What Griffiths did, I think very boldly and ... unashamedly, was to say, Look, these plays were written at a particular moment in time. They can't be divorced from their society and the political situation and context. So he went very clearly for the political interpretation — the all-of-Russia-is-our-orchard angle — which I thought worked marvellously. He took some liberties. He said he didn't, but he did. I think that's fair enough. I teach drama. I don't teach literature. My own training is theatre, not literary criticism as such. So it never worries me when somebody tries to make a living piece out of something that an audience goes to see. (Personal interview, July 1993)

Indeed, Gottlieb's support for the Eyre/Griffiths production had got her, famously, into strife with some of Britain's leading Slavists at a Cambridge Chekhov conference. Gottlieb's critical response to this fleshes out further the words that Senelick quoted in his book.

I think that the ... critical and audience reaction [at the conference] was in itself absolutely fascinating ... because they said, "Griffiths made him political." Well, Chekhov *is* political and *was* political. And I don't mean he was a member of the Bolshevik Party or a revolutionary. I'm not talking party politics. But I think it revealed the naïveté of the British or, in this instance, English idea that seventy years of Chekhov productions hitherto haven't been political. If you question the status quo [e.g., as Griffiths does], it is *seen* as "political," i.e., left wing. If you don't question the status quo, it's "not political." But I would argue [this latter response is itself] political by the very nature of not looking at issues and by not questioning them. That position is, in effect, actually quite profoundly right wing in its political assumptions. But it's pretending not to be political at all. And that's why ... I had a problem at the Cambridge conference on Chekhov, ... where people got very angry with me ... because it was a few months after a general election, and I started off the paper in Cambridge by quoting a Conservative Party political poster, a huge slogan ... "Take the politics out of education. Vote Conservative." I used that as an analogy to try and argue what I think has happened with seventy or eighty years of British Chekhov production, which is that there is somehow an assumption that the politics have been taken out [by Chekhov]. (Personal interview, July 1993)

Gottlieb, who, like Senelick, speaks Russian, did not agree with him about Griffiths's brutalizing of Chekhov's language and, far from seeing the importation of "English class lines" into *The Cherry Orchard*, believed that the production broke through the familiar Lopakhin as "bluff Yorkshire entrepreneur" to a more precise historicity, using the Scottish analogy to give a sense that Lopakhin "has really climbed a long, long way." Another British theatre academic, David Bradby, argued (in contrast to Senelick's view that the comedy is much reduced in Griffiths's version) that, by emphasizing the character interactions "on the basis of their place in the class order . . . far from making it a rather heavy piece, it actually emphasized a great deal of the comedy." For Bradby, Griffiths's version was "multiperspectival . . . releasing voices in the play that are often kept rather muffled" (personal interview, July 1993). It is significant that the academics who liked Griffiths's *The Cherry Orchard*, for example, Holland, Bradby, and Gottlieb, emphasized and remembered particularly the portrayal of Lopakhin, whereas Senelick, who strongly disliked the Nottingham performance, remembered most strongly the "ideological camp" represented by Trofimov.

Griffiths's new version of *The Cherry Orchard*, Eyre's production of the play within quite different theatrical and television conventions and innovations, Gottlieb's presentation of it (together with a similarly slanted piece at the Cambridge conference by David Allen), Gottlieb's appropriation by Senelick in his book, *The Chekhov Theatre*, Holland's and Bradby's discussion in interviews of critique of Griffiths's "positive" reading of Chekhov, Holland's discussion of the Griffiths production with his students (whom we interviewed), Senelick's printed riposte to Holland's academic writing on Chekhov, and our focus group interviews with students who watched Eyre/Griffiths's *The Cherry Orchard* are all "different kinds of text in different cultural circumstances" (AVCC Report, 1994, 17), with different constitutive authority at different moments and places.

The textual interaction of Senelick and Holland that I mention briefly here was part of our much broader textual analysis of Chekhov scholarship. By way of textual analysis as well as via long interviews with Chekhov scholars, our Chekhov in criticism research indicated that, by the mid-1990s, Shakespeare scholarship was considerably more involved than Chekhov scholarship in what the AVCC report referred to as anticanonical literary studies. It was perhaps no coincidence that it was Peter Holland's English course students (who studied both Shakespeare and Chekhov) who, as we will see, offered a greater range of "paradigmatic" readings of Eyre/Griffiths's *The Cherry Orchard* than other student classes (in Russian studies, for example) analyzed internationally.

The point here is not ourselves to control interpretations, despite Senelick's implicit accusations against Holland and Griffiths. It is not to establish here a surveillant reading (whether cultural materialist, poststructuralist, canonical, or any other). Rather, this approach of anti-canonical criticism focuses (as Kuhn also emphasizes) on the *institutionalized circulation* of Shakespeare and Chekhov via a negotiation of many other discourses. This must include the researchers' own discourses as well as those of Mary-Anne Gifford, Trevor Griffiths, Richard Eyre, Sue Fell, Geoff Feld, Howard King, Bill Paterson, Dave Hill, Laurence Senelick, Vera Gottlieb, Peter Holland, David Bradby, students at universities in the United States, Britain, and Australia (as presented in their questionnaire survey and focus group responses), theatre reviewers, and many other audience members at the Theatre Royal, Bath, the Belvoir Street Theatre, Sydney, the Q Theatre, Penrith, the Royal Shakespeare Theatre, Stratford-upon-Avon — all as part of the process whereby "interconnected social discourses . . . possess . . . greater constitutive authority at specific moments than others" (Kuhn 1987, 347).

Chekhov, Sociology, and University Students

When Peter Christensen noted that what "American students can connect to most easily . . . is a doomed class" (personal interview, May 1994), he added that what we lose in the doomed class view of Chekhov is a sense of the complex sociological negotiations and the alternative agencies of Russian history that the plays articulate. Instead of a dynamic, contradictory, and multilayered perspective, we settle for the dichotomy between a self-centered, self-defeating gentry and the revolutionaries (who, as we all know, were destined to win). Chekhov's own negotiation with the various movements of intellectual reformists (lawyers, doctors, artists, etc.; see Tulloch 1980) remains marginal, even invisible, in Chekhov academic writing, though at the time of the Chekhov in criticism project some academics interviewed were working through the implications of Chekhov, the first major nongentry artist in Russian literature, as part of a cohort of new intellectuals (Tulloch and Burvill 1996).

In the absence of this more complex sociocultural analysis, a simplistically sociological view of a doomed class *has* been a major component in traditional readings of Chekhov, especially of *The Cherry Orchard.*

Christensen is right: the notion of a stagnant Russia has been familiar in English-speaking academic Chekhov criticism for a long time (Tulloch 1985). In most of the earliest Chekhov criticism the emphasis was on Chekhov's naturalistic fidelity to a "frozen," undynamic, and stagnant Russia. When this view changed, the true-to-life naturalism of Chekhov continued to be an important template against which to measure the creativity of his art. By the time of the Bloomsbury group, Chekhov's genius was measured in relation to his ability to raise the pain of social loss, risk, and change to an aesthetic plane. "He is like a man who contemplates a perfect work of art; but the work of creation has been his, and has consisted in the gradual adjustment of his vision until he could see the frustration of human destinies and the arbitrary infliction of pain as processes no less inevitable, natural and beautiful than the flowering of a plant" (J. Middleton Murry, cited in Tulloch 1985, 192). We note here the common assumption of arbitrary risk and pain as inevitable and natural. Similarly, in the more layered and complex aesthetic of critics like Laurence Senelick, the all-enveloping and metaphysical layer tends to emphasize the comedy of inevitability and immutability of human beings trapped in the involuntary march of time and place.

Given this long-term tendency in Chekhov scholarship and teaching, in what ways (how and why) *did* university students attribute social meanings and sociological value to Chekhov? What kind of sociology was this? Given their true-to-life reading of Chekhov, what kind of social reading and "art with a message" was valued? To what extent was the "social inevitability" reading of Chekhov's plays that Peter Christensen ascribed to American university theatre departments widely held? And how was the Griffiths/Eyre interpretation of human agency and choice (especially in relation to the "dramatic disjunctures" of the vagrant, Trofimov, Lopakhin, and Firs's death) interpreted?

In the "Reading Chekhov" project a number of qualitative and quantitative methods were adopted to try and answer these questions relating spectator positions and social audiences. Initially, in the postscreening questionnaire a "topic of discourse" (van Dijk) discursive and qualitative analysis was adopted to analyze students' responses to "what was the *The Cherry Orchard* about?" These responses were also postcoded and quantified and compared with other open-ended qualitative responses in the questionnaires. Quantitative (postcoding and semantic differential) methods were augmented by open-ended survey responses to key scenes (e.g., Lopakhin's "poppy field in bloom" speech). Following Roland

Barthes's notion of a semantic "skid of meanings" in literary discourse, postcoding of open-ended survey responses examined the meanings that students attributed to Griffiths's vagrant, and this method was augmented by more straightforward (multiple-choice) quantitative measures relating to the television representation of the vagrant. Finally, students' responses to Firs's death scene were examined using a combination of quantitative (multiple-choice) and qualitative (open-ended) measures.

Analyzing The Cherry Orchard *Summaries:*
The Drama of Agency and Structure
At the beginning of the postscreening survey the students were asked, "What was the Richard Eyre/Trevor Griffiths version of *The Cherry Orchard* about?" This summarizing question was deliberately placed first in the questionnaire so that the later, more directed survey questions did not influence students' sense of the salient themes in the production.

The "summary" question elicited an open-ended response on one page and so was qualitative. However, it could also be quantified. This is because a summarizing question, as van Dijk (1984) had pointed out, allows respondents to both elaborate and enumerate cognitive macrostructures as their own reading of the text. This takes further Eversmann's notion (see chapter 1) of the relationship between cognitive responses to the theatrical event and audience members' memory of the performance. As van Dijk argues, the role of the topic of discourse as a device of understanding is as a category of *information reduction*, which both facilitates memory and yet at the same time is entailed by the text in full. As a "reading" device that refers to the text in full by reducing it to macropropositions, these topics of discourse can be quantified.

A clear example of this process of reducing the text to memorable propositions and yet at the same time attempting to release the different layers of the text in full can be seen in the following summary response by one of Peter Holland's Cambridge students. For this student, who gave her political affiliation as "Humanist," Eyre/Griffiths's *The Cherry Orchard* was about

The end of the old guard.
People pinning too much worth on material possession.
Lack of communication.
Self-enclosed words / minds.
The hope of youth.

Optimism from naivete.

Denial of responsibilities.

The transience of life.

Natural order of things / inability to prevent continuance of
monotony.

Ridiculous human nature.

Folly.

The actual layout of this student's response is reproduced here, as it illustrates well van Dijk's notion of summarizing discourse as a series of
macropropositions or topics of discourse.

It seems clear that some of Senelick's key Chekhovian concepts appear
here, for example, the transience of life, folly, and ridiculous human
nature. Indeed, these propositions could very easily be reworked *discursively* via the two aesthetic forms (symbolism and the New Comedy) that
Senelick foregrounds. But the propositions can also be *counted* to see how
often they occur across the student body as a whole.

If we approach this Cambridge student's summary syntagmatically (as
a narrative), we can see here topics of discourse that convey a social-
context-of-Russia reading that is close to the one that Christensen
describes among American students. In particular, the social emphasis is
on a doomed class ("the end of the old guard"), and the actantial focus is
on inevitability ("inability to prevent"). Thus, the sociology adopted by
this Cambridge student emphasizes the inevitability of stagnation and
monotony; the "ridiculous" and foolish (rather than agentive) quality of
human nature; the "self-enclosed words / minds" of human communication and "denial of responsibilities"; the inevitable "transience of life."

This emphasis on stagnation, transience, and the denial of responsibilities is in marked contrast to Griffiths's own macrostructural proposition that "freedom gets threaded through the play like a piece of tapestry."
When this Cambridge student does refer to hope, it is immediately tied
to youth and the optimism born of naïveté. In this audience member's
social discourse, it is "ridiculous human nature" (i.e., the "natural order
of things") that ensures the "inability to prevent continuance of monotony" as each generation changes to the next and "transient" life flows on.

It is possible to take syntagmatic, discursive analysis further by exploring this student's whole questionnaire response as itself a narrative generated by production-oriented questions. When we do this and turn to
the student's response to the performance of the various *characters* in the

production, we are not surprised to find that she liked the playing of Ranevskaya because "I believed in her lack of strength and resignation to the inevitable." The student also enjoyed the playing of Anya because she seemed "naive, immature, sincere, convincingly full of hope"; and she disliked the playing of the vagrant because of his "non-convincing performance," which was "not truthful."

In her response to a multiple-choice question about the vagrant (as to whether he represented a peasant, revolutionary, or deserting soldier in the production), this student read him as a peasant. But in her interpretation this was a peasant of the *past* who was introduced by the production as "a representative of an outmoded peasant class" in order to emphasize "Mme Ranevsky's frivolity, compassion." This was *not* Trevor Griffiths's vagrant of massive disaffection, who was one potential strand of a revolutionary future, but rather a peasant of a doomed class introduced to demonstrate "ridiculous human nature" (through Ranevskaya's mix of "frivolity, compassion"). This "peasant," it became clear from her open-ended comments, was interpreted by the Cambridge student as "not truthful" because he was too aggressive and oriented toward future change.

By contrast, a politically affiliated "Socialist" student, also in Holland's class at Cambridge, summarized the Eyre/Griffiths production as about

> the break-down of old social structures leaving individuals disoriented and unsure how to behave towards others. The wealthy family's position is threatened and then ultimately overthrown by Lopakhin, a peasant's son, buying the cherry orchard and literally displacing them. Related to this is the theme of memory, the yearning for an "innocent" past that Mme Ranevsky' talk and the rocking horse suggests. The way the actors inhabited the space seemed to create and enhance the apathetic heaviness that most of the characters are prone to — draping themselves over furniture, over-crowding each other, even Varia's accidental striking of Lopakhin with the billiard cue seemed to underline their isolation.

Some of the same topics of discourse that the humanist student recalled are evident here: the breakdown of the old social order (in both cases placed first, as the controlling macrostructural proposition), the failure and isolation of human communication, the monotony and apathy. But there is no emphasis in this socialist student's summary at all on the "folly" of the "natural order of things" and more focus on Griffiths's sense of a collectivity of alienated individuals who are "disoriented" and "unsure" as they engage with change ("literally displacing them"). In this student's discourse, the complexity of the characters relates to the ambiguous play between "insight" and "uncertainty," energy and desperation, social power and personal vulnerability. Thus, this Cambridge student liked the playing of Ranevskaya because "she was flirtatious but also care-worn, trying to take refuge in memories but had flashes of insight." The student also liked Lopakhin because "he showed that slight desperation beneath his enthusiasm by his wild gesticulating." She approved of Trofimov because he is "possessed" and liked Anya because she is "quite clueless, vacant — [she] has really surrendered herself up to playing the role of little girl and then Trofimov's follower." The student even likes the peasants for reasons similar to Griffiths's: "All [are] telling their own stories by what they say / don't say."

This Cambridge student's reading places the servants in their various local story lines, but each is perceived to be within a structure of exploitation. Thus, the student sees Firs as "a servant exploited by his masters" and interprets his death scene as the final discarding of a class-owned commodity. "He's locked inside the house; the place where he had done his duty finally betrays him. He wraps himself in his master's coat. He is as forgotten as the coat, only an object, spare furniture." In fact, in the TV production that this socialist student actually saw, Firs wraps himself in an old shawl, and Firs only refers *verbally* to Gayev's coat. But this is a student who (as her other questionnaire responses make clear) reads *The Cherry Orchard* in terms of property and possession: Gayev's coat and Firs are equated (in this "misreading") as "owned" commodities.

Like Griffiths, too, this socialist student reads the vagrant as a "dramatic disjuncture"; and, unlike a Loughborough student who disliked the vagrant because he seemed to have wandered onstage from the "wrong play," the Cambridge student liked this "other play" representation: "Monstrous figure — seemed to have wandered from another play." For this Cambridge student, the vagrant's role in the production was not to emphasize the "frivolity, compassion" of Ranevskaya as in the humanist Cambridge student response but was introduced as a "contrast with the wealthy party — Direct *deprivation*."

Third, a self-defined "socialist post-structuralist" Cambridge student provided the following summary: "*Change*. Did Chekhov believe in souls? Was the production about the conflict between historical impulses, which are grand narrative, and the specific, local [that] can involve our ideals and biographical circumstances; and the extent to which our *souls,* that is our transcendentally allotted qualities (fates/characters) hold us back in the fine details of the plot (which ultimately determine the greater)?"

Once again, the opening macrostructural proposition is about social change. But in this case there is a conscious and continuous play in the topic of discourse summary between category reduction (as "grand narrative") and the detail of the text in full ("specific, local," "details of the plot"). This playing between different epistemological positions is itself made the subject of interpretation and memory. The transcendental determination of author's/characters'/audience's "soul" is put into play with "the fine details of the plot, which ultimately determine the greater" in a kind of hermeneutic tension that actually challenges the very notion of cognitive macrostructures in her account — on behalf of the poststructural "local."

Like the others, this Cambridge student engages with the issue of change itself. But she does so neither through "inevitable" and "ridiculous" human tensions between "frivolity" and "compassion" (like the first student) nor through tensions between social agency and uncertainty (like the second student). Rather, her interpretation of the characters is via the tension of "local fine detail" and "grand narrative." She likes Ranevskaya because "her every utterance [is] charged with biography." Trofimov is admired because there is a "good indication of the way in which he simultaneously engages with grand narrative and evades smaller (emotional) plots." Lopakhin's performance is praised because his "voice/accent had beauty and dignity, where[as his] circumstances gave [him] less status." The servants were liked, "Firs especially for pathos encapsulated in failure of ideology." The performance of Varya was enjoyed for her "*splendid* physical artistry — [an] agonising portrayal of shattered nerves, yet tightly controlled."

In this poststructuralist reading of the production, detailed bodily "plots" ("utterance," "voice/accent," "physical artistry — shattered nerves") engage with and undercut the "transcendentally allotted qualities" of "status," "grand narrative," "ideology," and "control." Thus, in her reading the vagrant is both a "deserting soldier" and "an image of the coming revolution," but the character is not identified with either because that would imply a grand narrative of "inevitability." Rather, the vagrant represents a "simultaneous/transitory place between deference/obedience and threat of violent future."

"Transitory" in this poststructuralist account has a very different meaning from the humanist student's "transience." Rather than being based in the "order of things" inevitability of the latter, "transitory" is read by this poststructuralist Cambridge student as a *simultaneous* bodily presence and absence, control and change, deference and violence. The vagrant is a representation of things that *differ*. He is both "things falling apart" and "authority, order, his maleness/aggression [an] externalisation of Varya's fear of (sexual/political) 'nastiness.'"

The "return of the repressed" that this third Cambridge student also speaks about in an open-ended response discussing the Eyre/Griffiths production is thus both individual and social, both sexual and class based, both embodied and narrativized, since for this student the vagrant represents both Varya's "fear of nastiness" and "what the landowners are afraid of, yet [are] blocking from consideration."

This third among Peter Holland's Cambridge students reads the production's gender and class politics of *The Cherry Orchard* in a more sophisticated way than Rayfield's "betrayal of doubt" by "sociological rising forces, decaying forces" critique. The poststructuralist student focuses, precisely and theoretically, on "doubt" and ambiguity. Firs's death is read by this student in a similar way: "The script suggests his inability to escape from the story mapped out for him during the first years of his life, although the historical story has become dislocated from this. It is his determination (whatever it is that determines *him*) to persist in the same character which brings about his death." In this student's interpretation, story (script) and Firs's "his-story" are dislocated. Individual (local) and socially determining (grand) narratives diverge. Here Griffiths's cultural materialist play of choice, agency, and structure is fine-tuned, reread, and rediscovered within a poststructuralist socialism in a reading as radical as Griffiths's own rediscovery of Chekhov.

Despite this poststructuralist student's position, these three analyses of Cambridge students' summaries do indicate very clearly the layered macrostructural relationship between political/formal reading formations and audience interpretations; and their responses point also to the danger of quantifying in an oversimplistic way, since the same topic of discourse — social change / the passing of the old order — means very different things in three discourses pertaining to three distinct social audience positions: to the "futility" of life (student 1), to the commoditizing gentry (student 2), and to all "transcendentally allotted qualities," including the "ordering" qualities of Left conceptual analysis itself (student 3).

But how representative is the poststructuralist account we have just discussed among the larger student body? Or is it possible to generalize

Christensen's hypothesis about American theatre students across disciplines (Russian and drama) and across countries (United States, Britain, Australia)? Is the hypothesis of most academics that we interviewed internationally correct that the theorized (cultural materialist and poststructuralist) accounts would more likely occur in an English group (exposed to the current critical paradigm debate, as in Peter Holland's Cambridge class) rather than in Russian studies? The summaries were postcoded to assess whether social change was a topic of discourse (and whether, in addition, it was the *first* macrostructural proposition) and to examine whether these social change discourses were interpreted from an inevitability, human agency, or indeterminacy position or whether no indication was given of reading formation.

The indeterminacy audience position was postcoded specifically in the poststructuralist sense discussed above in order to distinguish it from the more familiar canonical indeterminacy of inevitable transience, miscommunication, and generational change. The inevitability audience reading in the summaries was postcoded according to emphasis on a fatalistic, nonagentive, or cyclical nature of change. Thus, the following were coded "inevitability": "Everyone is unable to do anything. In summation it's about life. Just as we are. Comic, tragic, noble and silly" (Florida State). "Desperation and helplessness. The characters were batted around by fate. There was a sense of inevitability and it was depressing" (Columbia). Summaries were postcoded "human agency" that recognized individual or political choices people made to change their own destinies within the "shift in economic structures" (Loughborough) or emphasized the force and energy involved in the dynamic of individual/social and intergroup conflict. Key words here included "Firs *regretting past inaction*," "*struggle to improve life*," "*exploring change*," "vibrant characters who *catalyse change*," "*hope towards a new future*," "bourgeois/socialist oppositions *demonstrating a need of action, for change*." Thus, "human agency" reading positions included emphasis on the politics of the production: "I felt it had a distinctly Marxist approach — emphasising the point about bourgeois/socialist oppositions. The emphasis was very much on the inability of the bourgeois to act . . . demonstrating a need for action, for change" (Middlesex). Agency readings also recognized Griffiths's act 2 subtext: "[The vagrant] points out to the audience the discussion of Trofimov and suggests a correlation between him and the vagrant" (Florida State). "Feeling of hope towards a new future — the wish to leave the past behind and be optimistic about the future. This was presented in contrast to destruction as inevitable, the feeling that one can never escape, that there is no hope to the future" (Loughborough).

Of the 122 students who responded to the summary question, 71 percent emphasized social change as a topic of discourse, and of these over three quarters used it as their first macrostructural proposition. The summary topics of discourse thus clearly reaffirmed the semantic differential data's emphasis on Chekhov's "art with a message" as sociological. His message is *about* social change. Of those who responded with social change as a topic of discourse, about a third gave an inevitability reading, and another third gave a human agency reading. Only one student gave an indeterminacy reading of the Eyre/Griffiths production. However, whereas only 12 percent of British social change students interpreted the Eyre/Griffiths *The Cherry Orchard* as inevitable, *47 percent of American students did.* The data support Peter Christensen's view that American students have a tendency to see the historical changes circulating around the sale of the cherry orchard as inevitable.

But, in contrast, the full range of inevitability/agency/indeterminacy readings appeared *only* among the Cambridge english/drama students. This link between theory and English classes was further supported by responses to the prescreening question: "Would you say you're impressed by any of the following approaches to textual or performance study?: New Criticism, Semiotics, Cultural Materialism, Marxist Theory, Feminist Theory, Post-Colonial Theory, Post-structuralist Theory, New Historicism, Psychoanalytic Theory, Other." The English students covered a far richer range of critical approaches than all other groups. For example, the Cambridge English students (year 3) had read virtually no standard analyses of Chekhov (and mentioned only Vera Gottlieb as "most interesting"). But in responding to the approaches to textual or performance study that they were "impressed by," they nominated semiotics (Barthes), feminist theory (Jardine, Newman, *The Feminist Reader*), psychoanalytic theory (Ellman), new historicism (Greenblatt), and poststructuralist theory (Derrida). In contrast, the Bangor Russian studies students had read a variety of books on Chekhov (mainly Peace but also Magarshack, Valency, Styan, Gottlieb, and Williams) but did not give a single example of theory that impressed them. The same was true of the Florida State theatre (master's) students, who strongly mentioned the influence of Robert Brustein, who is known for his "antitheory" position in drama criticism. Commenting in interview about the more extensive turn to theory in Shakespeare than in Chekhov studies, Brustein said, "I don't think academics make reputations on Chekhov the way they do on Shakespeare. Shakespeare's a much better object for parasites than Chekhov. And in fact, Chekhov, bless him . . . in *Uncle Vanya* was . . . highly satirical of the professors who later would be eating his remains . . . for the advancement of their careers. . . . I can't bear what's happening in scholarship these days. It's getting further and further from the humanity of literature, and more and more self-engrossed and narcissistic. And thank heavens the structuralists haven't found Chekhov yet!" (personal interview with Tom Burvill, May 1994).

The Agents of Change: Trofimov and Lopakhin

Would the Eyre/Griffiths Trofimov be read as a positive change agent? One "Left Wing" Hull drama student, for example, adopted the Mick Ford position, liking Anton Lesser's portrayal of Trofimov in the television production "because I have seen him played as rather ridiculous — a foolish crusader — but here he was credible — he believed and so we believed." Or would the students' dominant reading be that of the "Left-ish" Durham Russian studies student who described Trofimov as an "idealist, dreamer"? Or the "Liberal" Hull student who said Trofimov "captured the idealism of youth"?

Open-ended comments as to why Trofimov was liked/disliked in the Eyre/Griffiths production were postcoded[1] according to three main categories: (1) Trofimov as social force and change agent: the serious radical, working actively to change others (i.e., Griffiths's Trofimov, a man "to be reckoned with"). There were 13 percent responses in this category. (2) Trofimov as "eternal student": the rhetorician who preaches revolution but can't find his galoshes; sincere but comical, youthfully naive, slightly pathetic, and physically weedy (the canonical Trofimov). There were 26 percent responses in this category. (3) The sincere, positive idealist of passionate energy and serious thought who is nevertheless solipsistic because he does not act on other people and does not represent a connection with "the people." There were 30 percent responses in this category. (Two other postcoding categories emerged: responses to Lesser's professional performance, 15 percent; and "other," 16 percent.) The production did achieve a positive Trofimov: 70 percent of the students liked him, and 43 percent read him as an energetic, positive character. But only 13 percent read him as a serious agent of social change.

Both Eyre and Griffiths wanted to portray Lopakhin positively. In the postscreening questionnaire there were two semantic differential questions (on a seven-point scale) relating a series of characteristics in two of Griffiths's key scenes: (1) "When in Act III Lopakhin announces that he has bought the cherry orchard and then speaks to Ranevskaya, how would you describe him? sympathetic/unsympathetic; negative/positive; sensitive/insensitive; complex character / shallow character; greedy/generous?" (2) "When in Act IV Lopakhin talks about the fields of poppies, how would you describe him? lover of nature / oblivious to nature; mercenary/non-mercenary; unsympathetic/sympathetic; sensitive/insensitive; complex character / shallow character?"

In addition to the possibility of postcoding (and quantifying) students' reasons for liking Lopakhin, it was possible to draw on this semantic differential data to examine student responses to Griffiths's cherry orchard–buying but nature-loving "accountant." In the "I've bought the house" scene, Lopakhin was seen by students as a positive character overall. What is surprising is that he is seen so positively despite a tendency to find him "insensitive" and "unsympathetic" in that same scene. However, this apparent contradiction is explained by the fact that, in addition, Lopakhin was seen as a complex rather than a shallow character in this scene. In other words, as students also reported in focus group discussions, Lopakhin was viewed as crass and overbearing during his drunken dance in act 3, but he was also forgiven by many students because he has tried to help Ranevskaya first and has bought the orchard almost to his own surprise. In addition, some argued (like Peter Holland) that in this scene "you get the insight into why he did what he did — you find out about his father" (Charles Sturt). There were, however, significant quantitative differences between U.S. and British students on the greedy/generous scale, U.S. students finding the entrepreneur less greedy. British students also found Lopakhin significantly more positive than American students, but the latter found him significantly more complex.

A complex Lopakhin also emerged from the second semantic differential question (about the poppy field). But this complexity was not made up of the combined mercenary / lover of nature qualities that Griffiths looked for. Overall, 46 percent of students rated Lopakhin as mercenary (compared with 20 percent who did not), while only 20 percent read him as a lover of nature (compared with 50 percent who saw him as "oblivious to nature"). In addition, there was quite a strong *negative* correlation between the "lover of nature" and "mercenary" responses. In other words, only 7 percent of students saw Lopakhin in the poppy field scene as Griffiths would have liked them to see him: as both a lover of nature and an "accountant." Thus, correlations of weighted adjectives across the semantic differential scale suggest that the complexity of Lopakhin was *not* read in Griffiths's terms. So what qualities, then, did make up the positive complexity of Lopakhin for these students?

Quantified semantic differential scales reveal that Lopakhin was viewed "complexly" as a positive yet relatively unsympathetic, insensitive, and mercenary character in specific scenes. But this quantified approach doesn't take us far in explaining what, narratively speaking, that complexity consisted of. One further survey question could help with this matter. In the postscreening questionnaire students were asked to respond "yes/no" whether they liked the various *Cherry Orchard* characters and (in an open-ended answer) why. Overall, Lopakhin was liked by most university students. But what did "liking Lopakhin" mean, and how did this attitude relate to students' reading of Eyre/Griffiths's *The Cherry Orchard?* By tracing *individual students'* various responses to Lopakhin across the postscreening questionnaire, it is possible to get a more fine grained understanding of the complexity of liking Lopakhin than by simply quantifying postcoded responses.

In these open-ended responses, only one student — a female ("Socialist") drama student from Hull University — "liked Lopakhin *overall*" in terms of Griffiths's specific reading: "a combination of business interests and sensitivity." In responding to the poppy fields semantic differential question, she clearly read him the way Griffiths did, ranking Lopakhin strongly as both a lover of nature and a mercenary. She also found him in this scene to be both insensitive and sympathetic, and it was this combination of characteristics that contributed to her very high ranking of Lopakhin as a complex character in this scene. By comparison, a female ("Conservative") Russian studies student from Durham University indicated the difficulty in assessing readings of the complexity of Lopakhin only quantitatively. She liked Paterson's performance because he was "originally peasant status, he has worked hard to buy the estate. [This was an] HONEST — true characterisation." As one of the relatively few Conservative Party supporters in the British student sample, this student perhaps saw Lopakhin the way Bill Paterson tried to play him: as part of the new, 1980s generation of neoconservative entrepreneurs. Certainly, elsewhere in her questionnaire she underlined that this production was about "Lopakhin as a hard-working man." This could account for her reading of Lopakhin in the poppy field scene as both a lover of nature and strongly nonmercenary (while also being unsympathetic, sensitive, and complex).

If we cannot be absolutely sure of this 1980s reading of Lopakhin by the Tory Durham student, we can be certain of it in the case of a male ("Socialist") drama student from Loughborough. He liked Paterson's Lopakhin, though with "mixed feelings." This was because he was "an 80s character = Yuppie, but [he was] a yuppie with a heart. There was a terrible sadness to his life — past and present." His reading of Lopakhin's complexity was spelled out here; and, like the socialist student from Hull, this Loughborough student was one of the few who ranked Bill Paterson's poppy fields performance as both lover of nature and mercenary.

The difficulty, however, of trying to establish simple correlations between social audience positions (conceived politically, as in the case of these two socialist students) and spectator positions presented by the production of socialist playwright Trevor Griffiths is evident from the fact that one socialist student liked the production and one did not. And further, the one who did not like the production specifically stated that it was Griffiths's "alienating" act 2 that she disliked because it was "overplayed, sombre," and did "not gel with the rest." The socialist student who did like the production enjoyed act 2 for *nonagentive*/ non–social change reasons! "There is no long term hope. The play reinforced this for me."

Fine-grained analysis of this kind is essential if we are to avoid overgeneralized correlations drawing on simple quantitative data. But is there no way, then, to generalize about liking Lopakhin from this data? In fact, certain more general patterns did emerge through postcoding of openended responses to why Lopakhin was liked. He was liked by some (23 percent) because the complexity of Paterson's performance emphasized the *ambiguity and pain of his upward mobility*: for example, "[it was a] wonderful portrayal of a working class, peasant-stock man made rich. The lacking in breeding puts into heartbreaking relief his incongruous presence in the house" (Royal Holloway). In this category Paterson's Scottish accent was liked because it was "so important in showing class differences" (Cambridge). Overall, this reading primarily situated Lopakhin's complexity in his handling of the social disjuncture between his peasant past and the gentry world he inhabits now, and some respondents read this as heartbreaking, others as comic in the Senelick manner.

Lopakhin was liked by others (7 percent) as a *complex but driven agent of change*: "A positive force through the doom and gloom — the zest for life and driving for progress in terms of the real world which acts as a necessary contrast to the other characters" (Loughborough). This reading emphasized the strong, energetic Lopakhin and the realist of the future rather than the heartbreaking incongruous presence that relates to his peasant past. In this reading Lopakhin "crashed through the play" (Hull), "charged through the play" (Hull), and his "complexity" revolved around his action more than his status.

By others (5 percent) Lopakhin was liked (and sometimes also disliked) as the *economic individualist*. This general category contained the two political inflections mentioned earlier: the socialist's 1980s "yuppie with a heart" and the Tory's peasant who had "worked hard to buy the estate." One Middlesex drama student liked the "good representation of single minded capitalism." And a Bristol drama student liked the "sense of the economic individualist caught in the character's decisiveness." In contrast, a Scottish Russian studies student from Bangor disliked him because "I couldn't relate to him being a Scot. He was more mercenary and callous than [Lopakhin is in] my own interpretation." This purely *mean* stereotypical Scot, the "capitalist dude," was criticized by students at Columbia as well as by another Bangor student who disliked Lopakhin because the "Scottish accent was somewhat disquieting." In fact, this Bangor student disliked the entire production because the "use of Scottish accents . . . was an insult to Scottish people and totally inappropriate in the production of a Russian play." Nearly all of the (rather unexpectedly) low rating for liking Lopakhin at Bangor was due to this aspect of his Scottishness. (Perhaps a common devolutionist sympathy?)

To summarize: 61 percent of the students overall liked Lopakhin; he was seen as a positive but also unsympathetic and insensitive character in the "I've bought the house" scene; 46 percent read him as mercenary; 20 percent read him as a lover of nature; and only 7 percent read him as both in the poppy fields sequence; 23 percent (16 percent of total respondents) liked him for his "ambiguity" associated with social mobility; 17 percent for his drive, energy, and emphasis on change; and 5 percent for his economic individualism.

The Vagrant as Dramatic Disjuncture

In Griffiths's account of his translation of *The Cherry Orchard*, the vagrant is at least as important as Trofimov and Lopakhin as an agent of social disjuncture. Griffiths identified the vagrant as an "extraordinary menace" who "destabilises any notion the audience might have of a settled world, *their* settled world."

As directed by Richard Eyre, the entry of the vagrant in act 2 was, indeed, threatening. This was partly the result of camera style, as the series of extraordinarily long tableau shots — of Gayev, Ranevskaya, and Lopakhin on the bench, of the close-up interaction between Ranevskaya and Lopakhin, and of Gayev, Ranevskaya, Lopakhin, Trofimov, Anya, and Firs before the sound of the breaking cable — were interrupted by faster edits and violent movement in-frame as the vagrant enters and speaks. It was partly a matter of lighting, as the sun sets completely, and the silent tableau of cherry orchard people is confronted by a looming, dark figure shuffling slowly, ominously, and noisily (on the studio shale) toward them. The dramatic interruption was also partly the result of sound contrasts, as Yepikhodov's quiet guitar and Firs's plaintive recollection about hearing a similar sound ("an owl hooted") "before the misfortune" when "they set us free" are replaced not only by the threatening noise of the vagrant's slow, shuffling march into frame but also by his growling, angry voice: "Brothers, starving and suffering comrades, unite now by the river, let them *hear* your misery."

Focus group interviews clearly revealed that some students (for example, at Columbia University) could be "unsettled" by the set of act 2. Yet this was not perceived as being *politically* "destabilizing" in Griffiths's sense. What kind of sociological reading, then, would the students apply to Griffiths's most important destabilizing character? A number of students in focus group discussions said that they had hardly noticed the vagrant at all until the postscreening questionnaires had drawn attention to him. When "asked the question" by the research process students tended to reach for canonical interpretations that focused on themes of the "passing" old order and the societal place of peasants who were (or should be) sad and grateful rather than threatening and powerful. Where Griffiths's dramatic disjuncture *was* noticed it was often seen as either unfocused or "deviant" rather than revolutionary. In a multiple-choice question only 18 percent of respondents nominated the vagrant in the Eyre/Griffiths production as "revolutionary" rather than a "peasant," "escaped convict," or "returning soldier."

In fact, the survey asked six different questions about the vagrant. The resulting data indicated that a quarter of the students said they hardly noticed the vagrant in the production. Asked why they chose particular multiple-choice designations of what the vagrant represented, it was clear that in the production discrete images and words cued students to their readings far more often than Griffiths's "freedom" subtext did. Thus, the "escaped convict" multiple-choice response was nominated because of the interpretation of quite particular details relating to performance, script, bodily detail, timing, and intertextual reference. Here an "escaped convict" schema ("shaven head"/ "ball and chain"/ "dangerous, lack of respect"/ "ragged"/ "on-the-run"/ "cunning"/ "rough"/ "desperate"/ "thieving"/ "arbitrary arrival"/ "alien"/ "looked like Magwitch in *Great Expectations*") was constructed on the basis of textual and performance cues.

In contrast, the "revolutionary" was primarily constructed around his language: "he spoke of comrades," "he spoke about uprising," "he was scathing about the upper class," "his ramblings suggested he had a cause," "he questioned the politics of the assembled group," "he was at the end of his life, *shouting* for a new life." Consequently, Trevor Griffiths's controversial changes to Chekhov's text were important here (the use of "comrades" was noted and even generated misreadings that included students hearing things the vagrant *didn't* say about "uprisings" and the "redistribution of wealth"). For some students (as for Senelick) this authorial "talk" was an offensive authorial sign for Griffiths as "political activist."

Overall, discrete images and words far outnumbered references to narrative or Griffiths's subtext in explaining the students' choice of nomination for the vagrant. Out of 143 responses to this question, only 2 gave a (Griffiths) narrative-based explanation for one of the nominations in the multiple-choice question. While the "escaped convict" reading could draw on what Roland Barthes (1975) called a density of proximate "expansions" within a conventional narrative schema (e.g., the actor's trailing, limping leg could be read cognitively as dragging a ball and chain behind him), the "revolutionary" reading tended to emphasize, students said, the rhetoric of the director's "ramblings" about comrades and the redistribution of wealth. For example, one student wrote that the vagrant "seemed rag-tag yet educated — someone like Trofimov who could work but chooses not to, and lives off the efforts of others while he rambles on about change." These "ramblings" were not read by most students in terms of the broader context of "alienated" peasants, servants, and student intellectuals as Griffiths intended with his act 2 subtext. When the vagrant *was* connected with Trofimov, he was as likely to be embedded in a "dole scrounger / parasite" schema ("lives off the efforts of others") as in an "exploited class" schema.

Further, apart from the one example quoted above, nor did the "peasant" readings relate to the Griffiths subtext. Unlike the responses to the "escaped convict" and "revolutionary" multiple-choice nominations, which tended to draw on direct visual or verbal textual cues, the "peasant" identification tended to be nominated for more general historical reasons:

"because of situation in Russia at this time"; "because . . . he seems to match to the stereotyping image of the poor vulgar peasant of the time" (Middlesex); "how I felt peasants were behaving after emancipation — lost with no money" (Middlesex). Students, in other words, constructed three rather different schemas for "escaped convict," "revolutionary," and "peasant" (cued by visuals, language, and general historical codes), establishing different spectator positions, which were carried to their *next* vagrant question, which was "Why do you suppose he was introduced by Chekhov?"

This survey question asked about Chekhov's (rather than Eyre/Griffiths's) construction of the vagrant. Unlike the responses to most of the open-ended questions, there was an overwhelming similarity of responses here. Out of 125 responses to this question, no less than 57 percent of students gave the following kind of "outsider/insider" explanation: "to represent the infiltration of 'less desirable' elements into the once protected, sheltered lives of the falling aristocracy" (Harvard); "to bring an element of the *outside world* . . . into the claustrophobic atmosphere of the house and its grounds" (Hull); "to show the audience a picture of the outside world — what is really happening instead of their blinkered, claustrophobic family's visions" (Loughborough). Of the remaining responses, 14 percent said the vagrant was introduced "to emphasise Ranevskaya's frivolity," and 14 percent said "a representation of the future / social change."

These data establish very clearly just what most students meant by saying that Chekhov's is "art with a message": *it is about change associated with the social claustrophobia and blindness of a particular "complacent wealthy" class.* But there is another important inclusion here: both Lopakhin and Trofimov were generally seen as part of this claustrophobic "comfort and luxury" on the estate. Thus, students argued that Chekhov introduces the vagrant "to show . . . Lopakhin's and Trofimov's inability to deal with real examples of the people they talk about — [and the] whole family's inaction and recoiling from the unknown" (Columbia) "to undercut all the high talk by Trofimov." Accordingly, the vagrant was "an infringement on the self-indulgence of the gathering" (Loughborough).

The next question about the vagrant was "Why do you suppose he was introduced by this *production*?" thus focusing on Eyre/Griffiths's (rather than Chekhov's) meanings. Over three quarters of the students in fact perceived the television production as "true to Chekhov," which explains why most also answered this vagrant question with the response, "because Chekhov used him" or "to be true to the playwright." Only very occasionally a student responded with a point about the politics of this particular production of Chekhov: "the same [as Chekhov's reason for the vagrant] with some Red leanings thrown in (hindsight is 20/20)" (Florida State).

Overall, the reading of the vagrant in this question had the sense of "inevitable" class forces rising against the blind and "claustrophobic" cherry orchard people, among whom students included Trofimov and Lopakhin. Very few responses (7 percent) linked the vagrant to Griffiths's subtext (as in the response, "to point out to the audience the discussion of Trofimov and suggest a correlation between him and the vagrant" [Florida State]).

If the vagrant *was* seen as a dramatic disjuncture, this was of the "outside" into an "inside" that included Trofimov and Lopakhin. The students' reading of the sociological in the case of the vagrant was most often based on a combination of traditional reading formation (i.e., the noncommunicating world of gentry/intellectual claustrophobia) and a retrospectively perceived Russian history (the "inevitable" revolution) than on Griffiths's positive change agent valuation of Lopakhin or Trofimov.

Firs's Dying Fall: Mumbling, Muttering, Droning, and Speaking

For Trevor Griffiths, it was through Firs's words in act 2 that "freedom is unleashed in this text, and it resonates throughout the play." Equally, for Griffiths it was Firs's semirecognition at the end of the play of his own bad faith that emphasized the crucial importance of human agency in challenging social structure. The reading by students of Firs's death is thus highly significant in assessing what kind of sociological meaning they attributed to (Griffiths's) Chekhov.

In the postscreening questionnaire, students answered two questions, one multiple choice and one open ended, about Firs in the Eyre/Griffiths production: "When you watched the final scene of Firs falling to the ground, how did you interpret it? Just another helpless, hapless Chekhov character? A servant exploited by his masters? Just an old man 'ready for the knacker's yard' as Yasha says? Someone who has brought this all on himself — the curtain goes down, he gets up and life goes on? A sad but dignified ending?" and "What aspects of the performance, lighting, script or whatever led you to this interpretation of Firs at the end of the play?"

The students' strongly sociological reading of this production was again indicated, with easily the largest percentage (41 percent) of students choosing "a servant exploited by his masters" response to the multiple-choice question. But which aspects of production multimediality helped lead the students to a particular interpretation? The point of adding an open-ended survey question asking students which aspects of the production led them to their particular interpretation of "Firs falling to the ground" was again to generate topics of discourse. But unlike the earlier "what was it about?" questions, in this case the survey question focused these topics specifically on the "semiotic thickness" (Elam 1980) or multimediality (Eversmann forthcoming) of the television event by way of its wording (i.e., "what aspects of the performance, lighting, script . . . "). There is no guarantee that what respondents say is how (unconsciously and emotionally) they may have been affected by the television image or sound. But that is not the point of the exercise. The question is asking students how they *interpret* (cognitively) their response to Firs falling down (i.e., during Eversmann's postperformance cognitive phase). And what this exercise does reveal is the complex interaction of image/sound/text with a student's prior reading formation.

For example, the humanist Cambridge student who read *The Cherry Orchard* in terms of an "inevitable change" / "everything works in cycles" formation *saw* the woollen shawl that Firs picked up as a baby blanket. (The shawl had been dropped on the floor initially by Charlotta much earlier in the scene, after she had done her baby imitation.) In the open-ended response to Firs's death this student emphasized that the wrapping of the old man in a baby blanket signified both death and rebirth and that social change was thus captured in the inevitable cycle of generations. In contrast, the socialist Cambridge student who read the play in terms of exploitation saw the shawl as Gayev's overcoat, which Firs's *words* signify in this last scene. Thus, different semiotic channels of the audiovisual text were "called up" by these two Cambridge students according to different (canonical or socialist) readings of Chekhov's social meanings.

The final scene of the Eyre/Griffiths *The Cherry Orchard* was not only shot in an almost empty white set, but the camera was relatively static to allow a major focus on the performance of Paul Curran as Firs. The camera moved only four times in this final sequence, and there were only two cuts: one of them at the end, from the medium close-up of Firs falling toward the camera to the wide shot of him lying prostrate in the empty room. Throughout this "distanced" scene, the lighting was indirect, Howard King's cube of light. His indirect light played for the most part (as King told us) on relatively flat planes of Firs sitting in medium close-up with the white dustcovers over the furniture behind.

Analyzing this scene textually, one could argue that it was sound and acting rather than camera, lighting, or set design that created the dynamic quality of this otherwise static, empty scene. As Firs speaks of Gayev's forgotten fur coat ("He'll be wearing his thin one if I'm not there to see to things. These green young laddies"), the sound of the axe begins, motivating a facial change. Here Firs's mood adjusts from protective sorrow for Gayev to an almost blank incomprehension of his own personal loss. Firs speaks of his wasted life for the first time at this moment. "It's gone. It's gone, as if I'd never lived it. . . . You've no strength left, have ye, eh? You've nothing left. Nothing. You silly old nothing [sobs]. You silly old nothing."

Firs's ritualized, wistful shake of the head as he thinks of Gayev's coat changes at this moment to something visually new: an agitated forward and backward rocking toward the camera that, in its own sad way, assaults the viewer in a manner comparable to the entrance of the vagrant in act 2. Finally, Firs's rocking converts into his forward fall off the chair as the camera cuts to its final wide shot of the dead retainer in an empty room. The sound of the axe stops at the moment of Firs's fall, leaving the final image silent until the sound of the breaking cable, which ends the play.

The camera drama of this "new" Firs was interpreted very positively by a Charles Sturt theatre student: "It was stunning, I loved it, the way it was cut — like he falls into the camera, forward, and it is cut to a side shot and he's still falling." The open-ended survey responses to the death of Firs were analyzed in two ways. The different semiotic aspects of the production that students believed led them to their interpretation of the end of the play were counted. The main aspects of production and performance that students draw on to rationalize their response were, in fact, script and acting style more often than lighting, camera, staging, or sound. Out of 114 respondents to this question, 45 percent drew on aspects of the actor's performance, 39 percent referred to the script or storyline, 5 percent mentioned the lighting, 5 percent the set, 4 percent the camera, and 3 percent the sound effects.

Responses to the two Firs questions were then correlated to examine the relationship between the multiple-choice responses and the "semiotics of production" focus of the open-ended question. Here there was some tendency for students' multiple-choice reading of the meaning of Firs falling to the ground to be habitually linked to an aspect of production that they believed motivated it. Thus, students who believed "he has brought all this on himself" tended to relate this to Firs's earlier agency in the script (act 2) where he speaks of giving away his freedom. Those students who responded to the multiple-choice question with a "ready for the knacker's yard" reading related this to the actor's physical persona and performance: "looks like he had a stroke" (Columbia); "very decrepit" (Durham); "the frailty of the man led to a sad, rather run-down image —I was expecting it" (Bristol). The students who chose both the "sad" and "helpless/hapless" interpretations of Firs tended to draw on a symbolic "inevitability" reading via either the script or the sound: "the sound of the axe makes us think of fate, hence of dignity in front of one's own fate" (Sussex). Those students who adopted a "life goes on" reading of the ending of the play focused negatively on the theatricality of the acting. Thus, the multiple-choice answer "the curtain goes down, he gets up and life goes on" was drawn on by those students who wanted to criticize the theatricality of the television production: "the final, overdone dive from the chair.... I could not understand the need for such theatricality.... A stupid overstatement of what Chekhov showed in brilliantly sympathetic understatement" (Birmingham). Students who adopted an "exploited servant" choice tended to focus on the interpersonal relationships between Firs and the owners. For these students, the interpersonal "power" dimension might be conveyed by set and camera style ("space and emptiness of room," "close-up rocking," "isolation"), props ("master's coat," "furniture"), physicality ("lost his mind / body broken"), or script ("used and forgotten him").

Although "exploited servant" readings thus drew on a greater range of semiotic channels, a significant group of these were similar to each other in their use of agentive (and often violent) transitives: "they abused and mistreated him," "they exploit their power to command their lives," "they locked inside / betrayed him," "they had broken his body," "they neglected him," "they destroyed and used him." The relationship between the Trevor Griffiths chosen spectator position and the class-oriented social audience position is clear in the following open-ended responses: "The space and emptiness of the room [is] firstly seen as the camera shows the whole space and then pulls back to show a larger space with him within it. This helps you to see him *left* alone. The close-ups on his face also make you feel sadness for the fate of this character. Because of his elderly and fragile appearance and devotion to his masters you do not criticise him for allowing to be used like this but the blame is shifted to those who have abused and mistreated him" (Loughborough). "The close up on the way he was rocking backward and forward. It made me feel angry the way he died all alone after the years he faithfully served the family. They are sensitive to themselves and their own kind but not Firs — he is forgotten. A tiny man in what seemed a huge room by the lighting" (Middlesex).

The contrast between this group of "exploited servant" interpretations and other multiple-choice readings is also evident in students' description of Firs's last words. A "ready for the knacker's yard" interpretation was correlated with a reading of his last words as a geriatric "*droning* on [that] loses sympathy." A traditional "sad" reading was associated with Firs muttering symbolically; for example, "he seems contented muttering to himself, rather die in the house he loved than alone in hospital. He is symbolic of the old regime and so it is right he should die with it" (Sussex). In contrast, an "exploited servant" reading emphasized the former servant detaching himself from his past as he finally spoke out about the nothing with which he has been left.

Those students who complained about a Firs who "says too much," who should succumb to "a quiet death" and not die actively ("drops dead," "dives from the chair," "overacted," "melodramatic"), pointed to their own reading formation and to the lack of agency in the traditional canonical reading of Chekhov. In contrast, for Griffiths Firs *says* it all — and it is from his earlier words in act 2 that "freedom gets threaded through the play." So his final *speaking* (as contrasted to "mumbling," "droning," and "muttering") is important.

Bronwyn Davies has argued for "another kind of agency.... In a poststructuralist framework . . . agency can be thought of as: the discursive constitution of a particular individual as having presence (rather than absence), that is having access to a subject position in which they have the right to speak and to be heard; . . . a sense of oneself as one who can go beyond the given meanings in any one discourse, and forge something new, through a combination of previously unrelated discourses, through the invention of words and concepts which capture a shift in consciousness that is beginning to occur" (1991, 51). The spectator position that Griffiths was trying to establish in *The Cherry Orchard* was one that perceived Firs having "presence" (rather than social absence) for the first time in his last moments. In this last sequence, as recorded in the BBC production, Firs is also author of multiple meanings for the first time (both "these green young laddies" and "silly old nothing"). He is beginning to forge something new out of previously unrelated discourses. He has new "words" but no new "concepts." But the latter are conveyed by an aggressive camera style and a performance style that link Firs to what one student called the "political landscape."

In some students' "exploitation" reading, Howard King's cube of light was not read as individually imposed, generational, existential, or dignified social "fate." Rather, Firs's abandoned empty space was one of power and agentive neglect: "a larger space with him within it . . . helps you to see him *left* alone." These, however, were *not* the majority readings of Firs's death, even among the "exploited servant" readings. This social audience reading comprised 43 percent of the "exploitation" readings and only 14 percent of the total student responses. Much more typical than an angry reading was the following sympathetic and empathizing set of responses at Charles Sturt University: "That old man was great. 'They've forgotten me. They're leaving it all behind.' It symbolised the death of a whole life style, a whole era, and he was symbolic of it — and he was just beautiful. He reminded me of my dad." "Such dignity. He doesn't whinge when they've forgotten him." "I thought it was meant to be inaudible on purpose, while the sound of the cherry orchard being chopped down was fairly loud." "Maybe the mumbling helped."

In this "symbolic" reading the "inaudible" mumbling and the louder sound of the new reality — the destruction of the trees of the old order — are contrasted, leaving Firs in a position equivalent to Raymond Williams's Chekhov characters, where the new structure of feeling is turned inward and where consciousness is inarticulate and nonconnecting. In that audience reading, Firs's mumbling to himself "helped," because there was no one else to help or hear him.

Conclusion

This chapter has tried to find methodologies that can help explore both "spectators and social audiences . . . as discursive constructs" (Kuhn 1987, 347). As Kuhn argues, textual representations (constructed by way of a variety of vehicles of semiotic communication), contexts of production (and research), social audiences (in this case consisting of students and their reading formations), and spectator positions need to be understood "as a series of interconnected discourses, certain discourses possessing greater constitutive authority at specific moments than others" (1987, 347).

Research methodologies, no less than the processual (Elam 1989) circuits of production, performance, and reception, help give constitutive authority to certain moments; and in this chapter the "moment" profiled has been that of the interaction of spectator / social audience discourses.

The overall findings might be disappointing to Trevor Griffiths. From a number of different qualitative and quantitative measures, a pattern emerged where a relatively small minority of students who saw the Eyre/Griffiths production read it from the spectator positions that the producers tried to design. Topic of discourse analysis indicated that 71 percent of students said *The Cherry Orchard* was about social change, and 77 percent of these used social change as their macrostructural proposition. Although 33 percent gave an "agency" reading of change in their topic of discourse responses, 47 percent of American students gave an "inevitability" inflection to their social change macroproposition, supporting Peter Christensen's observation about his students. Semantic differential data indicated that only 7 percent of students read Lopakhin as both mercenary and a lover of nature; and postcoded qualitative data indicated that only 12 percent of students liked Lopakhin as an agent of social change. Similarly, only 13 percent read Trofimov as a sympathetic but also active agent of change, that is, not as the "eternal student" but as a politically positioned radical who is, in Griffiths's words, a "force" in the text. Multiple-choice data indicated that 41 percent of the students read Firs as "a servant exploited by his masters"; but postcoded data in response to Firs's death indicated only 14 percent who read the final scene as a broadly representative space of power, exploitation, and agentive neglect. There tended to be a feeling among many students that an *active* death, as against a dignified fade-out of Firs, reduced the "Chekhovian" ambiguity of the ending. Overall, the sociological Firs was related to a Chekhov still melancholically and pessimistically locked into the inevitabilities of social change. Postcoded qualitative data in responses to the vagrant indicated that only 7 percent of students linked him to Trevor Griffiths's subtext. Analysis of several questions related to the vagrant indicated that the sociological reading of the vagrant was a traditional one: that the social order was inevitably falling, driven on by its inability to change. A dominant insider/outsider reading of cherry orchard people versus the vagrant included Trofimov and Lopakhin as insiders to this outmoded gentry group rather than change agents in any dynamic way. The vagrant represented less Griffiths's wandering agent of enlightenment and social justice than the exploited "other," a figure who is more representative of the gentry's personal/socialized inadequacies and frivolities than of the positive quest for modernity. Among the majority of university students,

Chekhov remained locked into the past, into history as completed. A minority accepted spectator positions, seeing a Chekhov concerned with the dynamics of social forces as contemporary agencies of change.

NOTES

1. The researchers identified the predominant themes in the open-ended responses. Individual student responses were then classified under these categories independently by two coders. Intercoder reliability was regularly 95 percent or greater.

THE THEATRICAL EVENT

INNER AND OUTER AUDIENCE FRAMES

The outer frame contains all those cultural elements which create and inform the theatrical event. The inner frame contains the dramatic production in a particular playing space. . . . It is the interactive relations between audience and stage, spectator and spectator which constitute production and reception, and which cause the inner and outer frames to converge for the creation of a particular experience. —Susan Bennett, Theatre Audiences

This chapter returns to the live stage. It moves from the macro- to the micro-audience, following Susan Bennett's point that the symptomatic theatre audience consists of small groups of family and friends. It also moves from the "mediated" to the "live" audience. At this point, the "Reading Chekhov" project laid aside its larger-scale focus group and survey approaches for a more fine grained processual approach. This was for a production of Chekhov's *The Seagull* at a consciously (and reflexively) "anti-state theatre" company, the Belvoir Street Theatre in Sydney. Belvoir Street was chosen as a "postcolonial" Australian theatre site to examine the converging of Bennett's inner and outer frames, both in production and among audience members. What notions of Chekhov, Australianness, and modernity would be embodied, via acting, set design, costuming, lighting, and sound, at Belvoir Street, and how would these be perceived by audience members who came from country New South Wales to see it?

Theatre professionals who were involved in this Australian Chekhov production were not interested in some eternal essence of Australianness. This was not, as one of the actors emphasized, an Australian Chekhov in the sense of being set in deep-country New South Wales, near Wagga Wagga, with "To Sydney" in the place of "To Moscow." It *was* Australian in an important way in its translation, specially prepared by director Neil Armfield's Russian partner with particular Australian actors' idiosyncrasies in mind. It was also explicitly postcolonial in its Australian accents and speech rhythms, deliberately avoiding what both its actors and our audience group called the British "plumminess" of language that for so long had been a sign of Australian colonial status in the theatre.

There were also many other signs of the Australian in the production: in the weather-board walls of the set; in the props (e.g., the large box in lieu of Arkadina's traveling trunk, with "Enmore, Australia," an inner-city suburb of Sydney, boldly painted on it); in trivial aspects of the language (Yakov's "g'day," etc.). Sorin's actor, Don Reid, also pointed to deliberately Australian aspects of the costuming, for example, the "brown cardigan with old check dressing gown that so many old Australians in their eighties wear, Nina's pretty little dress . . . you saw heaps of them when I was younger in that Australian period of the 1950s / early 1960s" (personal interview, 1997). But, importantly, these signifiers of the Australian were all embedded in a specific Australian *theatre's* engagement with constructing an audience via its very particular leisure time and space. As the production team put it, "This is Chekhov, Belvoir Street, Surrey Hills in Sydney, 1997."

Points of Theory, Method, and Substance

The focus here is on a particular theatrical institution's embedding of an "Australian Chekhov" in aspects of language, costume, design, place, and time within specific audiencing practices. The chapter will examine the issue of audience construction in production and reception as a series of overlapping histories: of the theatre itself; of its sequencing of plays; of the Belvoir Street Theatre's acting space and its set design around that space; of the director's signature; of casting, acting, use of props, and so on.

My primary focus here is from Bennett's external frame inward. Consequently, I physically approached the theatre with my audience group: Jennie (an employment officer), her partner, Wayne (a prison officer), Anne (a part-time secretary and gardener), and her partner, Paul (a businessman), all from country New South Wales. And, successively, I accompanied them from sitting outside the theatre through the foyer into the auditorium, and I watched the production with them, discussing it with them in process, including during the interval and at dinner afterward. Postperformance discussion is often an important opportunity to reshape initial decoding of the production among small groups of theatre audience members. Consequently, an important "ethnographic" part of my audience study was this sitting over dinner at a local restaurant with these four theatregoing friends after the matinee performance of *The Seagull*, discussing as an audience member with them the production we had just seen.

Two methodological points are important before we proceed. One relates to a necessary reflexivity in this audience interview process. I was not simply a "neutral" observer, nor did I pretend to be. My interest was in how a small group of friends constituted itself as an audience and how it related in doing so to the audiencing frames constructed by the Belvoir Street Theatre and its *Seagull* production. The interviewer became part of this theatre audience group of friends and from time to time during the interview would make comments of an evaluative kind about the production, just as everybody else did. In a longer discourse analysis of this interview, it would be perfectly possible to analyze the turn-taking effect of this on the "interview-as-text" (see, e.g., Tulloch 1999a, chap. 2). But in this chapter, I will ignore the interviewer's interventions (which were relatively minimal), relying on the interviewees' insistence that what is quoted from them here was not especially predetermined by the interviewer's involvement. This audience group met for dinner like this customarily as "regulars" at Belvoir Street Theatre to talk about the performance they had just seen. Their own methodological point to the interviewer was that they felt their after-performance discussion of *The Seagull* perhaps went on for longer than it otherwise might have done but would not have been different in substance. The tape recorder may have encouraged them to elaborate points that normally would have been embedded in their shorthand communication as theatregoing friends; but otherwise, they argued, their views of the production were unchanged by the interview process.

The second methodological point is that this tracing of the lived leisure experience of four members of the audience was at the fine-grained end of our audience analysis for this play. Other parts of the "Reading Chekhov" project at Belvoir Street's *The Seagull* were more representative in approach to its audiences, consisting, for example, of focus group interviews with different generational groups who watched the production. But in this chapter my focus is primarily on Bennett's small self-constituting group of theatregoing friends and their process of bringing their external frames to Chekhov. This country group of audience members was chosen deliberately because of the country theme of the play.

The audience choice was a deliberate device to examine the converging of inner and outer frames.

However, in this particular case study, I do take Bennett's preliminary suggestions further into current cultural studies' audience theory by focusing also on the discursive and spatial frames of "audiencing" constructed by *The Seagull* production itself. This required an extended ethnographic study of the rehearsal/production process. By way of these two ethnographies of "audiencing," then, we could begin to examine how notions of performances-with-an-audience are embedded both as production strategies and as audiences' own lived experience.

This was a *particular* Australian theatre's Chekhov. I will begin with a brief comparison of the sites of performance of two Chekhov plays produced in Sydney during a six-month period: the New Theatre production of *The Cherry Orchard* in Sydney in December 1996 and the March–April 1997 production of *The Seagull* at Belvoir Street Theatre. These two theatres were similar in defining themselves as "not a State Theatre" company. Moreover, both productions established a "history" of Chekhov intertextually (via costuming) in relation to film and popular cultural styles. These two similarities then offer a productive shorthand for the purposes of this section in discussing the institutional particularities and organizational conventions of the specific theatre, Belvoir Street, where Wayne, Jennie, Anne, and Paul came to see Chekhov's *The Seagull*.

To tie together a number of interwoven external and internal spaces in a short case study I will use two linking devices. The first is to emulate the processual nature of the theatre audience itself, taking our small audience group sequentially from outside the theatre through its various spatially situated narratives and histories to the watched performance of the play and then to dinner discussion afterward. In this way we can trace this small group audience's own convergence of outer and inner frames. The second device is to weave through these different audiencing histories one signature motif from the production itself. This was what one reviewer called "Director Armfield's sustained experiment with old chairs and an empty Belvoir space" (Waites 1997).

Theatre Histories

Anne and Paul traveled about 210 kilometers from Bathurst to get to the Belvoir Street Theatre in Sydney to see *The Seagull* that day, and as subscribers they regularly got back home at 3 A.M. after evening performances.

Theatre in a housing estate. Belvoir Street Theatre, Sydney.

Their friends Wayne and Jennie traveled 120 kilometers to Sydney from Blackheath in the Blue Mountains, and prior to that, when all four lived in Mudgee, they would travel 360 kilometers by car (an eight- to nine-hour round trip over quite poor roads) as regulars of the theatre.

Why did they travel so far? Jennie said that when they lived in Mudgee, NSW, they "were *desperate* for something else, some newer ideas than Mudgee could provide, and we bought a subscription." So, in this rather Chekhovian sense, "To Sydney" was a cultural way out of country boredom for my audience group. But why did they choose this particular theatre out of Sydney's rich crop? Why Belvoir Street and not the New Theatre or the Sydney Theatre Company at the Wharf Theatre or at the Opera House? It was, Jennie argued, because of a theatrical "energy" at Belvoir Street that she saw as linked to "the history of Nimrod Theatre behind it, and everything *that* stood for" as Australian theatre. Particular theatre histories and the "moralities" they contained were therefore significant factors in the pleasures and expectations of this audience group; similarly, they were significant variables in the practices and discourses of the different producers of Chekhov.

A thumbnail sketch of the two theatres playing Chekhov in Sydney in late 1996 and early 1997 will indicate what I mean. The New Theatre in Newtown had a sixty-year Old Left history, going back to the 1930s movements for a workers'/people's "nonexpert" theatre with Communist Party links. During the 1930s and 1940s the New Theatre was strongly promoting leftist playwrights and during the Vietnam period was foremost in Australia in doing anti–Vietnam War plays. Although that strong political emphasis had waned with the political changes of recent years, and the theatre was no longer directly aligned to trade unions or to the Communist Party, the political and socially conscious edge of the New Theatre was by no means gone. The director of the New Theatre's *The Cherry Orchard*, Mary-Anne Gifford, was of Old Left parentage and was herself involved in the political movements of the 1970s.

In contrast, Belvoir Street Theatre's history was strongly associated with that of the Australian arts and its recent funding crises. As Jennie (an amateur actor herself) indicated, the theatre's history was embedded in the earlier history of the Nimrod Theatre, which had been in the forefront in NSW in presenting new Australian drama during the 1970s. In 1984 a syndicate of "more than 600 theatre lovers, arts, entertainment and media professionals" (including Australian international high achievers like Patrick White, Peter Carey, Dame Joan Sutherland, Mel Gibson, and Nicole Kidman) took action to save the Nimrod Theatre from demolition "rather than lose another performance space in inner city Sydney" (*The 1997 Book*, Belvoir Street Theatre, 32).

This ownership/event generated Company B under the artistic directorship of Neil Armfield, who argued that the "originality and energy of Company B productions arose out of the unique action" of 1984. From the start there was a sense of ownership by a professional family of theatre and media people, from high culture to soap opera. That sense of professional family ownership was carried on significantly, we were told, through Armfield's policy of equal pay for everyone, from internationally recognized actors like 1997 Oscar best actor winner Geoffrey Rush to front of house, bar, and cleaning staff. Shared vision was also as important to Company B as shared pay. As Belvoir scenic designer Anna Borghesi said, "Working with Neil Armfield and also with Tess Schofield [the costume designer], it's so often so hard to know where the idea came from, whose idea it was" (personal interview, 1997). In the case of *The Seagull* these three (and others) were cooperatively involved in planning from the earliest stages on (Tess Schofield, personal interview, 1997).

Armfield argued that if you have hierarchy off the stage, it shows onstage, and he wrote of the sense of "family belonging" that is present for audience and professional staff at Belvoir Street. "People often describe the experience of coming to Belvoir as an experience of family. This comes from a very particular sense of belonging: to the building itself, to the unique space of the theatre, and most especially to the Company B actors as we witness them grow and develop together from show to show and year to year" (*The 1997 Book*).

Armfield was right in this perception. For many Belvoir Street supporters there was a genuine sense of pride and ownership in seeing Cate Blanchett and Geoffrey Rush dominating the film *Elizabeth* (for which they were both nominated for Oscars). Many subscribers at Belvoir Street Theatre had seen their acting "grow and develop from show to show and year to year." As Anne said, "I've been thrilled to see Geoffrey Rush in two plays last year, before he acted in *Shine*.... He was brilliant. And also people like Hugo Weaving. It's good to recognize some of them are well-known actors, some of them aren't, and I think there's a bit of variety there."

This "family" sense — in relation to the building, to the history of its urban space, and to its actors — worked very strongly for my audience group of subscribers as well. Standing outside the theatre before the performance of *The Seagull*, Wayne said, "It's the galvanized-iron roof [laughs] that brings me here. I mean that seriously. There's a sense of 'it's not the Opera House,' and I've known this place from the days when we used to walk through the car park [to it], and they didn't really care how you got *into* the building. I feel it's part of Sydney, and it's part of our own history.... Look at that couple who have just come in, like the suburban mum and dad, you know. They're not here to be *seen*." Jennie added: "And they're not here to say they've seen it, which you do for, say, *Les Misérables* or *Phantom of the Opera* or *Miss Saigon*." Jennie had taken her two young children to see "*Les Mis*" just the previous week in Sydney, mainly, she said, because her children wanted to go. But this particular weekend the kids were being looked after, and Jennie and Wayne were making their own choice: "*The Seagull* at Belvoir Street, 1997."

In an interview, scenic designer Anna Borghesi elaborated the particular Belvoir Street notion of "audiencing" that Wayne was picking up and enjoying through his emphasis on the theatre's galvanized roof.

> Belvoir Street ... is for an audience who don't have a State Theatre Company background to theatre-going.... [At] the State Theatre companies ... people are paying an incredible amount of money to go and sit there to watch ... work that's beautifully finished with costumes that are immaculately put together, etc. And the fact is that you're not challenged when you go to see stuff like that. I think work here makes an audience go away and *talk*, because some people get really annoyed

Belvoir Street Theatre's galvanized roof.

that it's a bit scrappy [at the beginning of *The Seagull* where a large number of ill-matching chairs are set out for Konstantine's play], saying, "Look at that bunch of old bloody chairs — you'd think they could get six that match," and then it can start a discussion because maybe somebody else might say, "They weren't supposed to be matching.". . . I'm interested in making an audience ask questions . . . so that you don't just get in the car and go home and get into bed and forget about it. (Personal interview, 1997)

All of my audience group did in fact "ask questions" about Borghesi's ill-matching chairs after the performance, noting with approval that it seemed "a creative theme," along with the equally ill matching periods of costuming. Paul pointed to the institutional expectations underpinning their interpretation, saying that "if they'd done that at the Opera House . . . it would have jarred. You'd have thought, Somebody's slipped up here." Two of the group had actually given up Opera House membership for Belvoir Street, seeing the former as a "stereotyped" and "conventional" theatre of "plummy language for the over-fifties."

For this audience group, Belvoir Street's history represented *Australian* theatre in three senses. First, it was Australian in not being *English* Chekhov, with its "plummy language" as a long-lasting signifier of colonization. Second, it had preserved *Australian drama* through collective rather than state ownership (against which kind of theatre Belvoir Street defined itself). Third, its history was very much part of an urban time and space that "belongs to everyone" (the theatre is now physically surrounded by an inner-city housing estate), and Wayne spoke fondly of an earlier Belvoir production that threw open its back hatches and used the actual Sydney cityscape as backcloth. Moreover, unlike the theatres of the State Theatre Company at the Sydney Opera House and the Wharf Theatre, which are situated in the Harbour area of affluence and tourism, Belvoir Street is in strongly "ethnic" territory, with many of the best but cheap Lebanese restaurants a couple of minutes' walk away. It was there (or in the Spanish restaurant where we had our after-show discussion) that this group often ate and talked after the show.

Play Histories

As they walked in from the galvanized-iron-roof exterior through the Belvoir Street foyer to see the matinee performance of *The Seagull,* my

Another set of histories: Pinning up reviews for *The Governor's Family*, Belvoir Street Theatre.

audience group was confronted by another set of histories. This is where the reviews of the production are regularly pinned up, but there were none there that day (possibly because, as Paul pointed out, the earliest reviews had not been particularly favorable, though they were to pick up later). But what they did see in the foyer was a visual history of Belvoir Street productions. For instance, there was the photo of Cate Blanchett (who played Nina today) in her earlier role as Miranda in *The Tempest*.

The foyer photographs were part of a Belvoir display that constructed both past and future histories of the theatre's productions, augmented by the old posters climbing the stairs to the auditorium, and by way of the subscribers' yearbook, which my audience group had already seen and I was carrying with me. Jennie, Wayne, Anne, and Paul, as regular visitors, were also carrying in their memories a history of previous plays in the Belvoir season, and they would walk through this foyer again for later plays that would help reshape their initial interpretations of *The Seagull*. The chairs and set would reappear, for example, in Armfield's next play, *The Governor's Family*, and indeed the chairs had appeared, as the newspaper reviewer noted, systematically (and as some kind of signature) in earlier Armfield plays like Ben Jonson's *The Alchemist* (which Anne also mentioned favorably).

As we went through the foyer, Jennie pondered on what Armfield would do with the set this time. While representing a signature feature of

Armfield's productions, the chairs were not, as he himself insisted, inevitable or "mechanical," nor did they signify continuously the same meanings. In *The Seagull* the set designer actually began with the traditional Chekhov garden bench for the family watching Kostya's play. But, Armfield said, "in the first rehearsal I said, 'Everyone have a chair, and you're responsible for your own chair,' and that was related to Anna Borghesi's suggestion that everyone was so obsessed that each should have their own little shrine or little work station and come at [their part] from that. . . . Everyone is so separate in this play that the bench became too spatially straitjacketing and restrictive" (personal interview, 1997).

The chairs signifying that "everyone is so separate" derived from a blending of conventional readings of Chekhov with Armstrong's directing signature. The familiar Chekhov bench (inflected in Richard Eyre's *The Cherry Orchard* with John Berger/Gainsborough readings) was again here made to mean intertextually and interperformatively. In Belvoir Street's next play, *The Governor's Family*, Armfield's "sustained experiment with old chairs and an empty Belvoir space" continued but was inflected now via *The Seagull*. So in both *The Seagull* and *The Governor's Family* the chairs conveyed isolation and solipsism within the heart of these nineteenth-century fin de siècle families. The rows of chairs that we first saw in front of Kostya's little stage in *The Seagull* reappeared in *The Governor's Family* as each self-obsessed character's "own little shrine." In this later production they were shrines to the governor's daughter's socialism, to the European-aristocrat mother's laudanum-induced near-catatonia, to the son's effete decadence, to the British governor's white male guilt in the face of the literal rape of black Australia. And both here and in *The Seagull* the chairs were juxtaposed with a continuous roaming, wandering traversal of the theatrical space by displaced characters.

It was by way of these theatrical connections, of theme, of time, of set, and of actors, that Belvoir Street's postcolonialism spoke to Chekhov. 1997–98 was a key moment of public controversy over the Aboriginal land rights issue in Australia, and *The Governor's Family* played out its late-nineteenth-century history as a series of overlapping ownerships: between European empires (the father's British imperial culture against his wife's Austro-Hungarian one); between different classes (as the late-nineteenth-century Australian Labor movement was seen also to be compromised, patriarchal, and racist); between ages and genders (the mother's effete "European" decline, her daughter's naive "New World" socialism, each in the thrall of "their men"); between sexual preferences (the brother's homosexuality, the sister's sexual favors from the trade union leader); and between races (as the black servant turns out, via her rape and child by the governor, to be "the governor's family" too).

On their way to *The Seagull*, my audience group already had some sense of what Armfield was signifying conceptually with his "family displacement" theme. He had written about it in the 1997 subscribers brochure, which they had read: "The notion of family is central to our 1997 Season. Across the productions I am aware that the linking concern is with family and home on the one hand, and the tension of displacement and separation on the other. Pabst's siren of innocence, Lulu, is displaced in a foreign home, while Black Mary is displaced and hunted in her own. The governor's family of Beatrix Christian deliquesce in the strange heat of Australia and collapse from within, the Sorin family in *The Seagull* refuses to hear Kostya's desperate scream for *himself*" (Armfield, *1997 Book*). When writing about *The Governor's Family*, Armfield elaborated on the contemporaneity of this Belvoir Street sense of family and audiencing: "There is a wonderful sense in *The Governor's Family* of two kinds of truth. One is the risk of judgment — which involves respect, trust, love, kindness — inviolable and unchanging and the basis of human certainty. The other is like shifting sand, affected by situation, opinion, expedience, tradition, loyalties, the historical accident of time, [and] prejudice. It is in the shifting ground of this kind of 'truth' where that vicious fool Pauline Hanson is currently floundering" (Armfield, 1997 Book).

Pauline Hanson at the time was regarded by many as one of Australia's most racist politicians. She was held responsible by many Australians for an antimigrant backlash in the country that was threatening its tourist and trade relations with Southeast Asian neighbors, whom the recent Labor government under Paul Keating had been assiduously courting as part of Australia's growing Republican move. This tension between a centered "family and home" and the shifting ground of historical time, national racism, and local prejudice, which was also a tension between tradition, modernity, and postmodern fragmentation, was powerfully inflected as white imperialism in *The Governor's Family*. In this Armfield production the fading matriarch was played by the same actress, Gillian Jones, who performed Arkadina in *The Seagull*, and there were strong continuities in the set of the two sequential plays also. What the set designer described as the "rehearsal room" wooden floor of *The Seagull* was reproduced for the next play, as were its off-white papered walls. But in *The Governor's Family* the white civilization signified by the wooden floor struggled to contain the dust and dirt of an inner square of "aboriginal" earth, while the white walls were scrawled with a threatening black graffiti.

In an important sense, then, the politics of Belvoir Street's "family" series of plays were contemporary Australian. At the same time, like Mary-Anne Gifford's *The Cherry Orchard* at the New Theatre, Belvoir Street's Chekhov played between two periods, "then" and "now." In her program notes for *The Cherry Orchard*, Gifford wrote (referring to the new conservative government's attack on the welfare state), "There is nothing solid to hold on to, things have been taken away we thought were solid." Like Gifford's 1970s Left, the Australian Left had a similar problem at the turn of the twentieth century in Belvoir Street's play *The Governor's Family*. Here the socialist-inclined daughter of the British governor of New South Wales seeks the love of the Irish leader of the revolutionary movement but is rejected on class-imperialist grounds. Neither of these class enemies and potential lovers, however, supports the part-white Aboriginal woman at the center of the play who has been raped and tortured by the Irish socialist leader's brothers. In this play, as Armfield says of his season generally, the family was the center of theatrical attention, particularly the governor's family, which was self-destructing from within its white imperialist, patriarchal traditions. In *The Governor's Family* the family center was always being displaced (via geography) and separated (via generation, class, race, and gender). The periphery-center relations of coloniality were embedded in the interperformative themes, sets, and acting of a particular Australian theatre, which, at the time of the research, was playing Chekhov.

Regular Belvoir Street audiences were encouraged by the subscribers brochure (as well as the overlap of key actors and of set design between the two plays) to interpret *The Seagull* and *The Governor's Family* in this kind of family/temporal/political displacement continuity. Like the governor's son (who affected an Oscar Wilde decadence) and his daughter (who adopted soup-kitchen socialism), the young people of *The Seagull*, Konstantine and Nina, also were engaged in parent-child rivalry for new forms that were familial and political as well as theatrical. Armfield wrote that *The Seagull* "could have been written yesterday." *The Governor's Family* was indeed written "yesterday," and the associations *The Seagull* invoked for its audience (in sequence with *The Governor's Family*) were strongly contemporary.

Focusing on Konstantine, scenic designer Anna Borghesi "read in" an audience relevance for the families of contemporary (especially rural) youth. She asked her audience to "please have an opinion . . . when you look at *The Seagull*. Youth suicide is an *incredible* issue in this country. . . . *The Seagull*'s not about presenting answers . . . but it's setting the wheels in motion for an audience to go away and talk, . . . and hopefully something will happen. That's part of the idealism of doing the work, I suppose" (Borghesi, personal interview, 1997).

This particular contemporary inflection was not one that my audience group responded to personally. Their children were too young for them to worry directly about teenage suicide. However, Armfield's "family displacement" theme did help cue one of Wayne's main pleasures in this production, which he was to speak about both during the interval and after the production. This pleasure of recognition came via a very recent "generation clash" for Wayne, not with the young suicide but with the old man, brother of Arkadina. Seeing Sorin sitting in that other temporally "ill matching" chair in the Armfield production, the shiny new 1997 wheelchair, Wayne was reminded of his own difficult father, who, after years of distance, came to die with him in Mudgee. Wayne's father was "old Australian" and, unlike his son, racially prejudiced. But he was a father who had come to his son to die. Wayne was visibly moved from early on watching *The Seagull* and even by the interval was saying that he would not have enjoyed it prior to that experience of generational tension, displacement, and reconciliation within the family.

Stage Histories

As Wayne, Jennie, Anne, and Paul moved from the foyer into the auditorium, they encountered Yakov slowly putting out Armfield's ill-matching chairs on the acting space. Wayne liked this aspect of Belvoir Street's informal acting space: "I enjoyed that because it gave you the feeling that you were going into a play that wasn't set up on a separate stage. It was trying to connect to you coming into the theatre, and whether Chekhov had done that or not, I felt they'd done it well so you could feel 'yes, I'm in the theatre, yes, they're about to put on a play. But we're all connected.'"

If the *theatre's history* emphasized the political economy of "family" ownership, and its program of *play histories* in 1997 dramatized family displacement and a center-periphery modernity, the *stage history* of Belvoir Street was designedly all about reintegration: between Armfield's onstage chairs on the small thrust stage and the very close up seats where the audience sits.

As Armfield described it, the key to Belvoir Street's play-making history has been in workshopping a particular relationship between actors and audiences. It has been a relationship between "your own life and experience and associations," on the one hand (e.g., an audience member's media-related experience of racism, or Wayne's personal experience of his father's racism when he came to Mudgee), and the particular sense of space around Belvoir Street Theatre's thrust stage, on the other. "The 'architectural aspect' . . . is fundamental — the playmaking corner of the Belvoir stage is the starting point of all our work. It is a space in which prejudice, cliche, vanity, and above all fear, can be surrendered in the spirit of trusting human interaction. It frames the action, it amplifies the energy of the stage and it connects audiences and performers into a single, unified space — a room. . . . [I]t is the Belvoir corner that is responsible for that simple, un-rhetorical yet detailed and focused style of production and performance that Company B has become famous for. That is why when we go on tour we have to take our corner with us" (Armfield, *The 1997 Book*).

As Schofield said, all the production staff at Belvoir Street emphasized this approach to theatre, "which means that you're honest about the space that you're in. It's 1997, it's Surrey Hills [Sydney], it's Belvoir Street, we're doing a production of Chekhov. We aren't a group of Russian actors or production designers putting on this thing. So we talked about the rehearsal room approach and how the low-tech approach is also very suited to Belvoir Street" (personal interview, 1997).

Similarly, prior to walking in to see *The Seagull* our audience member Jennie said, "I would expect something more than a conventional stage and period setting." In his *The Seagull* program notes (which Jennie at that point had not read), Armfield spoke of ways of "*relaxing* the production, of letting it feel as accidental as the play feels. . . . And so the Belvoir St corner for *The Seagull* resembles the corner of our rehearsal space, and we have worked against the straight-jacketing of characters into specific realities of period and illusions of particular scenic constructions in favour of a loose collection of clothes and artefacts and furniture gathered together for the telling of this story."

The reviewer that noted "Armfield's sustained experiment with old chairs and an empty Belvoir space" was pointing to an important aspect of this postmodern signature as director. Together with actors speaking out to the very close up audience, this rehearsal room concept was part of his antinaturalist, anti–State Theatre Company repertoire of "finished work but . . . giv[ing] the sense of . . . kind of stuck together here and a bit of hot glue there . . . [so that] the audience [members] . . . are not kept away by the elite idea that they could never be part of it" (Borghesi, personal interview, 1997).

All the Belvoir productions were striving for this, but *The Seagull*, as a play about new forms, allowed Armfield to foreground the rehearsal room concept as a device (as in the film *Vanya on 42nd Street*) at the beginning of the actual rehearsals. However, as the production developed, the rehearsal room concept began to be rejected, since it was seen to be just as "straight-jacketing" as any specific time period would have been.

But the idea of foregrounding theatre remained. Set, props, and costume histories at Belvoir Street productions were significantly self-referencing. Scenic designer Anna Borghesi, in rejecting "the Russian drawing room" with all the real period pieces audiences would expect to find at the State Theatre Company, said, "We did have a samovar [in *The Seagull*] — in the cupboard as a little joke. . . . I like the idea of *that* kind of history onstage, so that having a cupboard with all that stuff hidden in it was like it was Belvoir Street's cupboard. . . . It was saying, 'This is Belvoir Street. This is the reality of where we are. Even though there's all these Russian characters . . . still, it's 1997 and here we are, here's the samovar from our earlier production of this or that, here's the little dolls from *The Alchemist.* '. . . It's a constant reminder that . . . everything that happens up there is a manufactured thing. There's truth in the lie" (personal interview, 1997). The same "reminder" was conveyed by the packing case stamped with a local inner-city suburb's name: "Enmore, Australia, . . . was definitely related to the idea of them being rehearsal props, so that one day when you went into the big 'real' [State] theatre you'd get the real ones, the beautiful leather trunks. . . . The packing case was actually bought for the previous show, for *Lulu*, and we didn't use it. . . . When I went down to rehearsals it had 'Enmore' written on it and I thought, That's fine. . . . It *represents* 'luggage'" (Borghesi, personal interview, 1997).

Similarly, the ill-matching chairs represented not only Chekhov's famously solipsistic characters nor only the displaced family theme of that year's season. They also signified "this is Belvoir Street. We are workshopping another play with you — Chekhov this time — in our corner." However, this Belvoir Street reflexivity about its stage-audience relationship could have unexpected results. The proximity of audience and acting corner at this theatre meant that anyone could actually see characters and other audience members in the same visual "frame." Anne, who liked to look around the intimately connected audience "about a dozen times" during a Belvoir Street production, said, "Contrasting those women down below me in the audience with their wild hair or their unusual, strong dress sense in comparison with those women on the stage . . . I thought, Oh my god, how pathetic. . . . We've got the beautiful . . . country lass, Nina, who floats around in little lime dresses, lovely figure, and pure skin . . . whereas the men were the geniuses, they were the creators." So here Neil Armfield's intention of a close audience / acting corner interchange actually worked against his thematic intention that it was Konstantine not Nina who was the tragic seagull. And Anne's very reason for subscribing to Belvoir Street rather than the Opera House (i.e., that the former was full of "strong young women" rather than the "blue rinse" middle class) was now subverting what she "saw" on the stage.

Yet Jennie and Wayne engaged very positively with the audience-player "intimacy" of act 1's ill-matched chairs in front of Kostya's stage within Belvoir's stage. Wayne only agreed partly with Anne. "I looked at the audience. . . . A lot of women in there probably are strong in the sense that you are saying. They are the young ones. But I saw women in the audience too who had been through everything that was on the stage." Wayne and Jennie also remembered pleasurably their *own* audience experience with "new forms" theatre narratives. "There was this fringe festival in Sydney. We went down this back alley and up to this theatre at the back of Redfern . . . and a painter and her boyfriend put on this play — it was almost a copy of [Kostya's play]. . . . We didn't know what it was about." But they had the memory of that experience as an intimate, "back alley" actor-audience event. Now they felt there was something of that feeling at the beginning of *The Seagull* too.

Costuming Histories

Soon after taking their seats, my audience group was confronted with virtually the entire cast of *The Seagull*, some of them engaging the audience quite directly with their eyes. A signature of Armfield as director was to introduce his cast to the audience at the start. In Patrick White's *Night on Bald Mountain* they were all on set at the beginning as mountain goats. In *The Seagull* they gathered for Kostya's play, enabling Masha to say directly to the audience, "The play is about to begin." This foregrounding device also allowed *The Seagull* audience to contemplate at the start the temporally disparate range of costumes, which, as Jennie noted as we sat there, were as eclectic in styles and periods as the "loose collection" of chairs.

My audience group was already familiar with these actors as part of Armfield's policy of audiences witnessing actors who "grow and develop together from show to show and year to year." So at Belvoir Street there was not only the rather familiar back-to-back *Hamlet/Seagull* intertextuality operating for our audience group, having seen Gillian Jones play Gertrude prior to this Arkadina, Richard Roxburgh play Hamlet and now Trigorin, and Cate Blanchett previously as Ophelia, which she consciously worked against as Nina. But this audience group also intimately knew these actors via other Belvoir Street performances such as Cate Blanchett's Miranda in *The Tempest*.

Blanchett described their invisible acting "masks" in *The Seagull* as being "egg-shell thin . . . almost as though we have been asked to play ourselves" (*Sydney Morning Herald*, May 10, 1997: 3S), and Neil Armfield revealed this to be a key aspect of his casting and thus of the costuming. Clothing the actors at Belvoir Street was the result of watching already-known Belvoir actors in rehearsal to see how "they took their character and sat it on themselves" (Borghesi, personal interview, 1997). Thus, the "diva" that Armfield saw in Gillian Jones was inflected in *The Seagull* as "a film actress . . . of the 1920s/1930s . . . the floatiness, the girlishness, the frivolity, and the superficiality — those clothes of that time, all that flouncy, printed, summery chiffon seemed to exemplify what Chekhov was getting at in the visuals of this character . . . kind of sexually overt" (personal interview, 1997).

As a result of this perceived fusion of actor's body and character, Arkadina was denied her "period" bustle in *The Seagull* "because of who Gillian is. We thought it would be horrible to strap her into some Victorian nightmare" (Schofield, personal interview, 1997). In *The Governor's Family*, on the other hand, Gillian Jones *was* "strapped into the Victorian nightmare" of a bustle, since this, dragging through the "aboriginal" dirt that partially overlaid the same "rehearsal room" wooden floor as in *The Seagull*, embodied her multiple identities of displacement and defeat. There was defeat in her intraimperialist displacement (as an Austro-Hungarian aristocrat) from her British governor husband and defeat in her class, generation, gender, race, space, and place displacement from all of the other characters in the play. In the end Jones collapsed, aged and supine, in the heat of that Australian dirt, in contrast with her Arkadina in *The Seagull*, who continued to *display* her "youth," which she liked to compare with Masha's ageing. In *The Seagull* it was Masha who trailed around, drug soaked, in a bustle. But in both plays Jones was still costumed as Armfield's diva, and my audience group disliked this diva aspect of Jones, whom they had watched several times before and felt would be "as domineering at home as she was on the stage."

In the case of nonregular cast also, such as Noah Taylor, who played Konstantine, an actor-character fusion was attempted. Well known for his "oversensitive adolescent" parts in recent Australian films (and later as the "young Hitler" in the 2002 Hollywood film *Max*), Taylor had been encouraged into his first professional stage role by Belvoir Street regular (and co-star of *Shine*) Geoffrey Rush. So though Taylor was new to the Belvoir Street ensemble, his mentor was not. Taylor (as Armfield knew) identified closely through recent personal experience with the suicidal Kostya. Tess Schofield emphasized Taylor's screen and personal fragility, costuming him "like a Newtown uni student [but also] a . . . kind of bohemian, the slightly French Left Bank look, the little French striped top and the beret. So I was playing on stereotypes and classic looks but personalizing them to fit the body of Noah Taylor and the character" (personal interview, 1997).

Similar considerations informed the costuming of Rebecca Massey's Masha as "a bit of a teenage protest costume. . . . The blackness is in mourning for her life but also dressing in sympathy for Kostya [whom she loves] and trying to demonstrate her allegiance, and then using a kind of deconstructed period look, the bustle, in the same way that Goths in Newtown wear medieval things. . . . And with the little Greek op-shop knitted tops . . . I was playing on the look of a fifties beatnik, a kind of intellectual" (Schofield, personal interview, 1997). The women in my audience group noticed Masha's mixed costuming, and Anne clearly liked this characterization, laughing a lot when Masha appeared.

> Jennie: That woman in black, she had a period-style skirt, but I've seen women with tops on like that now.
> Anne: Absolutely, but her character was so unusual. It's so brave to say, "I'm bored. I'm depressed."
> Jennie: No, I know thousands of teenage girls who do that.
> Anne: But they're not going to admit it, except to each other maybe.
> Jennie: No, I think they do it all the time. You should see Year 11 and 12 — you know, they're going "Ooohhh, I'm utterly *bored* with life."

Anne: Well, I did the Queensland equivalent of Years 11 and 12. . . .
My parents didn't understand me, but I can't remember saying I
was bored. I was good at school but bored at home. My father
kept telling me, "You'll never win."

Jennie was more interested in Nina's outfit, noting that when Nina first
ran between those ill-matching chairs to perform in Kostya's play she was
wearing riding jodhpurs, signifying country Australia. But she also signified for Jennie, as an actor, the retro-style first-year acting ingenues at the
national drama training school, NIDA. Costume designer Tess Schofield,
said, "Jodhpurs and the little forties jacket was very much the uniform of
first-year NIDA graduates when we were there, so we sneaked that in"
(personal interview, 1997). Nina was also dressed in a mix of country gear,
"those little tailored fifties looks, you know, Elizabeth Taylor in *Black
Beauty*, kind of middle-class and trim, a little bit sporty but still very much
being representative of the family from which she comes," but also "the
NIDA student. Acting students all over Australia wear these funny little
mixed up outfits that are a kind of combination of retro clothes and stuff
they drag out of their school dress-up wardrobe stocks" (Schofield, personal interview, 1997).

Thus, what Armfield jokingly described to us during rehearsal as his
postmodern mix of costumes and historical styles was in fact an effect of
a policy that he and his actors called "bringing the character to the actor."
This was Chekhov in the casting histories of Belvoir Street. Quite deliberately it was Chekhov positioned in the spaces and places of a particular Australian theatre, with a translation specially prepared for the
idiosyncratic voices and rhythms of these same regular actors. It was not
Chekhov in Russian history.

Different aspects of this composite Australianness combined in my
audience group's pleasures in the production. So, for instance, all four of
the audience group read Nina, in her Alice hairband and jodhpurs, as a
particular "squatter's daughter" they had known in Mudgee. Even Anne
and Paul enjoyed this aspect of *The Seagull*, and Anne reacted to her first
sight of Nina with a great shout of laughter, which I was to ask her about
later. *The Seagull* had taken them full circuit back to their country
Australian home. Because of Jenny's own amateur acting background, she
recognized the "Sydney acting set" in the costumes of this play generally,
not only in the case of Nina. She enjoyed this recognition a lot, and it was
the first thing she mentioned as we came back down the stairs to the foyer

at the interval. "It's very Australian in that it reminds me of the Sydney scene . . . the acting world. It reminds me of when I was doing acting classes. . . . There are so many things in it that remind me of things that have happened to people I know. . . . And they've also lost the [English] plumminess of acting. It's very natural, especially Nina and Trigorin, they're just like people that you know talking."

In the New Theatre's *The Cherry Orchard* also a range of early-twentieth-century popular theatre / film costumes constructed it as a visually nonnaturalistic, "not State theatre" performance. But at the New Theatre the director, Mary-Anne Gifford, was signifying with her postmodern mix of costumes a very specific moment in (her interpretation of) Russian history, when social orders were in flux and "with nothing solid to hold on to." The Belvoir Street Theatre's Chekhov was also non-naturalistic ("not State theatre") and postmodern but in a very different way. It was emphasizing the self-reflexive audiencing of a "family-connected" season of plays to subscribers by way of the bodies and costuming of an intimately (and intertextually) known company of actors.

By way of its use of its intimate acting/audience space, its recognized actors, and its reflexive costuming policy, Belvoir Street Theatre established an ongoing movement between outer and inner frames, where audiences (and especially subscribers like Wayne, Jennie, Anne, and Paul) could move forward with the play and backward with their memories. This clearly worked in relation to the costumes, as we have seen here. But in fact entire sequences of the play itself could be caught up in this audience movement between inner and outer frames.

A clear example of this became apparent as we went back outside the theatre at the interval and responded to Jennie's immediate observation that it was a "contemporary" production of "the Sydney scene" and "people I know." Wayne immediately recalled his brother, and Jennie added, "Wayne's brother, and his mother and Auntie Gell — the actress is like Gell and his mother together." Wayne chipped in that his brother would have been the Kostya figure in this family context, and then he and Jennie devised their own displaced family memories. Wayne said that watching Konstantine's play and thinking of the relationship between his mother and brother, he had been reminded of the father of a musician friend who got involved as a drummer in his son's musical gig in a pub in Katoomba, country NSW. Thus, during the interval, Wayne was reconstructing, by way of his own real-life drama, the scene in act 1 where Kostya destroys his play in front of his uncomprehending mother, who has talked all the way through it.

The Gearins Hotel in Katoomba, we knew this fellow Mitch who was in a band, and we were asked to go along and see the band. . . . The drummer had a break and went out and got so stoned that he didn't turn up again. . . . So . . . Mitch's father, who was an old jazz drummer from years ago, said, "Well, I'll fill in," and he got up the back and was trying to fill in the beat and was going pretty well. And the audience at the Gearins was so drunk and off their faces that they didn't care. They were dancing and didn't notice any difference whatsoever. But Mitch did. Mitch said, "God, he can't get the beat. . . . " Anyway, the band was playing on and the audience was dancing and nobody was noticing anything different, even though they had a man who was fifty up there. And suddenly Mitch just stood there and threw his guitar to the ground and said, "I can't do it. This is crap, it's not real music." And he picked up the speakers and threw them and wrecked the whole band and stormed out of the pub. And the audience is standing there, saying, "What's the matter, where's the music?" And the father was doing quite a good job, but Mitch was so pure about his art.

Wayne's inner frame reference for this outer frame memory was, of course, Chekhov's play within a play, where Kostya also was so pure about his art and where his mother could simply not understand all the commotion she caused by talking through it. But the reference was also directly to the outer frame of Wayne's own family and friends. Jennie responded to Wayne's account of the musical gig in Katoomba by bringing the narrative back to his own family. "The mother in the play was in a different situation. Your mother wouldn't talk through something *you* did. But those two situations did come to my mind in there — your brother would have put on a play and done something, and your mother would have made comments, and he would have thrown things." It was clear that a particular personal history, of Wayne's mother's different responses to her two sons, was being played out here during the interval by way of Konstantine's play and the memory it evoked of a musical gig in Katoomba.

Performance Histories

This chapter brings together two ethnographies, of audience and of actors in rehearsal; and it was during the latter that we learned of some of the actors' own outer frames brought with them to the production. Cate Blanchett, who played Nina in Belvoir Street's *The Seagull*, spoke of the "masks being very close to the skin" in this production; and this was especially apparent when Noah Taylor, who played Konstantine, was interviewed. Earlier, I had encountered Konstantine via the outer frames of Wayne, his brother, and his mother. But Taylor too had — as Neil Armfield knew well — his own outer frames to bring to the part of Konstantine. In interview he spoke of how close his identification was with the part, especially emphasizing his own near-suicidal feelings after breaking up with a girlfriend.

Although well known in Australian cinema for his portrayal of sensitive male teenage roles, this was Taylor's first stage part; and it was Cate Blanchett, much more experienced as a stage actor, who was able to conceptualize via more "professional" memories her own feeling of these parts being "very close to the skin." "When I did *The Cherry Orchard* at NIDA it was all about putting on a mask — a very truthful mask, but the reason why you do Chekhov as a student is to blow apart and explore what it is to create a character. And it feels like in this production we've been stripping things away to reveal ourselves, which has thrown what I perceive to be Chekhov on its head. . . . I think it's because . . . the way the play is written it blew apart a formula, and I think Neil also tried to blow apart a formula of how one approaches Chekhov. So the line we walk is even thinner, and so sometimes I think we lose trust in that" (Blanchett, personal interview, 1997).

Armfield, as director, elaborated on this policy in terms of his pleasure in directing Chekhov, "because the behavior [in Chekhov] is so extreme but the atmosphere is so normal. . . . Like that scene with Trigorin and Nina. It is a scene of high performance, but you can only get to that point by allowing everything else to drop away. That's why it varied so much in performance, and sometimes it didn't work at all, which was when they were trying to cook it up in some way or cook it down. It was really when they were just kind of breathing it [that it worked as both] strange and completely normal. Then the action of desire in it is so strong that there is a way in which those things get turned into poetry by the play all the time just because [the actors] *are* so exposed" (personal interview, 1997).

Clearly there is a very fine line to tread between an actor's outer and inner frames on stage: the connection, for example, between the diva role onstage and in "real life" that my audience group felt sure they could see in Jones's Arkadina, or between Taylor's typecasting as a sensitive male and his own deeply experienced personal memories and emotions. Armfield spoke about this also as an important aspect of his casting policy.

It's about seeking a . . . cross section between the energy of the character and the energy of the actor. It's when they meet at a really interesting point inside the actor that they're good in the part. It's not about typecasting, because typing is to do with the conventional mask that you always see the actor in. But it's to do with my perceptions of people and perceptions about the character. I think to play Chekhov you have to just live in it in such an exposed way, and to make sense of it, it is not about theatrical types but about types of people. I think that Gillian [Arkadina] has got a diva inside her, even though I don't think she's like Arkadina at all. And I don't think Cate's got that tragic selfishness or whatever that Nina has, though maybe she has a bit. Noah's identification with Kostya was embarrassing at times. . . . With a character like Polina . . . when I thought about the play I thought about Lyn Curran because it needs someone with a lot of sexual energy . . . on the surface and someone who has easy access to their anxiety.

Cate Blanchett found this "very close to the skin" way of playing Chekhov precarious and felt that a more Stanislavskian approach in rehearsals might have made for a more even and comfortable production. For her, it was made doubly complicated by her interpretation of Nina as both victim and strong woman.

[Another director] said to me that he had never seen a Nina who was impelling her own destiny, that normally Trigorin was the lovable villain of the piece who seduced the innocent. For me, I think [Nina's part] lies somewhere in naked ambition tempered with a self-conscious sense about her selfishness. . . . There's probably a curiosity or a love of risk. But also she probably has a sense that she's not that [much of] an outsider, in that she sits with everyone else in her quest for fulfillment and completion through a love experience. . . . There's a key direction that Neil gave about the delivery of the line "one day a man comes along and sees her . . . and says it's an idea for a little story." He said that that was a moment of clarity for her when she says "No, it's not that, that is not my destiny." But then after that she says, "I love him," and so she hasn't lost her hope. She still hopes, and so she is still able to feel. . . . It's the whole thing about leaving her father, leaving the home, being rejected by the family, her child dying, and having no one. . . . She has to believe that she loves him and that that was real, it wasn't constructed, it wasn't part of a story. . . . "It's not that. I have *done* this. I'm stronger than that, I am separate from that, and I'm not going to be what he said I'm going to be"…because for me, that's what he tried to rip away from her, that he didn't love her.

Cate Blanchett's "submission" to Trigorin was embodied in the same way that Karen, our eighteen-year-old teenager watching *A Midsummer Night's Dream* (chapter 2), understood the playing of Helena's attempted submission to Demetrius in the woods. It was as an active choice of will, a decision to love, have sex, and yet still not be what the man projects her to be. Cate's part, though, was worked through a different "everyday" from Karen's, and in the end she seemed herself ambivalent about this submission to Trigorin. On the one hand, there was her intertextual memory of playing *Hamlet* prodding at her part, and here her sense of the "positive" Nina had to remain strong. But, on the other hand, there was the memory of her *own* mother and father.

> [Nina has to be] separate from that, and believe "I'm not going to be what [Trigorin] said I'm going to be." Because otherwise it becomes a mad scene, which it probably frequently does. It becomes Ophelia…. I've played Ophelia with Richard [Trigorin] as Hamlet, and those resonances are definitely there. But it's an Ophelia who has lost everything but doesn't go and kill herself. *Konstantine* does that…. When Nina says, "If you ever need my life, come and take it," I remember a lot of women who know exactly what they want, but it's not in their thinking that they can clearly state what they want. So they play the victim and give themselves over to someone. Then that person can give them exactly what they want. But they can … feel that they've had to make a decision … and it feeds a romantic ideal…. I suppose the way I'm playing it is "I better give this to you quickly because you're going to know exactly what I mean…. So you come and take me away." So the way you survive, like my mother [did] in a country town … like Mudgee, is that you say, "The sailor's going to come and rescue me." … It's that confirmation of your greatness. It's "take my life and do something with it." But it is sacrificial…. My mother was brought up in the country, so I've heard about life in a small country town and the need to escape…. My father was an American sailor. (Blanchett, personal interview, 1997)

The convergence of outer and inner frames, in Susan Bennett's sense, was very complex here, both for actors like Blanchett and Taylor and for audience members like Wayne and Jennie. But it seems clear that it was

Armfield's view of Chekhov as "so extreme but . . . so normal" that made it all so "very close to the skin" for Taylor, Blanchett, and the others. Coincidentally, Cate Blanchett had her own "Mudgee" story in interpreting Nina, just like Jennie, Wayne, Anne, and Paul, who, by way of *their* country model for Nina, saw only the victim. Yet in some part of her performance, Cate Blanchett embodied that same active tension as her mother (and my audience group) of both being in and escaping from the country into the city. Her jodhpurs, signifying both "country" and the "retro" sophistication of a city art set, were a nice representation of that.

In positioning itself within this sequence of the contemporaneous by refusing the alibi of "Russia, late nineteenth century," Belvoir Street's production of *The Seagull* engendered new risks. Anne and Paul were to reject the play for being long, dull, and "out of date" in its gender politics. In the long discussion of the play that we had at dinner after the performance, all four of my audience group read Nina's final speeches as a defeat at the hands of men, despite the intentions of the director and of Cate Blanchett. So even though Anne preempted her viewing of *The Governor's Family* by positioning Nina in "the squattocracy [who] stole the land in the first place," neither she nor Paul enjoyed this production of *The Seagull* at all.

In our final discussion of the play at dinner, all the issues discussed earlier were raised again: Belvoir Street as an informal, intimate theatre that, as Paul said, had a "light atmosphere" so that just entering the foyer "almost makes you feel like you're a student again"; the sense of closeness to some actors you knew well, like Geoffrey Rush and Cate Blanchett, and others less well known to this theatre's audience, like Noah Taylor; the eclectic, postmodern mixing of styles in both sets and costumes; the playing between this and earlier Armfield productions at Belvoir Street; the contemporary Australianness of the production; the outer frame of family associations called up by the play; the gender politics of women's roles; and, regularly, a return in their thoughts not to Moscow but to Mudgee.

Final extracts from that dinnertime conversation with Jennie, Wayne, Anne, and Paul give some indication of how these different responses to the performance of *The Seagull* they had just seen were woven together discursively.

Paul: I think you've got to admire the actors on that stage, because there's nothing hiding them, they have to act, they can't hide behind anything. You know, some people are sitting as close as a couple of feet [away] . . . and it really shows, warts and all. If they can't perform, it shows up straightaway . . .

Wayne: The acting was good. . . . I almost enjoyed everybody else except the guy who committed suicide — Konstantine, Noah Taylor. . . . I was trying to work out whether I was irritated with his acting or whether he was acting a part that irritated me. . . . He was the only one I was conscious of the acting, so I couldn't decide why I responded that way to it . . .

Jennie: He was just like an amateur actor, that Noah Taylor, in that role. He just didn't have the energy. When you say something onstage it has to be full of intent.

Anne: The problem was that the acting didn't have the energy you usually see at the Belvoir.

Jennie: He didn't, the others were fine . . .

Paul: I thought the acting was good, it's just that I felt the play was dated, slow.

Wayne: I actually thought the opposite. I thought they made it very contemporary, very relevant. Actually, I went there expecting to see a European or Russian play that didn't sit easily in Australia. But I found that it did, and I liked it very much. . . . That was because of a few of the little things that they did, like the fellow when he went for a swim, the towel around him, there were conscious Australian affectations in it. I thought about that afterward. . . . I don't know if I understood the play, but it was very good because I felt it spoke about things that had happened in my life, and . . . I could feel and understand people that were relevant to me. . . . You know, in the second half, where the character's in a wheelchair, and he looked very much like my father, it almost brought tears to my eyes, because it was like I was looking at my father asleep in the chair. . . . I was imposing on to the play a lot of my own personal experience. . . . It also related to me because of the text of [Konstantine's] play in terms of the artist and the mother. I could relate to people and types, like my brother Stephen and my mother . . .

Paul: I found the end of the play quite moving. I've never felt this way about a play before. But I reckon I could have a go at it. I think I could cut an hour out of it . . .

Anne: Nina's a typical silly female who doesn't know what she wants, and you didn't believe she was going to be an actor.

Jennie: I didn't think silly female. I think it's just a woman who has fallen in love, and he betrayed her.

Anne: But he's gone on with his life, she hasn't . . .

Paul: I thought she was going off to a life she didn't want. I thought she was a bit . . .

Jennie: Yes, with the bourgeoisie [in those remote towns] fawning upon her, all these men that she doesn't want to know about. . . . I think she's a tragic figure. I don't see her in a bad light.

Anne: She's dressed tragically!

Jennie: Her hair was tragic, her face was tragic, there was nothing to give her hope or that said to us she was going to go on to pull herself together and be her own woman.

Wayne: We actually agree, Anne!

Anne: That's why I thought the play was outdated . . .

Paul: I think it's relevant. That thing of unrequited love and of people doing things for a living they don't want to do.

Jennie: Even the artistry thing, you know, "How will I write this? Am I doing a worthwhile thing?" . . . I liked [the set] because it's unfussy. It's practical but it's interesting, and it allows the actors' space to be . . .

Anne: If anything, I thought it was too fussy, fussier than a normal set. Their costumes were fussier than normal too.

Jennie: Their costumes were interesting really, weren't they. They were out of period in a way.

Anne: I didn't quite understand the significance of the costumes. I couldn't work out whether they were trying to be contemporary or they were trying to be historical or they were trying to be eclectic. I kept watching them all the time. . . . The lady who was always in black, she was obviously historical.

Jennie: And yet the skirt was and the top wasn't.

Wayne: That's why I thought it was related to Australia today. I saw her almost as the inner city, black-dressed . . .

Anne: I really related to the woman in black, so many things she said I thought, Oh my God, I've said that.

Interviewer: "I'm in mourning for my life"?

Anne: Oh yeah, as a teenager I used to be like that.

Interviewer: You laughed a lot at her.

Anne: Yeah, it's because I could recognize that.

This extended extract of the after-show discussion also indicates major strengths of this small-group ethnographic method of audience analysis. First, it gives us access to individual audience responses in ways that focus groups and surveys can seldom do. Second, it illustrates how individual audience members nevertheless operate as "social audiences." They are still, as Susan Bennett has argued, social constructs. Within and between individual audience members, inner and outer frames are drawn on in equal measure to establish "contradictions, oppositional readings and varying degrees of discursive authority" (Kuhn 1987, 347).

Paul had some personal investment in Belvoir's "warts and all" performer-audience intimacy. He had recently given up his subscription at the Sydney Opera House because he found it too formal there, with a "stilted" atmosphere and audiences "dressed to the nines." He said he felt younger at Belvoir Street, and this encouraged him to come to *The Seagull* despite reviews he had read that "bagged the wooden acting." Because of his investment in this "light," "informal" theatre and its actors, he needed a rationale, during the conversation over dinner, for his disappointment at this particular play, and he found it in the "overlong," "out-of-date" text itself, to which his comments continually returned. His discursive authority for this position were the same reviews he had ignored to come here in the first place.

His partner, Anne, was the most critical of the play among this group. Almost everything "irritated" her about it: the actress who played Arkadina because "she is always cast in those types of roles, she never plays anything else"; Nina as a "typical, silly female who doesn't know what she wants"; the schoolteacher because "you would have self-pity with a husband like that — he was pathetic"; the "revolting" fiberglass tree used for Konstantine's play because "in those days they would have had an actual treetrunk," even though it was only a prop. Yet, like Paul, Anne rejected the Opera House because it was "so authentic, so predictable" and had previously come for an enjoyable year of casual visits to Belvoir Street with Jennie (who was already a subscriber) before taking out her own subscription in 1997 for the first time. For Anne, the focus on friendship in her small-group theatre visits was important: "This subscription sort of makes you come, and it's nice to go with somebody you want to see again, that you don't see that often." Belvoir Street had not let her down. She had, for example, thoroughly enjoyed Armfield's earlier production of *The Alchemist* and liked seeing close up well-known stars like Geoffrey Rush and Hugo Weaving. But, like Paul, she was disappointed in *The Seagull* and turned to her feminism for discursive authority in the aftershow discussion. For her, the play was "irrelevant" and "out of date" because "I was offended by the roles the women had ultimately."

Wayne was the audience member least likely to return because he was not a subscriber and preferred concerts at the Opera House. Yet, even before going into the theatre to see *The Seagull*, he had been speaking enthusiastically about Belvoir Street as "owned" by the community, with its unpretentious location and tin roof. Wayne's Left political values were important here — as was his recent experience with his dying father — in authenticating his pleasure in the play. Linked to this was his own rather larrikin identity as an Australian. He simply loved the servants who had built Konstantine's stage greeting the rather pretentious young artist with a "g'day" and then "nicking off in their bathers" for a quick dip in the "enchanted lake."

Jennie was the actress among them, and the "professional" comments about the production in the dinner discussion tended to come from her: about Noah Taylor as an "amateur" on the live stage, about the creative use of stage space, about Cate Blanchett's NIDA retro-gear, about avant-garde performances that she compared with Konstantine's play. She was the longest-term subscriber to Belvoir Street and saw the theatre in its much longer history of promoting Australian plays. Jennie liked to "get to Sydney to see good theatre," and for her *The Seagull* worked well on all levels, including her vicarious pleasure in seeing the relevance to Wayne's "brother, mother, and Auntie Gell."

But for all of them, despite their differences, there was one common factor: Nina — and Mudgee, which they returned to talk about at length over dinner. Anne had picked up only the "Ophelia" Blanchett.

Anne: I think her mind's going.
Jennie: She's just having trouble hanging on to her life.
Anne: . . . the "seagull" girl, Nina.
Jennie: Her costumes annoyed me.
Wayne: They annoyed me. But I thought they were clever, in that
she was the young country girl, she had her Alice bands on . . .

Jennie: All the country girls in Mudgee wear them.

Paul: They wear them in the shearing shed so that their hair doesn't get in the wool [laughter].

Anne: Well, I just thought *Mudgee*. What did they say? . . . It was hot, there was nothing to do, and I forget the other analogy. Wayne and I just burst out laughing. But it was just so typical.

Wayne: It was definitely true.

Anne: It was so true it made me feel uncomfortable. All the nice country girls wear these headbands. Wayne said "Susie Wood," and I burst out laughing . . .

Wayne: She's a Pittwater girl that married into country gentry . . .

Anne: Susie Wood wouldn't have [had the affair with Trigorin]. That's where Nina lost [out with me]. . . . I don't think she changed convincingly. I kept seeing her as the country girl. That's why she wasn't convincing enough. I sort of thought she was Susie. . . . She just didn't convince me — I don't know whether it's because I had this Mudgee image in my head . . .

Interviewer: How much do you think the Mudgee image helped you to interpret her character?

Wayne: I think it worked really well because it had that country . . .

Paul: I like the country.

Anne: Mudgee's not typical, it's strange.

Jennie: It's typical . . .

Interviewer: Were there other country characters for you then, or just this Nina/Susie girl?

Anne: No, they were all there, but Nina was the best. . . . It was close to experience. It was actually frightening. I thought, if a raffia hat appears, that's it, I'm leaving . . .

Jennie: The country women like her wouldn't go out to work unless they had to.

Anne: No, I don't agree. I'm not saying they'd work. But they'd have to have some pretense that they do something else than domesticity. . . . Susie Wood would do landscape gardening or something. She would not just say, "I'm a housewife."

Of course, to some extent this Mudgee finale to the postperformance discussion was an effect of the research method, in that I had particularly chosen a country audience to follow through this country play. But clearly Mudgee, or country places very like it, had also figured significantly in the minds, concepts, and bodies of the professionals who produced *The Seagull.* Insofar as the bush and the country continue to figure significantly in the minds of many urban Australians also (Tulloch 1981, 1985), it is very likely that many among *The Seagull's* audiences at Belvoir Street also recognized Nina's Alice headbands. But they would have brought multiple subjectivities to this recognition, just as Wayne, Jennie, Anne, and Paul did, with their varying political, feminist, familial, acting, and other "authorizing" discursive positions. And this is the main point of this chapter, that the converging of inner and outer frames at the theatre takes place according to multiple identities of both productions and audiences, with, as Annette Kuhn would argue, "representations, contexts, audiences and spectators . . . as a series of interconnected social discourses, certain discourses possessing greater constitutive authority at specific moments than others." The "contradictions, oppositional readings and varying degrees of discursive authority" (Kuhn 1987, 347) have been a marked feature of the recognition, interest, and enjoyment of Anne, Paul, Jennie, and Wayne as they traversed the spaces from Mudgee to the auditorium of Belvoir Street Theatre to see Chekhov's *The Seagull.*

Part Three

Theatrical
Event Studies

6

CONTEXTUAL THEATRICALITY
THE THEATRICAL EVENT AS OCCASION AND PLACE

*The artistic, organisational and structural
conventions, in which a theatrical event takes place,
are . . . theatrical contexts. . . . [E]ven the most
traditional production relates to these contexts.*
—Willmar Sauter, The Theatrical Event

I was initially drawn to the Theatre Royal, Bath (TRB), because they were producing three very different versions of Chekhov within three months, between March and June 2000: Janet Suzman's political setting of *The Cherry Orchard* within the "new citizenship" of postapartheid South Africa; the state-subsidized Royal Shakespeare Company's performance of *The Seagull*, directed by Adrian Noble; and the English Touring Theatre's *The Cherry Orchard*. This provided an unusual opportunity to compare three different productions of Chekhov in one local theatre "place" in front of many of the same audience members and thus to explore comparatively the structural, organizational, and artistic conventions that, as Willmar Sauter points out, are integrally related in performance.

Sauter's own example for illustrating this "contextual theatricality" is Brecht's theatre in the postwar German Democratic Republic. This theatre relied integrally on a fusion of state-subsidized structural (and conceptual-ideological) conventions, the particular organizational configuration of the Berliner Ensemble, and Brecht's own artistic innovation of a bare stage and gray backdrop that gestured outward to the still-devastated streets of Berlin. As Sauter says, "For Brecht it was neither possible nor necessary to show the destruction of war on stage while the ruins of Berlin outside the theatre were familiar to every spectator" (Sauter, forthcoming).

A similarly artistic convention was employed at the end of Janet Suzman's "response" to *The Cherry Orchard* in her play *The Free State*, where the abandoned old black retainer was left alone on a bare chiaroscuro stage with the deafeningly loud sound of chainsaws destroying the (unseen) world outside. But here the performer-audience communication was different. In Brecht's case in 1950s Berlin, his audience came into the theatre from those destroyed streets. His audience lived in those streets. There was no need to signify the civic destruction onstage. In Suzman's case, her Bath audience entered the theatre from some of the finest "heritage" streets in England, which, unlike Brecht's Berlin, had survived for two centuries and, unlike nearby Bristol, had been untouched by German bombing during World War II. Brecht was bringing to his audiences *their* occasion and place. Suzman was bringing to these Bath audiences *other* places and occasions: Chekhov's Russia, 1903, via South Africa, 1993.

The object of the research at the TRB was to examine the interfacing of structural, organizational, and artistic conventions in the three Chekhov plays in order to explore just why audiences were, for example, so visibly shaken by the ending of one production performed there (Suzman's) and not particularly moved — or certainly not moved in the same way — by others, particularly the English Touring Theatre's *The Cherry Orchard*. At the same time, it was important to think through Sauter's notions of contextual theatricality and cultural contexts in terms of actual *audience* analysis.

Contextual Theatricality: Structural and Organizational Conventions

The structural/conceptual and organizational conventions of the Theatre Royal, Bath, were those pertaining to a leisure economy. As Susan Bennett notes, contemporary "Western industrial societies . . . assign a specific role for leisure and this supports an economically important entertainment industry. In this way, there is a pre-determined need [for theatre] to seek out and maintain audiences for the arts" (1997, 93). Sauter's own local example in his discussion of contextual theatricality, Brecht's Berliner Ensemble, was very different. The Berliner Ensemble was fully state subsidized, had a company of its own, and produced plays only chosen by Brecht himself for specific political/ideological reasons, and these were all performed in "ensemble" style with a "long" perspective. In contrast, the Theatre Royal, Bath, relied on a wide variety of touring companies, was increasingly driven by market competitiveness, and chose its plays according to a star-driven commercial policy.

Working within a market economy, the TRB had to differentiate its geographical position within the local leisure industry quite precisely. Bath's neighboring city, Bristol, is less than thirteen miles away and is one of Britain's most prestigious theatre cities, with a variety of levels of quality theatre and show venues. In this theatre-rich region, the TRB theatre manager Danny Moar saw his own theatre's audience niche in presenting top-quality, West End–led productions, often prior to their London run. He believed that potential audiences living in the Bath/Bristol area were very well served. "They've got Bristol Old Vic doing home-produced work, they've got Bristol Hippodrome doing big lyric theatre or big musicals, and they've got us doing glossy touring product" (Moar, personal interview, May 2000).

"Glossy," however, still meant "quality," because the TRB touring events often featured the local appearance of either a major star (Penelope Wilton and Richard Pasco in *The Seagull*, Prunella Scales and Frank Middlemass in *The Cherry Orchard*, Janet Suzman in *The Free State*) or a major touring company (the RSC, the National Theatre, or, in 1999, the sell-out Lithuanian *Hamlet*, with its fire/ice theme led by a Lithuanian rock star and with chandeliers made of ice that melted onstage). We are, said Moar, a 'name' theatre. If it's got a big name, it will sell." Even with their few home-produced plays, the star/event formula still operated. In this case, Moar said, the theatre was "even more pragmatic and cynical. It's really a question of persuading a star that he or she wants to act in a play, ... then finding out what they want to be in ... and packaging it for him or her." For the TRB's own productions, Shakespeare was "beyond them" because of the large casts, and Chekhov was "a bit high. But it would depend on the calibre of the person that wants to do it. If Maggie Smith or Judi Dench said she wanted to do *The Cherry Orchard*, then it wouldn't matter."

Actors' agents were the point of contact in the case of the TRB's own productions. Then the stars were "just commodities for their agents, because the agents get a percentage of their work. So ... they want to place them in lucrative projects.... There are so many dodgy producers around who run off without paying their bills. But there's a feeling that the Theatre

A "name" theatre: Prunella Scales's *The Cherry Orchard* poster
and Bath's "charmed circle" audience at the Theatre Royal.

Royal Bath is . . . going to honour all its financial commitments. . . . So
that's what makes us an attractive proposition for agents" (Moar, personal
interview, May 2000).

For most of the year the theatre relied on touring companies, and
Danny Moar's preferred contacts were his equivalents at the RSC and the
National Theatre (i.e., "quality" theatres). In addition, he dealt with a very
few commercial West End companies like Triumph Proscenium
Productions, whose producers were sufficiently influential to match top
stars with preferred directors and who were also prepared to do a pre-
London tour.

There were two features of local TRB audiences that ensured the theatre's attractiveness to quality companies and to agents of star performers. First, said Moar, "we must be the most expensive regional theatre in
the country. We're in such an affluent area, and it's not a big theatre. We've
only got six hundred to seven hundred decent seats, so they're all at a pre-
mium. It's expensive coming here." It was the mix of full houses with an
intimate heritage theatre space that attracted major actors, as Richard
Pasco emphasized in his preshow chat with *The Seagull* audience. Second,
the TRB had a very loyal and regular audience. In 1982 the theatre almost
closed because of enormous restoration requirements. The renovation
was funded mainly by theatre patrons' car-boot sales and other small-

scale activities. So, as the marketing manager, Anna Farr, emphasized, "there's no doubt that they really feel they are part of this theatre, and they really do support it well.... People love the starry cast in Bath. That's probably why the RSC *Cherry Orchard* did so well here after a rush of very mediocre Chekhovs.... It was a very strong cast, and it was the RSC, and it was a very good production" (personal interview, May 2000). Danny Moar confirmed this view. "Bath has a reputation for high-quality drama with well-known stars in them. So there's no particular brief for doing Chekhov or Shakespeare. We are much more casting-led than play-led. So if a Chekhov came up that has been produced by the RSC, yes, we'll take that. It's more because it's the RSC than because it's Chekhov."

The TRB's audience tracking system enabled the theatre to trace every individual who had come to a play there and thus could "build up individual audience profiles for targeting purposes." It was this sophisticated tracking system, reviewed and redesigned over twenty years, that had convinced the marketing people that the Bath audience wanted star-led productions. They also knew that their audiences would travel within a thirty-plus-mile radius of Bath, from Swansea and Cardiff in the west to the Swindon/M4 corridor to the east, from Gloucester and Cheltenham in the north as far as Southampton and Dorset in the south. My quantitative research confirmed this: audience members typically visited a number of theatres in different towns and cities, but these tended to cluster relatively locally, always including the TRB. The response of a woman who traveled sixty-five miles from Weymouth to see *The Cherry Orchard* reminds us that even in the much smaller spaces of southern England, theatre fans have, like the Australians Jennie, Wayne, Paul, and Anne (chapter 5), their own Mudgees to escape from. "The Theatre Royal is very important to me. Living in Weymouth has many advantages, but it cannot be described as a cultural centre. Bath is easily accessible by rail and the theatre is not too expensive. It offers the opportunity to see good plays and actors, *The Seagull* and *Macbeth* being two recent examples."

The TRB was quite aware of the sense of importance and ownership it had built up for both its traveling and local audience, and there was a specific sense of citizenship built into this.

The sense of ownership does make [Bath theatregoers] feel part of the building, so that can be exploited as far as your audience is concerned.... Also ... ensuring that the arts — especially the art of theatre — is made as accessible as possible and giving something back to the city from a cultural and art point of view, that's very important to us. . . . [Our aim is] to break down any barriers that . . . theatre "isn't for them." . . . And as for the educational aspects of a theatre based in a particular city, the idea is to educate that audience not to perceive the theatre as elitist and therefore continuing a new generation of theatregoers. So although our basic aim is to provide bums on seats, which gives us revenue, the other angle is to make sure that people appreciate theatre as an art form and for us to encourage a slightly less traditional theatre-going habit . . . to come down and have a go at something they would not automatically pick out.

The "whole new face to the Theatre Royal, Bath," philosophy about education and citizenship was able to work in two ways. This kind of marketing approach could encourage the regular but more "low-brow" TRB audience member to "take a risk with Chekhov." Alternatively, it could encourage new, younger audiences to come to the theatre for the first time; but, by its own admission, the TRB was (like many British theatres) much less successful with this strategy than it would have liked to be. Still, since opening its less formal studio theatre, the TRB had achieved significant successes with younger audiences by producing *Shopping and Fucking, A Clockwork Orange, Popcorn,* and *The Rocky Horror Show.* And not just with young audiences: as Danny Moar pointed out, for the sellout *Shopping and Fucking,* "32 percent of the audience had never been to the theatre before." On the face of it, he said, this play had nothing going for it with the Bath audience: no stars, no "known" author, and "very rude" action. But, he added, though Bath is very "moneyed middle class, it has a kind of hippie past as well," and some of the new theatregoers were in their fifties. Although the heritage town of Bath is traditionally conservative, it also has, politically, a strong small-l liberal population as well, with currently a Liberal Democrat member of Parliament. It was some of this left-of-center audience sector that was to provide a very appreciative audience for Janet Suzman's *The Free State.*

Nevertheless, *The Free State* was at the "slightly less traditional" edge of the "serious theatre" market for the TRB and at the time of interview was not doing quite as well at the box office as they had hoped. Moar had expected better but now opined that the play "sounds hard work basically, and Janet Suzman is a respectable actress but I wouldn't say she's a big commercial draw." Farr, whose job it was to put together the seasonal brochure, "picking out the features that make it more exciting," said that

The Free State "probably sounds like an *even* more difficult version of a difficult play as far as a member of the public goes. They've . . . complicated what might be seen as a difficult play by adding this other . . . South African aspect." Her task was to convert "a very wordy, rather intellectual sounding piece of copy" that "for our audience was just too highbrow" into something a bit lighter. "Now we call it a 'version' of Chekhov's *The Cherry Orchard*, whereas I think Janet Suzman calls it a 'response' to *The Cherry Orchard*, which is slightly different."

As Farr wrote these brochures, she was engaging daily in what Pertti Alasuutari calls "audiencing": constructing the brochure's perception of the Chekhov play in terms of what she knew about her Bath audience. As such she tried to offer a "packaged entertainment event."

> We try and sell it not just as an evening sitting in that auditorium, it is the whole entertainment *event*. For example, we have on Wednesdays a couple of the company talking about the show at lunchtime, so you can come along, have a glass of wine and a sandwich, and ask them questions about the production. . . . Also, lots of shows will have . . . a postshow discussion . . . [with] the cast or the director. . . . For *The Free State*, the Education Department has got a master class with Janet Suzman that is suitable for adults experienced in amateur dramatics . . . while *The Seagull* is running an "Introduction to Stanislavsky" workshop for teachers that encourages people to see both *The Free State* and *The Seagull*. (Farr, personal interview, May 2000)

If we reconsider the points I made earlier about Bennett's approach to theatre audiences, we can see how important occasion and place were as "signals for art" at the TRB. Theatrical events here were situated socially (in terms of the TRB's "Bath citizen/consumer" concept of its audience), economically (the primary bums on seats policy of star-led productions), organizationally (the TRB's reliance, as a non-state-funded theatre, on touring companies with their own artistic conventions), and geographically (the TRB's particular signature in the context of the Bristol Old Vic and other local theatres as well as the further-off state-subsidized Stratford and London theatres from which many of their "quality" productions came). These constituents of the TRB's "contextual theatricality" helped determine the interplay of artistic (primarily but not exclusively naturalistic) conventions, organizational (star-led) conventions, and the political/economic-rationalist conceptual conventions of the posteighties "free-market" Britain in which this theatre had to work.

It is with this particular, local theatrical/cultural interface that the economic, formal, and sociohistorical centering of canonical theatre took place at the TRB.

Contextual Theatricality: Artistic Conventions and the English Touring Theatre

Both *The Cherry Orchard* produced at the TRB by the English Touring Theatre (ETT) and Janet Suzman's *The Free State* were produced within this same set of structural/conceptual, organizational, and artistic conventions. Both were touring productions, both had to put bums on seats, and both were conventionally naturalistic. But audience members interviewed responded to them very differently. This and the following chapters will examine varying audience pleasures in the two productions. First we look at quantitative surveys of audience responses to the ETT's *The Cherry Orchard*.

The ETT had been together for seven years when they played *The Cherry Orchard* tour of Malvern, Oxford, Crewe, Cambridge, Guildford, Manchester, Bath, Richmond, and Greenwich. During those years the company had picked up Barclays Theatre Awards, Shakespeare Globe Awards, a *Sunday Times* First Prize, *Manchester Evening News* Awards, and *City Life* Awards for its productions of *Hamlet, As You Like It, Hedda Gabler, The Seagull, The Importance of Being Earnest,* and *Rupert Street Lonely Hearts Club.* These and the regularly good newspaper reviews they received provided the ETT with the kind of quality image that the Theatre Royal, Bath, liked. For example, the *Guardian* reviewer, Lyn Gardner, described the ETT's artistic director, Stephen Unwin, as directing Ibsen "better than anyone else in Britain." His *The Cherry Orchard,* Gardner added, provided "not a showy evening, but a true one" through "attention to detail" and clever negotiation of that "tricky Chekhovian tightrope between the ridiculous and the sublime" (*Guardian,* May 11, 2000, 20). Although Prunella Scales herself strongly rejected the notion that she was either a "comedy actress" playing tragedy or in a "star part," reviewers (and the TRB) partially disagreed. Christopher Gray, in the *Oxford Times Weekend* (May 5, 2000, *Arts* 17), for example, said, "While it would be impudent and inaccurate to label so versatile a performer 'a comedy actress,' it is undeniably the case that she is best known as a laughter maker, certainly in her television appearances. Her very presence in the cast reminds us that Chekhov intended this to be his funniest play."

This "comedy/star" perception of Scales could then be blended into the director's particular take on *The Cherry Orchard*. The ETT's *The Cherry Orchard Education Pack* emphasized the comic qualities of the play, despite Stanislavsky's original "elegiac and lachrymose" approach. But the *Education Pack* also noted the "tragic undertow" of the play. "Chekhov's characters stand as effectively types for an entire society in transition . . . it is the passing of a world we are witnessing, the extinction of a species." Director Unwin, cited in the *Education Pack*, noted that "everything is put into context by the arrival of the tramp, with his song of the Russian poor: a new world is arriving in the form of an urban proletariat who will confront the landowners, and sweep them all away." But unlike the Eyre/Griffiths version of *The Cherry Orchard*, which also emphasized the significance of the vagrant, the ETT's spin on the play was more or less fatalistic, a sense of "setting out the deckchairs on the *Titanic*" as "the clock ticks down through the lazy summer months." Rather than connecting the arrival of the vagrant with "progressive" social change (as in Griffiths), in the ETT version he was subsumed within Chekhov's "arrival-sojourn-departure" major-play scenarios, which were activated by a newcomer arriving and bringing about "a series of changes, generally for the worse." In Stephen Unwin's interpretation, "Chekhov achieves an unprecedented level of dramatic objectivity, in which the fragility of all human endeavour is glimpsed, and is placed beyond the reach of moral judgment. . . . Life is laid out on Chekhov's anatomist table and is shown for what it is" (English Touring Theatre 2000, 11, 7, 10, 5, 7).

Interestingly, this "objectivist doctor" ascription, which has been very common in Western interpretations of Chekhov (Tulloch 1985) and which tends to deny much thought of changes "for the better," was in some tension with the ETT's own reformist intentions and achievements. Like the Theatre Royal, Bath, the ETT emphasized that "at the heart of everything we do is the passionately held belief that quality theatre does not have to be elitist, and that people everywhere expect and deserve the best" (ETT website). Again on the website, we read that "the English Touring Theatre believes that great classic and contemporary drama should be available to all. Through its dynamic education programme, the Company seeks to develop the role of theatre as a vibrant force in the lives of young people and adults alike." Under the title "Access for All," the ETT Website also advertised a "broad and wide reaching programme of workshops, talks and special events" accompanying "every tour that we produce" as well as "venue-based events for the general public, special interest groups

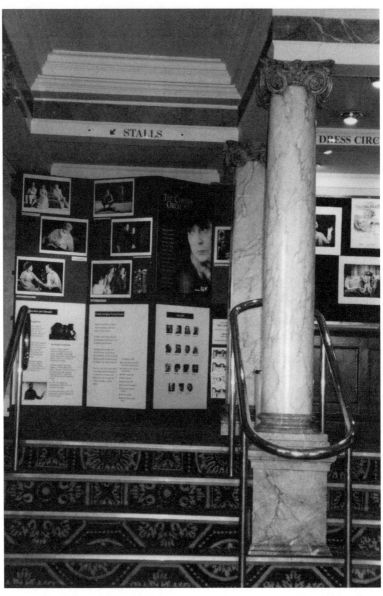

The English Touring Theatre's dynamic education program: foyer display for
The Cherry Orchard in the intimate heritage space of the Theatre Royal, Bath.

and the business community." From their home base in Crewe and with funding from the Crewe and Nantwich Borough Council, the ETT ran a theatre outreach program, including Infant and Junior Children's Theatre Workshops, Youth Theatre (where "groups have the opportunity to be involved in the running of the work through the annual election of their own Youth Theatre Committee"), and their annual playwriting course. During July and August 2000, for example, the ETT was involved in a summer school for children, a tour of Youth Theatre performance work, a training course in drama techniques for youth workers, and other projects associated with Young People at Risk.

As a tireless worker for youth and the underprivileged, Chekhov would have admired all of this (Tulloch 1980), and all at a theatre company that, for the *Guardian*, "produced the best *Hedda Gabler* of the decade — and did the same for *The Master Builder*" (ETT website). Possibly it was because of this deeply held educational brief that the ETT produced a lot of "classics," defined by Prunella Scales as plays that "generation after generation have [been] found . . . relevant and enjoyable" (English Touring Theatre 2000, 13).

Like the two other Chekhovs produced at the TRB, the ETT's *The Cherry Orchard* was naturalistic. Its artistic team, headed by Pamela Howard, emphasized "an overall design concept combining textual and historic accuracy" (English Touring Theatre 2000, 14). Howard herself produced a detailed "you-are-here" map of the cherry orchard estate to provide the audience with a naturalistic understanding of a "real space" that was only alluded to onstage. Thus the map established the exact position of the estate in relation to the river ("jetty — Grisha died here"), to the town (where Anya and Trofimov, in act 2, "see the future: 20th C: Industrial"), and to the little houses across the river of "The First Summer-Folk." In a preperformance talk at the theatre, Howard spoke of both her sets and her drawings of the estate and of actors in rehearsal as "helping the audience see with your eyes what you are not hearing — the little things that will help fill Chekhov's gaps. In that gap, your eyes will take in something that helps you understand. The smaller, perfect-replica sofa in the nursery [is there, for example,] to teach children how to behave. The paint peeling off the shutters tells you the house really is poor and about to fall down." Consequently, the rather minimalist schematic set (designed for easy transportation on the ETT's tour) was filled out with Howard's naturalistic details.

Her drawings of actors during rehearsals were also used, Howard argued, for greater naturalism and authenticity. For example, her drawing of an exhausted Frank Middlemass (Firs) "gave him an idea how to stand." She gave particular naturalistic attention to "authentic" costumes. She spoke of getting old silk in Macclesfield ("old colours that you never see now"), finding genuine old clothes in Bath, and "sometimes adding little bits of old clothes on to a new base because of the touring company's need for toughness." This was, then, primarily a naturalistic vision, though with an emphasis also in *The Cherry Orchard* on relatively minimalist sets that were both useful for a touring company and, via skillful juxtapositions, could point up the poignancy of a character's context, as, for example, in one of Howard's rehearsal drawings of an actor uncomfortably asleep on the child-sized chairs. Howard said she enjoyed working with the ETT because of its "unique interest in how something looks — its quality" and argued that though budgets at the ETT were small, she "wanted for nothing on the production" and "would not have put more on the stage, even if there had been more money." It was through this creatively naturalistic visual aesthetic that Howard saw herself "making a great classic play like *The Cherry Orchard* seem a fresh play." And it was around this set, and around the TRB's preferred "star" acting, that a significant amount of audience reaction ranged.

Contextual Theatricality: Artistic Conventions and the Audience

Despite his emphasis on theatre as "an event in which two partners engage in a playful relationship," Sauter's account of contextual theatricality gives little weight to an audience's everyday conventions (or reading formations) in relation to "classic" theatre productions. In other words, while Stephen Unwin, Pam Howard, and the ETT were establishing preferred spectator positions through a variety of "quality" and "educational" conventions, this tells us little about the actual conventionalized responses of social audiences. In the case of Chekhov, audiences often have quite particular sensory, artistic, and symbolic expectations of the production (as we have already found with the university students' data in chapter 4), so that the English Touring Theatre's aesthetic/organizational emphasis on "combining textual and historic accuracy" may be seen as part of a much broader set of audience expectations of "performing Chekhov." Because, of the three Chekhovs at the TRB, I obtained most audience access to the ETT's *The Cherry Orchard*, both qualitative and quantitative methods were used to study its audiences.

Methodology

The survey method here consisted of leaving fifteen hundred questionnaires on all seats at the theatre over three performances of *The Cherry Orchard*: the Wednesday matinee (immediately after the preshow talk by Frank Middlemas, who played Firs in the production) and the Wednesday and Friday evening performances. At an earlier preshow Wednesday talk for *The Seagull*, Richard Pasco, who played Sorin, spoke of the special pleasure they got as actors playing to matinee audiences, and I assumed (rightly) that a larger proportion of older people who do not want to travel at night would attend the afternoon performance. The theatre staff said that Friday night was usually a "good" night (i.e., a full house) as the penultimate performance of each touring play's run.

Two hundred and fourteen questionnaire responses were returned by stamped addressed envelope. These survey forms also contained questions about *The Free State* and *The Seagull* and a request for audience members who had been to *The Free State* to be interviewed about it. This formed the basis for my second-stage audience analysis of *The Free State* audience members via long interview (chapters 7 and 8).

This survey was looking for an "everyday leisure" account rather than the kind of quantitative/demographic focus that Bennett rightly describes as "of limited value" and that would have provided the kind of data the TRB marketing department already knew anyway. The questionnaire thus began with a "Why did you come to this particular production of *The Cherry Orchard* today?" question.

Responding to what Eversmann calls the multimediality of theatre, audience artistic conventions will work with a range of semiotic cues, from acting performance to set design, lighting, sound, and costume. So as well as a question about whether they liked or disliked the production (and why), there were questions also about these aspects of semiotic communication. I was also interested in the meaning for audiences of these communicative layers of the "semiotically thick" theatre event, so as well as quantifiable yes/no questions, there was, after each "Did you like it?" question, an open-ended (three-line) "Please expand" opportunity. Similar questions were asked of *The Free State* and *The Seagull*. I was also interested to know whether any particular audience member was a fan of theatre as an entertainment form to the extent of going to several other theatres and for what reason. The request to list these theatres provided also a sense of the geographical scope of their theatre activities.

There followed a multiple-choice question: "In the case of this particular Chekhov play (or either of the other two at the TRB — please name) were you attracted to the performance by any of the following (please tick): leaflet/poster image; newspaper reviews; word of mouth from family, friends, etc.; a particular actor; the fact it was Chekhov; the theatre itself; because you go to most plays here; some other reason. Please expand on any of these." (I encouraged the theatre marketing staff to help us construct the questionnaire, and the "leaflet/poster image" choice was added by them.) Finally, after a question about availability to be interviewed about *The Free State*, there was an "Any other comments?" blank page.

The opening question ("Why did you come to this particular production of *The Cherry Orchard* today?") was postcoded according to the respondents' own categories. For example, the first questionnaire received simply said boldly "I love Chekhov." Similarly, another respondent said, "Whenever possible I see — whether on the stage, film or TV — Chekhov's plays"; another said, "Love Chekhov — usually have a Chekhov 'fix' annually!"; and another, "Because we love Chekhov and *The Cherry Orchard* in particular, and have seen at least 5 productions over recent years." These were categorized as "Chekhov fans."

By contrast, some people's response to question 1 was very different. "Knowing little of the Scandinavian/Russian playwrights I chose a well-known piece as a tactic. This visit to Chekhov was in the form of a discipline of duty! To myself!" Another respondent described it as "a sort of education." These were categorized, together with those who said they felt it was high time they "risked" Chekhov and those who said they wanted to keep up with "the classics," as "doing culture."

A third conventional audience response was also quite straightforward: many went to this production because they were attracted by the star cast, especially by Prunella Scales. These were categorized as "star fans." This is the local (TRB) "niche" audience position adopted by marketing manager Anna Farr when she said: "If a Chekhov comes up that is well cast, we'll have it. This theatre is star-driven, not playwright-driven."

The Theatre Royal, Bath, also had its fans, as indicated by a response to question 1 that said, "Love Chekhov and love Theatre Royal." (This latter category was often also elaborated at length in the "Any other comments?" section.) A fifth postcoded category was audience members who were especially drawn to the TRB by the company producing *The Cherry*

Orchard. Thus, some tourists from Dorset said, "We saw the English Touring Theatre's production of *The Master Builder*, which we enjoyed very much — so thought we'd try a Chekhov."

A sixth conventional category of response was the "special social event factor": the anniversary night out, the surprise ticket from a boyfriend, a "special treat from a friend," "bought ticket for wife's birthday — thought she would enjoy it," "special Xmas present." Sometimes, of course, the categories overlapped, as in "birthday present because I'm a big Chekhov fan"; this was coded both as "Chekhov fan" and "special event." (As respondents sometimes gave more than one reason for the visit, as in "because I love Prunella Scales and like Chekhov very much," numbers of responses to each category were added, and percentage scores do not equal 100 percent.) As predicted by the theatre staff, tourists did not compose a quantitatively significant category on their own. Accordingly, the "we like a visit to the theatre when on holiday" response was categorized as "special event" also.

A seventh category, getting closer to Eversmann's cognitive orders rather than to the pleasures of fan affect, was "formal education." This was composed primarily of school students studying Chekhov for A level (and told to go by their teacher). Eighth, and even more draconian, was the "because mum said" or "husband chooses" category, which was labeled "under orders." Included here, for example, was the rather plaintive "I was with a group of retired clergymen and clergy widows and it was considered a 'suitable' play for this group," because this (and other coach group members) sometimes indicated that they did not actually choose which play they were going to or indeed which theatre they would end up in!

A ninth category was "happenstance." Here, for example, were included the audience member who went only because the show's wardrobe mistress lodged with her and she got a complimentary ticket; the woman who had gone shopping in Bath for the afternoon and on the spur of the moment chose to "take in the theatre"; and the audience member who saw the poster and went in out of "curiosity." Finally, there was an "other" category that included, for example, two deaf people who went only because the Wednesday matinee performance was sign-interpreted.

What thus became apparent is that the TRB audiences went to particular plays at "their" theatre for conventionally different (even if sometimes overlapping) reasons. These broad "everyday leisure" audience categories were *conventions* of everyday leisure activity that impacted in different ways on audience pleasures in *The Cherry Orchard.*

Results

There is space here only to examine the very rich data generated by the TRB survey in three ways.

1. The gross (quantitative) figures via the postcoded responses to the open-ended question 1 ("Why did you come . . . ?") shown in table 1 can be compared with the multiple-choice "Were you attracted to the performance by any of the following . . . ?" question shown in table 2.

Table 1. Percentages of postcoded responses to the open-ended question "Why did you come to this particular production of *The Cherry Orchard*?"

Q1 "Why did you come . . . ?"	N	%
Chekhov/*Cherry Orchard* fans	82	38
Prunella Scales/star fans	57	27
TRB fans	24	11
Special event	22	10
Doing culture	21	10
Likes ETT	14	7
Formal education	6	3
Under orders	7	3
Happenstance	7	3
Other	5	2

Table 2. Percentages choosing multiple-choice option to the question "Were you attracted to the performance by any of the following . . . ?"

"Were you attracted . . . by . . . ?"	N	%
The fact it was Chekhov	148	69
A particular actor	114	53
The theatre itself	110	51
Because you go to most plays here	65	30
Leaflet/poster image	41	19
Word of mouth	26	12
Newspaper reviews	18	8
Some other reason	17	7

It is immediately apparent from these two sets of figures that the data support the TRB marketing staff both in terms of the popularity of star performers with *The Cherry Orchard* audiences and in terms of their perception of ownership of "this lovely theatre." However, the fact that the "Chekhov" response topped both lists suggests greater popularity of this *playwright* than the TRB perhaps acknowledged and tends to support the ETT's touring of "classics" such as Chekhov and Ibsen. Question 1 responses revealed the 38 percent of Chekhov fans as the leading category as to what the event was that primarily attracted the audience to this performance on this particular day. Similarly, the multiple-choice question again had "Chekhov" as the lead attraction at 69 percent. (Quantitative differences between these two "Chekhov" percentages are explained by the self-generation of "reasons for going" in question 1, as against multiple choice, so that significantly fewer reasons were given by any one respondent; and the "Chekhov" responses to the multiple-choice question no doubt included headings categorized separately in question 1, such as "doing culture" and "formal education.")

2. Conventional expectations as to why audiences went to the play on that day can be correlated with "like/dislike" responses to *The Cherry Orchard* production. For example, to take some of the more significant "why I came to *The Cherry Orchard*" conventional responses, table 3 indicates the "liking" ratings for each category.

Table 3. Percentage of respondents indicating liking the production for each category of audience attandance

"I liked this *Cherry Orchard* production"	%
Chekhov/*Cherry Orchard* fans	56
Scales/star fans	81
English Touring Theatre fans	69
"Doing culture" audiences	58
Special event audiences	91
Happenstance	0

In other words, audience members who had gone to see the ETT's *The Cherry Orchard* as part of a special occasion night out (anniversary, birthday, etc.) or because they were fans of the particular performers enjoyed the production significantly more than those who went to see Chekhov.

3. Reasons given for liking or disliking the production could then be examined across all responses in the questionnaire. These data reveal individual profiles that differed according to the convention of artistic or symbolic expectation brought to the theatre by audiences. A few individual examples taken from five of these audience leisure categories illustrate this.

Anon 1 (who came to see his "favourite play") disliked this version: the choreography was too busy (as was the set), there was too much shouting, and there was a consequent loss of Chekhov's pathos/humor balance. There was also an "almost total lack of 'Russian' feel," and the "dialects didn't work." Meanwhile, there was "insufficient attention to the relationship *between* characters."

Anon 2 (who, with partner, was an admirer of "Chekhov and . . . *The Cherry Orchard*" in particular) disliked the production, particularly feeling let down by "Mdme Ranevskaya, as Prunella Scales was too low key and dull" (though Simon Scardifield's Yasha and John Quentin's Gayev were "brilliant"). "Awkward sets, lighting uninspired — the production lacked inspiration. The director could have had more movement — and the music lacked Russian 'angst.'" This pair didn't go to *The Free State* because "Chekhov is essentially Russian — atmosphere etc. There are plenty of good African playwrights."

John (who loved Chekhov and needed his "annual fix") disliked this production. "The actors appeared bored, poor diction, over-acting." The interpretation "failed to convey the changing times in society, the 'fin de siecle' theme within the play."

Harry (who liked Chekhov and had "enjoyed the play immensely" when he had seen it before) disliked all aspects of the production. "Frank Middlemass was the only convincing performance." The interpretation was "totally lacking in authentic detail." The "set was *not* a Russian home. Only the lighting was adequate." In contrast, RSC's *The Seagull* was an "excellent production all round."

James (who went because of the combination of his liking for Chekhov and Prunella Scales) disliked all aspects of the production. The acting was "automatic and barely considered: for the first time while seeing this play I didn't feel it was a well-written play!" There were "long, pointless scene changes and poor lighting, especially in Act 1," so that it was "difficult to establish characters." In contrast, James liked *The Free State* (though not Janet Suzman's performance). "Despite the 're-setting,' it was much easier to identify characters and to sense their feelings and motivations. . . . The 'adaptation' was minimal, and could perhaps have been more daring." Above all for him, there was RSC's *The Seagull*. "A class apart from the other two — superb playing from a genuine ensemble. If there was a flaw, it was that so much thought led to perfectly judged silences, which lengthened the evening beyond an ideal length of attention span. It felt like it had dragged — a real shame."

What is evident from this (and the rest of the) detailed sample of "Chekhov fans" who disliked the English Touring Theatre's production of *The Cherry Orchard* is that, as fans, they came to a performance with very clear expectations of the kind of artistic and symbolic conventions for which they "love Chekhov" and that when they failed to find these their sensory relationship with the actors did not rescue the situation. There seemed to be little sense of theatrical play with actors who "appeared bored." "Fan" preconceptions can thus lead to disappointments when confronted with the actual production's acting, directing, sets, music, and design. Although, as Sauter emphasized from his own audience research, the sense of theatrical play with actors is extremely important in audience evaluations of a performance, in the case of Chekhov fans it was not necessarily the most crucial aspect they were looking for. Or, at least, the actors were expected to provide a sensory point of contact with the writer himself.

These expectations led to disappointment among the wider sample of 44 percent of Chekhov fans who didn't like the ETT production for a quite specific cluster of reasons. They didn't like the absence of an expected emphasis on Russian atmosphere and history, which was, in part, an effect of the schematic touring set. There were complaints of a missing Russian angst, the ignoring of historical conflict and the writer's fin de siècle feel, the actors' use of northern (English) country accents as anachronisms, and, despite Pam Howard's best naturalistic efforts, that the home was not Russian and had no lived-in feel. There was disappointment over the loss of Chekhov's emotional mix of pathos and humor because of overbusy sets, over-the-top shouting, and otherwise flat, mechanical acting. Similarly, they disliked the loss of Chekhov's depth via routine, unsubtle performances by "bored" actors: the "actors ACTING," "just speaking their lines," "automatic," "just a performance of the plot," "poor diction." Others noted a failure to achieve Chekhov's ensemble effect and integration because of the mix of overbusy and flat acting, minimalist yet overfussy sets (like a "cheap American hotel"), and poor characterization (particularly, it was felt, by Prunella Scales as Ranevskaya and Michael Feast as an over-the-top Lopakhin). Issues of mise-en-scène and technical proficiency were also regularly mentioned, with the lighting of act 1 frequently criticized for making it harder to work out the characters, and the set and very long scene changes attracting the most criticism of all.

These last mise-en-scène points were made fairly generally by respondents across all categories. By and large, audiences were left uncomfortable with Howard's rather minimal set, which included a central doorway with no attached walls, so that actors who went off through the door could still be seen as they exited. But what distinguished the critical Chekhov fans from other audience members was their perception of the company's failure to meet their own expectations for Chekhovian artistic conventions. For example, respondents complained about the inadequacy of the set to convey the lived-in history of the house that Ranevskaya and Gayev loved so much. The almost universal acclaim by these Chekhov fans for the Adrian Noble/RSC *The Seagull* also indicated the very strong assumptions of Chekhovian naturalism underpinning their evaluations of a production. For example, Cassy (who also disliked *The Cherry Orchard*) said *The Seagull* was "brilliant. . . . I was completely drawn into this production. There wasn't a moment in the play when you weren't aware of what was going on in their minds. The set made you feel there was no one really looking after it. It was impermanent, which added to the discordant element. The costumes looked like the characters had lived in them for the last 20 years." Even where *The Seagull* was (marginally) criticized, it was via a knowledge about Chekhov's "pauses" or "silences" (e.g., James), the prolonging of which was a noted feature (which newspaper reviewers also emphasized) of Adrian Noble's *The Seagull*.

These examples indicate that Chekhov fans drew on very specific cultural competences relating to (sometimes displaced) sensory, artistic, and symbolic conventions and thus could be very severe critics (e.g., the ETT would not have had the touring funds for the kind of sets the RSC could produce for *The Seagull*). This is *not* to suggest that there were no supportive Chekhov fans for the ETT's *The Cherry Orchard*. On the contrary, the majority of Chekhov fan respondents *liked* the production (though proportionately far less than some other categories of audience). I am drawing attention to the (close to half) negative responses from Chekhov fans simply to indicate the rather set aesthetic and symbolic conventions with which this audience group approached the play. This is indicated also by the fact that the Chekhov fans who liked the production drew on the *same* sets of expectations of Chekhov as the more negative ones.

Thus, the ETT's *The Cherry Orchard* was also liked because of its Russianness ("never better than when in Russia"), the symbolism of the passage of time, the conflict between old and new orders, so that sets, costumes, music, and lighting were appraised in relation to this particular sense of atmosphere. It was also liked because of the touring company's ensemble style, with particular performances pronounced strong or weak according to their ability to portray a particular character's contribution to this ensemble (thus Ranevskaya's need to be "mercurial," "generous," and "feckless" was emphasized, as was Lopakhin's "mixture of humility and pride and passion and arrogance which makes him destroy those he loves"). Fans who liked the production also pointed to the portrayal of Chekhov's emotional balances between "humour and inevitability" and the "eternal conflict between young hope and desire to hold to the past."

Being faithful to Chekhov's intentions was, like his naturalism, a key theme in a Chekhov fan's pleasure in a particular performance (though this was not necessarily always the case in the evaluation of "versions" of his plays, like *The Free State*). But this cultural competence in Chekhov meant that even when saying they liked the production, Chekhov fans tended to add strong reservations. Thus:

Chris (who, as "an admirer of Chekhov," enjoyed "seeing any Chekhov play") liked it generally. "I felt overall that the production . . . captured the themes and symbolism so evident in Chekhov's play. Good use of costumes which reflected the passage of time and also symbolised old and new, and the demolition of the old order — symbolised by a superb performance by Frank Middlemass as Firs. Mrs Ranevsky is the principal character and the play can only succeed if it builds up around her. But I felt perhaps she was played with too much vulnerability and lacked perhaps the elusive mercurial essence of temperament which I believe the part demands."

Deirdre (a teacher who "loves Chekhov" and did the Stanislavsky workshop) liked the "splendid ensemble work" (thus supporting Prunella Scales's own view of the production), the emotional "contrast twixt the inevitability and the humour," and the "atmospheric simplicity of design." But she was "disappointed with Ranevskaya."

Like popular culture fans, these theatregoers tended to have very clear sensory, aesthetic, and symbolic ideas as to *why* they liked their fan object so much, and these clear notions of interpretation flowed through into their appreciation and liking (or not) of any particular production and also to their understanding of its meanings.

Several respondents said they went to this *The Cherry Orchard* production because they "adore Prunella Scales" or "to see Prunella"; and many others listed this actress (sometimes together with the other "outstanding cast") as their primary reason for going to the theatre that day. For them, the star was the major feature of the theatrical event. This category of respondent was proportionately far more positive about the ETT production than the Chekhov fans. It is evident from the "star fan" comments that for them the TRB was achieving its policy of entertaining both its loyal members and visiting tourists and travelers with its star-led policy.

Unlike the Chekhov fans, the star fans were close to unanimous in their pleasure in *The Cherry Orchard*. What is most noticeable is that, *except* when they actually overlapped in individual cases with Chekhov fans, they tended to use rather different measures for excellence. Star actors tended to be contrasted with their *personal* performances in other parts rather than critiqued or praised intratextually in terms of a prior expectation of the *character* within the ensemble. There were a number of references to Prunella Scales's other parts, with one of the small minority of star fans who *didn't* like *The Cherry Orchard* commenting that "bringing in famous TV actors doesn't always work in the theatre." As regards interpretation, star fans tended to be happy if the production was uncomplicated, direct, and easy to follow (an effect, probably, of expecting Chekhov to be difficult, as Anna Farr said, and indicating that this cognitive dimension of the theatrical event varied more according to the aesthetic conventions of an audience member than Eversmann suggests). This audience group also saw sets more functionally, giving stars the space to move, and (like the ETT followers) tended to point to the difficulty in having anything but minimal sets when touring. Lighting and music for these respondents should be expressive, perhaps atmospheric, but otherwise unobtrusive to be effective. Similarly, physically functional were some of the (few) criticisms of the acting: not being able to hear Prunella Scales's voice in the back of the theatre or, conversely, "hearing everything beautifully" from the Royal Circle. Diction was important, and this became an increasing feature with older people who were hard of hearing. More traditional values were evident here, too, with comments about swearing and shouting reflecting one aspect of why some people liked this "nice" and "intimate" theatre. But this was very much a minority reaction.

A larger number in this star-led category than any of the others enjoyed going to the big-name musicals at the Bristol Hippodrome. But others were as keen on classical drama as the Chekhov fans, both groups often being very specific about the particular *place* they enjoyed theatrical events at: "the Swan at Stratford," the "RSC Barbican" in London, and, of course, the "nice atmosphere, small in size" Theatre Royal, Bath. Not being Chekhov fans, postshow talks (either the ones by the performers or with friends on the way home) were often drawn on by members of this audience category to explain some hermeneutic issue ("why did the governess wear men's clothes?") or the symbolism of using strong English regional accents in a play set in Russia.

C. DOING CULTURE

Usually separate from the Chekhov fans, the star fans and the touring company followers were the "serious" theatre audiences who were "doing culture," often with a sense of feeling slightly guilty that they had never been to a Chekhov play, or that it was "high time" to see one, or that they would "risk Chekhov" in this particular version. Here is a selection of individual profiles of respondents seeking "a little culture."

A.D. (who went to the local theatre sometimes "to enjoy [and benefit from] a little 'culture'") liked all aspects of the production: "Great cast, great acting, easy to understand — though names get a little getting used to." The costumes, set, and so on were "All 'in period' — though the set was a little sparse." A.D. had also gone to *The Seagull* for the same "benefit from a little culture" and liked it for the same reasons. Other than the TRB, A.D. hardly saw any theatre. But the Theatre Royal, Bath, was valued as a regular venue. "What is so nice about the Theatre Royal is that you always have such a rich (and varied) selection on offer in each season — there is always something for all tastes." It is that inclusive, not exclusive, aspect of the TRB as an organizational context that fueled A.D.'s pleasure in "a little culture."

Carol said, "I'm ashamed to say that I know very little about Chekhov or Ibsen and this seemed a straightforward start for me" (especially, perhaps, because the ETT was already renowned for its productions of Ibsen). Prunella Scales had attracted her also, but through "curiosity, not because I am a fan." Carol liked the production but felt she didn't "know enough about Chekhov to judge" or make too many comments other than "all very good." Similarly, she didn't go to *The Free State* because "being ignorant about 'straight' Chekhov, I didn't think I would appreciate a more complicated version" (thus confirming Anna Farr's concern about the Suzman play). But there was another reason that she didn't go to *The Free State* or to *The Seagull*. Carol was "a bit limited by finances," and, although she loved the TRB, she could only afford to go once or twice per season. "I love going to Bath Theatre Royal and have seen some super things there. The main drawback for me is price. The cheapest way I can do it is to get the train to Bath £3.10, a standing £5 theatre ticket, and take my own interval refreshments! To enjoy it in style (and see all on the stage) you need to pay at least £18 per ticket and pay a fortune for a g&t with no ice." Carol's own theatrical event came about once a year, without "style," and reminds us (as other pensioners did in these audience responses) that the theatre can be a special event with very different constituents for different people.

Jane spoke of her reason for going to *The Cherry Orchard*. "Knowing little of the Scandinavian/Russian playwrights I chose a well-known piece as starter. This visit to Chekhov was in the form of a discipline or duty! To myself!" She was, at best, ambivalent about what she saw. "As an interpretation of an unfamiliar genre, the actors probably were as required but one or two unfortunately were OTT." The music was "unmemorable," the sets "spartan but effective," the "costumes effective (and Miss Scales' costume outstanding)." Jane only occasionally went to other theatres but "very much enjoys the Theatre Royal Bath and am delighted with the refurbishment. The variety of performances and actors is of high quality and appeals to most people." This ninety year old had impaired hearing and began to think the cost of the theatre unjustified. However, "we have now decided to invest in higher priced seats and come less often!" As a "lifelong learner" Jane had "wanted to see the *Cherry Orchard* with Prunella Scales in it to rationalize my deep distrust of the playwrights previously mentioned — why do I find them tiresome and tedious?" But her experience of this particular *The Cherry Orchard* was unlikely to change that view or attract her (given her new pricing policy) to come again to see this particular playwright, so she was probably going to continue "to pass Chekhov by."

The "doing culture" audience members were circumspect and probing in their engagement with Chekhov. True, they were ashamed to say that they were only just now catching up with, tasting, or risking Chekhov and tended to emphasize that it was as a "sort of education" or "discipline or duty." But there was also a strong cognitive desire here: to find out more about the Scandinavian and Russian playwrights, for example, or to allow Prunella Scales and company to "rationalize my deep distrust of the playwrights previously mentioned." Compared with the 91 percent "special event" audience members who liked *The Cherry Orchard*, only 58 percent "doing culture" ones did so. They frequently came to Chekhov with a considerable general theatregoing knowledge and background, so they were often there to assess Chekhov (and Ibsen and Turgenev) against the author's time ("I felt that some characters were too odd — as distinct from being prisoners of their time and culture"), their own time as audience ("Chekhov was very original in his themes and insights in his time, but they have been substantially overlaid since"), and the times and works of other "great" playwrights they knew better, especially Shakespeare ("Given a choice between Chekhov and Shakespeare, Shakespeare wins 'hands down'! And will do every time for us").

D. SPECIAL EVENT AUDIENCES

Of the audience members in the "special event" category, 91 percent liked *The Cherry Orchard*. For example, ticking his reasons for being attracted to the play, Lee mentioned in passing the *Guardian* review, "Frank Middlemass, Prunella Scales (of course!)," "not seen the play on stage before," and "do like the Bath T. Royal, small + elaborate," but he concluded, "It was my b'day!" That combination of place (the much-favored TRB), occasion (Middlemass and Scales "of course!"), and "catching up" with Chekhov was blended into the extra-special event of a birthday day out with his wife.

This kind of personal "packaging" of the theatrical event was quite familiar among the special event responses. Jane from Devizes emphasized the celebration of her wedding anniversary as the major reason for ·going but added that she liked Frank Middlemass, Prunella Scales, and the theatre. Although she "really didn't know what to expect" and "has suspected it would be rather 'high brow' and the 'play would seem long,'" in fact, "the time went in a flash," and she was "pleasantly surprised" by the "very professional, lively and enthusiastic actors." (Her husband, who was more knowledgeable about Chekhov, also complained more while still liking the "very professional" performances: "Not enough meditation on loss and hope, memory and destiny.")

And Yvonne, whose boyfriend organized the theatre visit as a surprise and didn't "know how Chekhov should be interpreted," also emphasized the "very professional actors" and the TRB as "a very nice venue — comfortable, friendly staff. I have enjoyed most productions I have seen there." Although she was much more of a fan of the big musicals and variety at the Bristol Hippodrome, for Yvonne, as for many of the other special event audience members, it was the combination of occasion (well-known stars), place (the comfortable, friendly, and nonthreatening TRB), and professional (not "high brow," "over my head") performances that made this an enjoyable celebration.

E. STUDYING CHEKHOV

The doing culture audiences were self-educating, even at the age of ninety! In a way, they were an important part of the ETT's ambitions, although many of them already went to the theatre. On the other hand, the ETT was particularly interested in bringing young audiences to the theatre. Doing the play for A level, of course, helped bring the young audience in. So although there were few school A-level students among the Bath *The Cherry Orchard* respondents, their reactions to the production are interesting. There is space here to look at just two of the six A-level questionnaire responses as a contrast to the doing culture ones.

Clare was doing A-level theatre studies and saw "a lot of theatre so that I can write about a 'contemporary' production." She was particularly attracted on this day by the pre- and postshow talks. For example, she appreciated the highly informative preshow talk on set design and costumes by Pamela Howard. In her talk Howard spoke about the "creative democracy" at the English Touring Theatre, each artist bringing her or his own talents to "make a great classic play like *The Cherry Orchard* seem a fresh play." She also spoke of how details of her estate map and details of her set design were there to "help see with your eyes what you are not hearing — showing little things that will help fill Chekhov's gaps," and she emphasized that, after her drawing during rehearsals, the key to costuming success was to design each piece to the individual actor, "building each character up looking in the fitting room mirror." There was plenty of excellent material here for an A-level student writing about contemporary production, and Clare emphasized both her enjoyment and increasing knowledge as a result. "Not knowing anything about the play — I was given a clue during the pre-show talk as to the use of space and how Pamela worked alongside the team from the beginning with drawings and map. Just after the show, I realised that for once I actually understood a play with a complicated story-line. I feel this was due to my awareness of the use of the set and artistic influence. . . . Because of the pre-show talk, I was aware of the silk being a 'free-be.' Yet it was beautiful." This was the ETT's educational outreach policy working at its best.

But it was not only Pamela Howard's talk that gave Clare such pleasurable access to *The Cherry Orchard*. Liking all aspects of the production, she said of the acting: "Prunella Scales played a 'Mother' which I related to with my own." As for the interpretation, Clare liked it, "as I know no different." But she had known, personally and professionally, a great deal that pleased her about this Chekhov production. Lacking her own "expert" knowledge, Clare drew on that of Pamela Howard to illuminate the play and also on the kind of lay knowledge that Eversmann calls "recognition": drawing on the perceived similarities of her mother and a character onstage.

Madeleine went to *The Cherry Orchard* "as part of Theatre Studies A-level, so that I could write about it if I wanted to in the paper on 19 June for critical analysis of a live production." This was a very immanent exposure to "learning," with the A-level exam about one week away! She came mainly because it was her teacher's idea, but she said she liked Chekhov anyway. However, Madeleine disliked the production, enjoying only the performance of Gayev. "Liuba wasn't convincing, Lopakhin didn't wave his hands around till the end — the characterization wasn't strong enough in many individuals. The emphasis on the changing society of Russia was lost, through bad set design. The extravagance was missing. The SUBTLETY of Chekhov was missing. The lighting was brash and seemingly unrelated to the dialogue 'the sun is setting' — with no subtle diminishing of light. The set was too bleak and not extravagant enough. No sense of era. Costumes okay, but not noticeably more extravagant in the ball scene. The music was random, and inappropriate because of this at times. The sounds: unconvincing."

Madeleine was a very critical young student indeed (reviewers, in fact, complimented the production for its setting-sun effects), but one who was used to theatre (in Salisbury, Oxford, Bristol Old Vic and Hippodrome, the London Globe, and the RSC at Stratford). She liked Chekhov and "loves Theatre!" But not this time around. Instead of the fulsome praise for the TRB that we received in most respondents' "any other comments," Madeleine remarked tersely: "Theatre Royal, Bath needs air conditioning."

These were two quite distinct A-level responses. Both were doing the same Theatre studies A level, which emphasized study of plays in production and performance. Clare drew closely on this demand of the course to sit at the feet of one of Britain's foremost sceneographers, so that "for once I actually understood a play with a complicated story-line." The preshow talk at the TRB was crucial to her considerable pleasure in the production. Madeleine had not been to the preshow talk, but she did bring another kind of competence to the theatre: her knowledge (and liking) of Chekhov and of theatre generally, being a far more active theatregoer than Clare. Her response to *The Cherry Orchard* had all of the critical engagement and knowledge of the Chekhov fan together with the knowledge of someone currently doing a detailed academic scrutiny of the text ("Lopakhin didn't wave his hands around till the end . . . 'the sun is setting' — with no subtle diminishing of light").

The differences in response to the same play in the same theatre by two female students of the same age doing the same A-level theatre course indicate very clearly two of Susan Bennett's main points. First, theatre "communication" can never be purely individualized, on a one-to-one basis. Rather, both production and reception are "positioned within and against cultural values." It is the interaction between live performance and audience of these "multiple horizons of expectations" (in this case, the different daily competences and theatrical conventions that Clare and Madeleine brought to the performance) that creates the play of meanings and pleasures in live theatre. Second, the processual relationship of meanings pre-, during, and postperformance is often crucial in determining the negotiation of these varied horizons of expectations. Clare's positive response to the ETT preshow talk was a clear indication of that and a strong vindication of the touring company's extensive educational program. But at the end of the day, the friendly ethos of place and occasion that Clare found at the TRB was simply not the same theatre that Madeleine found so hot and inhospitable.

Contextual Theatricality at the TRB

This chapter has related a particular Chekhov production to the everyday *leisure* choices of its audiences. It has also focused on a particular place, the Theatre Royal, Bath, and on a particular occasion, the arrival in town of the English Touring Theatre's *The Cherry Orchard* "star-led" by Prunella Scales and other well-known actors. Here structural, organizational, and artistic conventions were repositioned as audience pleasures and meanings, which I endeavored to measure quantitatively as well as qualitatively.

Although the methodology here contrasts strongly with that in chapter 5, it has, nevertheless, still told some local, small-scale "tales from the field." Even simple questionnaires can reveal such tales: for example, of the lady who waits for the train to Bath, queues for returns, and takes her own refreshments for the interval (instead of the expensive "g&t with no ice" that would be more "in style"); of the A-level schoolgirl who was entranced by the famous sceneographer's preshow talk about costumes, sets, and acting spaces so that she felt she understood a play better than ever before; of the audience members who were puzzled by details of the production (e.g., the "north country" accents, or "why did the governess wear men's clothes?") and then spoke of the animated discussion about these and the production values of the ETT on the one-hour drive home; of the retired clergyman who felt "stuck" in a coach with other clergy and clergy wives going to a play he had not chosen and didn't enjoy, so that only the rather avuncular, anecdotal preshow chat by Frank Middlemass and one detail of the performance (the lively dance scene) caught his attention at all; of the ninety-year-old lady who nearly stopped coming to the theatre altogether but instead chose to severely ration her visits and chose Prunella Scales's appearance to give Chekhov "one last chance."

There have been other local tales told here and many others in the survey that there has not been space for. These daily events *can* be exposed by a survey questionnaire method. But it was important not to ignore the macroeconomic aspect of all this either. At the TRB the citizen-as-consumer "bums on seats" need had been most obviously articulated in terms of a star-led policy, and we have seen how this generated both individually and socially conventionalized responses to the play, to the touring company, and to the theatre itself. Also part of this "macro" aspect is the related issue of the expense of the seats, and we have seen how individual people have negotiated that. Probably the most remarkable point here is that most people didn't mention seat prices at all (though quite a number complained of ancillary high costs like programs and even ice creams). This narrative "lack" (of cost of seats) in so many of these ministories is, of course, just another indicator of the comfortable middle-class nature of much of this audience.

But not all audiences members were in this position. Quite often a group of pensioners would club together to share petrol to travel, four to five together, in a car. I met at lunch after *The Cherry Orchard* preshow talk one such group of older ladies, ranging from late seventies to late eighties, who drove together the forty miles from Marlborough. Like the pensioner Carol and the ninety-year-old Jane, they had also cut back on the number of shows they saw, as declining hearing and increasing seat prices made it all that much harder.

Aging, expressed as declining physical and financial resources, were part of the risk equation for several of these audience members. In the case of Carol and Jane it was also a matter of weighing up affordability against a particular learning curve intention (Russian and Scandinavian playwrights) that was much more part of this year's theatrical event than particular stars. So the particular nature of the theatrical event may vary from year to year within any one individual narrative, and then stars are selected to help rationalize or to provide curiosity as performative guides and bonuses toward the major endeavor. It is this spatial-temporal relationship and mix of Chekhov with everyday leisure conventions ("doing culture", Chekhov fan, A level, etc.) that provided the very particular micro/macro, production/audience set of relationships of most people's contextual theatricality at the TRB.

CULTURAL CONTEXTS

THEATRICAL EVENT, LIMINALITY, AND RISK IN *THE FREE STATE*

The theatrical event must be understood as a process as much as it is a happening. . . . Every theatrical event has a socio-political aspect, both in relation to its content and in the way it is presented. —Willmar Sauter

I started off from act 2 because I was wanting to politicize the play in the sense of setting it in another political atmosphere, another political event, which is postrevolutionary South Africa. Acts 1, 3, and 4 are, if you like, in a generalized sense about letting go, trying to stamp out nostalgia, trying to disembarrass yourself of possessions, all of which carry resonances of an old order of apartheid, of that sort of possessiveness. But act 2 postulates another world. . . . It's immensely striking how strongly Chekhov feels about the stranger in act 2, for example. The stranger is one of the people from out there, and that is what I wanted my stranger to be as well—the people who are not in this charmed circle of those living in the house. So really, it was from act 2 that the web of political changes that affected Trofimov and Lopakhin had their beginnings for me. —Janet Suzman, personal interview, June 2000

Janet Suzman's *The Free State* was conceived in the South Africa of apartheid. In this national context, in a harsher version of the scientific "bads" of Beck's risk society, science and technology were frequently used as repressive tools: life destruction, surveillance, social control, and the kind of torture that accounts for Leko's damaged hands, which he waves around "too much" in Suzman's play. *The Free State* has not yet been performed in South Africa, but it was conceived there in a theatre struggling for an alternative South African politics. The play has twice run in Britain, which, at the turn of the twenty-first century, was still facing its own deep racist violence. At the time of playing *The Free State*, overt racism was evident in British streets, on football terraces, in prison cells (where racist murders still occurred), and even within the British Muslim religion. In research interviews I conducted at this time (Tulloch and Lupton 2003), first-generation migrants to Britain spoke about racism and risk, sometimes agreeing that things are getting better on the surface but that there were covert, indirect risks to face now. There were the risk of one's children growing up too fast in their mixed-race schools (drugs and violence were a current worry here), and there was what Beck calls "risky underemployment" as first-generation migrants whose economy had been based on family-run corner shops and small business were squeezed out by supermarkets and the microelectronic revolution.

The Cherry Orchard is, of course, about economic risk, primarily to the "outmoded" Russian gentry class at the turn of the twentieth century. But it details also the economic, social, and personal risks of other classes in that process: of the "underclass" stranger who storms on to the scene amidst the philosophizing of act 2; of the old serf, Firs, who proudly remembers how he refused his freedom; of the generations of exploited serfs who, Trofimov tells Anya, stare out from her cherry trees. Also in act 2 there are the personal and economic risks of Dunyasha, seduced and betrayed by Ranevskaya's upwardly mobile personal servant, Yasha; of Charlotta, who has no passport, no name, no lineage, no heritage and whose fate depends entirely on the gentry for whom she is governess (and who are as adept at losing their children as they are at making losses on their estates); and indeed of Lopakhin, who loves Ranevskaya, whom he cannot have, and has the economic resources either to save or destroy her. Suzman reworks this web of class, economic, and sexual risk in the context of South African racial and ethnic risk as she draws on black actors to play most of these "at risk" roles.

So act 2 of *The Cherry Orchard* is profoundly about risk, as Janet Suzman recognized in making it central to her theatrical setting of the Mandelan "political event." It is also, as she says, the act where "the web of changes that affected Trofimov and Lopakhin had their beginnings." The similarities are striking between Suzman's concept of *The Cherry Orchard* as political event within the broader context of postapartheid South Africa and Trevor Griffiths's reworking of the play to face the new conservatism of Margaret Thatcher (chapter 3). Both understood Chekhov's play as a tension between two spaces: the inner "charmed circle of those living in the house," where nearly all the action takes place, and the "out there" of act 2, where the rest of the people are.

Chekhov himself lived the contradictions of class mobility and hybridity. From a serf background and professionally socialized as a doctor, he also "lived in the house" (of various gentry friends). But, as well, he traveled and worked "out there": as a zemstvo doctor, as a social analyst of the penal colony at Sakhalin Island, as a writer of short stories about peasants and of reflexive plays about "this charmed circle" of intellectual, professional, and artistic middle-class folk (Tulloch 1980). It is because both Griffiths and Suzman read Chekhov's play as a political tension between inner circle and history happening out there that act 2 became so important in each of their productions.

Victor Turner speaks of theatrical performance as structured experiences that "probe a community's weaknesses, call its leaders to account, desacralize its most cherished values and beliefs, portray its characteristic conflicts and suggest remedies for them and generally take stock of its current situation in the 'known' world" (1982, 11). Undoubtedly, both Griffiths's and Suzman's reworkings of *The Cherry Orchard* do just that by engaging with the "new worlds" of Thatcher and Mandela. Turner's notion of the theatrical event as "society speaking to itself" is, however, too functionalist. It is people (individually and collectively) not societies that speak. And they do so, whether they are theatre producers, audiences, or indeed an author's socially constructed characters (like Trofimov and the vagrant), both performatively (within circuits of communication) and in their everyday lives. But Turner's notion of *liminality* — of the estranging of spectators from their everyday experience, of theatrical event as the transformative or liminal phase that generates new and unfamiliar experiences, and of the reincorporation of the audience within the social world — is still of considerable interest.

Chekhov, Griffiths, Suzman, in their different historical and geographical local situations, introduce an audience to the charmed circle of the country house. They then convey both characters and audience to that liminal space of act 2, to the people from out there. Choices are finally made (and not made) in act 3, the charmed circle breaks up in act 4, and all take their separate paths as separate agencies resonating in performance, as Griffiths says, between "time then" and "time now." These greater time-space coordinates, of history and sociopolitical theatrical event, are further inscribed in the place and occasion of the sites of performance (the charmed circle, for example, of the Theatre Royal, Bath) and thus in the everyday lives of their audiences. This chapter looks at the interaction of these various charmed circles: in Chekhov's text, in the (historically and geographically) situated production team of Janet Suzman, and among some members of the Theatre Royal, Bath, audience.

The Free State was performed in Bath: a "little hedgings" (as Suzman would say) sanctuary of England far from the city centers and suburbs of racial congregation like East Ham or Oldham, where prejudice and harassment was increasing at that time, but not far at all from the streets of Bristol, where violence had burst out in Thatcher's years. So, for the (all-white) Bath audiences that watched The Free State, it may have been a case also of charmed circle against those out there. With Suzman and Griffiths, this chapter looks at the interaction of geography then and now but also here and over there. It is through these time-space coordinates that a charmed circle audience's local, everyday life interacted with the more risky "global."

Cultural Context as Presentation:
Acting and Set Design in The Free State

In Trevor Griffiths's case, BBC Television's The Cherry Orchard was intended to interrogate British television's generic event of the year, Brideshead Revisited. Thus Griffiths's work with the televisual event was itself a matter of genre, reworking not simply the canonical text of Chekhov but the class constituents of the country-house genre itself. As such it was part of Griffiths's career of generic reworkings for television: of soap opera, miniseries, hospital saga, political speculative drama, the "well-made play." This is what Sauter means when he refers to the theatrical event as a process (in addition to being an individual "happening").

In Suzman's case, there was a significant professional history and biographical process behind her production of The Free State in Bath. Central here was the sense of her own charmed circle within the progressive theatrical community during the darker days of apartheid in South Africa. In particular, she was committed to the memory of Barney Simon, late artistic director of the Market Theatre, Johannesburg. It was he who, in the mid-1970s, had first suggested reworking The Cherry Orchard to her. Suzman described two juxtaposed events just twenty years later.

In 1994 South Africa held its first democratic elections — and on 30 June 1995 Barney Simon died. His heart gave out. Twenty years of running an open theatre in a closed society had taken its toll. It was shocking and it was tragic — he was far too young a man to die. He was a great man and had a profound influence on my thinking, as he did for many other people. "An unnecessary death," as Athol Fugard angrily put it at his graveside. And so, perforce, there remained unfinished business to attend to for Barney. I was somehow determined to complete what we had first mooted together — *The Cherry Orchard* seen through South African eyes — and to play a latter-day Ranyevskaya under his direction. (2000, xxiii)

Thus were the everyday events and the cultural context — the living and working professionally for change, the dying associated with open and closed societies — of the personal, professional, political, and societal risks embedded in Janet Suzman's theatrical event, *The Free State*. It played first at Birmingham Repertory Theatre in 1997 as *The Cherry Orchard* and then (called *The Free State* and with some new writing) went on an English tour in 2000, including the Theatre Royal, Bath.

Suzman was highly conscious of place and occasion in relation to this play. First, there was the South African occasion, mediated by Chekhov's own charmed circle:

The play, to obey the seasonal aspect of Chekhov's play . . . must start in the spring and move towards autumn. That dictated the September after the first [South African] April elections, when the cherry blossoms would be at their full beauty and the bright optimism of the elections would still be vibrating in the air. A window of time of six months, not yet dissipated by the carping and questioning that the ensuing years inevitably brought, would cover the journey of the play. Real revolutions, however, take longer than that. As Barney Simon had said: "Freedom through legislation has come suddenly and swiftly, and that is cause for great celebration. But freedom of the heart and mind is lagging far behind. It is that freedom that has always been [the Market Theatre's] concern, and remains it. We know that for a time we will continue to live in contradiction and confusion. . . . We struggle every day to *realise* the difference between what was and what is." Chekhov's pre-revolutionary Russians also struggled in contradiction and confusion, dreaming of better times. Our better times had come and yet on the surface nothing had changed. The political satirist, Pieter Dirk Uys, tells the story of an angry young black man on a recent voter-education tour shouting out: "We fought for freedom and we got democracy!" (Suzman 2000, xxviii)

Thus the charmed circle of a particular moment of South African politics, of Mandelan "harmony and . . . a benign optimism" (*The Free State* program notes), was to intersect with that of Chekhov, and two societal temporalities of occasion overlaid each other. The South African place had also to be re-created on stage, and so language, embodiment, and set design were very important to Suzman: "A play is dialogue, not merely an interesting political thesis, and so a familiarity with the speech rhythms, the social nuances, the sense of humour, the complicated interplay between the races of such an ethnically vexed country does not come amiss" (2000, xxii).

For myself, as a member of *The Free State* audience in Bath, there seemed to be an embodied sense of place and occasion throughout the play, from the first interaction of the play between Kele (Dunyasha) and Leko (Lopakhin) to the moment in act 4 where Kele (played by Marva Alexander), who, like Maria (Varya), is liberated by *escaping* her man, slaps Lebohang Elephant's Nyatso (Yasha) in the face. It was what Sauter describes as the sensory level of theatrical play — as the "spectator perceives the physical and mental presence of the actor and reacts to it more or less spontaneously" (2000, 7) — that affected me immediately and that I realised later I was trying to understand by way of artistic and symbolic conventions.

I was aware in interviewing Janet Suzman, to a degree that was not apparent in any other interview I conducted for this book, just how much of my own cultural context was operating as I talked with her about the play and yet at the same time how much I needed her understanding of that sensory "African" embodiment performed in *The Free State*. For this reason, the following extracts of her interview with me, during which Suzman describes how these embodiments of class and color were deeply but very specifically embedded in locations and histories other than the ones in which *The Free State* was being performed, are presented in dialogic mode.

I was discussing with her my own, unformulated sensory response to the opening scene of the play and to the arrival onstage of Anna (Anya), who, in Suzman's version, has been educated in the radical atmosphere of Witwatersrand University.

JT: I think that one of your successful characters is Anna. Strikingly different physically, strikingly positive . . . as against these wishy-washy Anyas that we so often get, where presumably we have a

young actor just working through the individualizing of the
character in some Stanislavskian way and not relating to
anything that was there in the Chekhov.

JS: I *so* agree with that. . . . Some people ask me, Why did you bring
South Africans over to do it? It is because . . . they bring a
baggage with them of a relationship with their own poverty, with
their own political landscape, and with the landscapes one is
trying to talk about in the play. And you are so right — the first
reaction . . . of English actors . . . is to the character, which from
a Stanislavskian point of view is very correct indeed. They try
and build the character but the character without . . . a
knowledge of poverty. (Personal interview, June 2000)

Suzman described how, in her own production, the outer and inner
frames of actors' experience and of the part they were acting had to converge. But it happened with difficulty during rehearsals.

I remember having an extraordinary crisis with the little girl who
played Dunyasha in the first version in '97 in the Birmingham one. Now
here was a smart Johannesburg street kid, very chic, very pretty, very
up-to-the-minute. Dead trendy. She was playing Dunyasha. And there
is this whole backlog of resentment about the master-servant relationship in young South African blacks, understandably. She says,
"You're patronizing Dunyasha; she can't have been as stupid as that.". . .
I said, "Look, somewhere in Russia is a little girl your age who will never
play with the Internet, who will never shop at Next, who will never be
popping into cinemas on a Friday night and clubbing, who will never
know a modern world but who nevertheless has a life, which the author
wishes to honor in some way. Who had her simple parameters of marriage as the attainment for a young female. Who got blinded for a second by somebody who was basically a shit, and who then had to take
stock of herself at the end, a sadder and wiser creature." And I said, "In
a way you have to split yourself into two. You have to bring with you
your own life, your own political upbringing," which in South Africa
was fairly hefty. As with most of the youngsters . . . she came of age . . .
as apartheid was dying, so she wasn't at the blunt end of it. . . . She real-
ized that although she could bring to it a kind of sassiness and a kind
of native cunning and a kind of enchantment and cuteness of her own,
she also had to take on board Dunyasha's limited little existence, her
blinkered little life, which was never going to be as rich or trendy or

cosmopolitan as hers. And that probably is a problem for a lot of actors. They have to leave behind some of themselves and honor the character with another part of themselves.

Given this degree of sensory, artistic, and symbolic complexity in the acting of Kele/Dunyasha, it is not surprising that a white audience member sitting in Bath, as I was, struggled with the emotional and intellectual theatrical playing of it.

> JT: And yet the Kele/Dunyasha actor [Marva Alexander] whom I saw I thought was extraordinarily strong. It was something to do with embodiment, to do with the way she carried her body and spoke, and I can't define that.

> JS: Well, I had to modernize the idea of it. In Chekhov's day a little girl who had been seduced by a Yasha . . . needed to find a husband and needed to have babies because that was the only way to go, both for Varya and Dunyasha. The proper end to a young girl's life was marriage. Now in modernizing it, it's quite clear that those two will survive very well without their suitors. Both Maria in my production and Kele in my production are going to be okay without marriage, which is why the one, Kele, can slap his face at the end — "How dare you have treated me like that" — and the other one, Maria, can say, "I feel free." . . . So she is not just a crybaby.

> JT: Just thinking about Kele/Dunyasha for a moment, what you describe there is a sort of conceptual understanding as to why she slaps his face. But, in fact, it comes as no surprise anyway because, as I say, right from act 1 there is something about her (and others') embodiment, the way she carries herself, her particular voice, the use of language. It is very hard to describe what that is. But it's so, so different from what you see on the English stage normally, playing Dunyasha or any of them. Was that something you worked on in rehearsals?

> JS: Yes. But I think there again, probably one of the most important things is this white-black, if you like, the master-servant relationship, which . . . Russia also understood very well, as a feudal system . . . this strangely close relationship of servants in a household. Whereas in England — I don't want to be too . . . simplistic — but it's much more upstairs, downstairs. . . . It's the nanny figure in English society that takes the place of the old

Anfisas, the old Firs, and such. But actually in South Africa every white child has been brought up by a black nanny. They receive their first hugs and kisses . . . on the backs of warm black skin, in sunlight and sunshine. And every white child knows the sort of lifelong symbiosis, that the first warm person in your life was a black servant. And so that whole feudal idea, if you like, is very deeply understood by white South Africans, and so they understand that . . . rather bantering interdependence between the two. Whereas in England it's shot through with class. . . . Things happen in a drawing room and things happen in a pantry, and never the twain shall meet. But that scene in *The Three Sisters* where Natasha is so unbearably rude to the old lady and Olga practically faints with the discomfort of it- that too could be understood by South Africans because of the history of South African households, the delicacy of those relationships, but also the closeness of them, which don't usually happen here in England.

What Suzman was clearly describing is the *sensory* underpinning of a white South African audience's potential involvement with the characters of her play, since they received "their first hugs and kisses . . . on the backs of warm black skin, in sunlight and sunshine." And that intuitive, sensory understanding would then flow through to an understanding of the the-atrical play — the communicative banter — between her characters across class divides. That could never be felt by an English audience, which in any case had been schooled in rather different artistic conventions for playing Chekhov's young people.

And if that was the problem of actor-audience theatrical play (of his-torical place and performed interactions) within the charmed circle of those living in the house, there was also an out there to establish. Here set design was very important to Suzman.

JT: What sort of relation did you have with the set designer?
JS: I had worked with him often before. He's a South African called Johan Engels. The first production we did together was *Othello* in the thick of apartheid, actually. I did that in the Market Theatre in '87. I absolutely wanted to use a South African, to know even the *smell* of those old houses . . . and the landscapes, that *feeling* in act 2, is where he came into his own. Most especially, I think, with the veranda in act 3, that huge reversed

veranda. So you got those pillars and porticoes and animal heads, African animal heads, and *out there* is the dark: a huge sky and a huge darkness. . . . South Africa is full of verandas, stoops, as we call them. I wanted very specifically for it to be a South African house rather than an English country house or even a Russian dacha.

JT: It occurred to me that there is that sense of space all through it, even in bits of conversation, such as when Lulu is talking about looking down on South Africa on the plane and how she wept. I have that sort of relationship with the Australian landscape from the plane. And it's occurred to me that one of the energies of your play is that not only are you replacing the "sad farewell" history of Ranyevskaya et al. with this very current history of South Africa, but you also have got a very strong geography. Is that fair? And I think that is coming not only through the words but also through the set design very strongly.

JS: Very strongly, yes. You know, one of the first things that strikes you about why somebody from Africa should respond so strongly to a play from Russia . . . is the sheer size of the place, which you will understand as an Australian. There is nothing remotely like it in continental Europe, certainly not in these [British] islands. Just a sense of unending land [in South Africa]. You know, you can see forty miles, and then when you get to that far mountain range there will be another forty miles of nothing, *but nothing*. And I remember understanding act 4 of *The Three Sisters* so well when I flew once from Moscow to Tashkent. It was March or April, and we flew for five hours, which is like going across the Atlantic, over nothing but snow and snow and snow and snow for five hours. And you think how big this country is, it's so gigantic. And so when the garrison says good-bye at the end of *The Three Sisters* they ain't going to Catterick. They are going forever, to the other end of the land mass, and they will never see them again. So it's awful, and you can't really genuinely play that in an English setting, as it just doesn't work, as people just don't understand distance in that way. So that was certainly a strong "binder" [in the play], and then this passion that people have for land. It's not *landscaped*. I always think that England, this country, has been sculpted over hundreds of generations into a jewel of a place. But it's man-made really. . . . The little hedgings, the *idea* of a landscape, like Capability Brown actually fashioning your view. As you know, that is so out of the question in Africa, Australia, and indeed Russia. It's way out of your hands, which is why the idea of . . . the cherry orchard itself seems to represent a security and a stability that is now way past its sell-by date. It's the *out-there-ness*, beyond those orchard fences, those limitations, you know, that both exhilarates and frightens people.

I have included this "dialogic" aspect of the interview transcript where I discuss body and place in *The Free State* with Janet Suzman because it is the only methodological access I have to a process that must have been occurring for other white British audience members for her play. But, of course, for each one of us the theatrical play of sensory, artistic, and symbolic levels would have been different. I, too, as a member of British colonial history, received many "first hugs and kisses . . . on the backs of warm black skin, in sunlight and sunshine" from my Indian ayah and still have the photographs to prove it. But the subsequent English history was so different from the South African (and the cross-class and race communication I observed as a young child in India so different too) that I had little intuitive purchase on the sensory play between black and white characters in Suzman's *The Free State*. But much more recent, immediate, and strong was my sensory contact with the vast space of the Australian landscape, and it was that which allowed me into aspects of the sensory and artistic play of Suzman's direction, as she clearly recognized in this interview.

Bath, with the Theatre Royal at its center, is situated in that landscape of "hedgings . . . sculpted over hundreds of generations into a jewel of a place" that Suzman describes. Indeed, one audience member described the TRB as "a jewel of a theatre in a jewel of a city." Many in the audience for *The Free State* would have driven — from Marlborough, from Devizes, from Frome, from Bristol, from Gloucester and Chippenham — through that hedged landscape and down into the Avon valley to Bath. The "jewel of a place" — the landscape, the town, the theatre, all "jewels" — then both contained (as charmed circle) and ostended Janet Suzman's "out-thereness," her play *The Free State*.

JS: Clearly, what happens in *The Cherry Orchard* is interior/exterior. And obviously Chekhov wanted something fairly spectacular. I mean to set act 2 out in the sticks, as it were. In nature rather than in possessions.

JT: Except that he talks about there being a township in the distance or some sense of modernity. . . . I think Trevor Griffith did have a township actually. . . . In fact, the poster for the Nottingham Playhouse *The Cherry Orchard* was a telegraph pole bursting into the blossom of the cherry orchard.

JS: Well, that's right, Chekhov does combine these old and new elements all the time in the play. There is a continual battle between those who can't let go and those who can . . . the new and . . . the old. So I think visually that is probably right. Our homage to that was a wind pump, which in the first production of the play in '97 was actually onstage. It was a proper wind pump, with its head turning and clanking where the dam was where the boy drowns. Because it was a touring set in the revival, we had to paint it on the back lot. So it is a *working* landscape. You know, it wasn't just a beautiful African landscape. So the wind pump was there and was much more present in the first production because . . . just before the strange sound, the head stopped moving. So for a moment, there was a complete strange silence before the twang.

This was Janet Suzman's explanation to us in Bath of her "other" theatrical event, conceived with Barney Simon, about the political events in South Africa post-1994. As Sauter says, the sociopolitical aspect of a play's cultural contexts is important both in its content and the way it is presented (through acting style, set design, etc.). And those aspects of cultural context were worked through the everyday working lives, family lives, and leisure lives of Janet Suzman and Barney Simon and through the "native cunning" of actors in *The Free State*. Then they were renegotiated in the daily lives of her audiences. But how did her British audience respond to Suzman's tale of two cultures?

Cultural Context as Content: *The Free State* Characters

Janet Suzman's symbolic emphasis on the charmed circle of "benign" white-black relations within the revolutionary South Africa led by Mandela had a number of key performative and semiotic "content indicators" onstage. These included

a portrait of Lulu's (i.e., Liuba's) husband, Johan, which was large and center-back stage in act 1. The picture was actually of Nelson Mandela's defense counsel, Bram Fischer, who was himself impris-

oned and died during apartheid. He represented here the Left-
liberal tendencies in South African life (e.g., as in Suzman's own
family), which, in the play, had impacted on Lulu, on her brother
Leo, on Leko (the merchant), on Pitso (the student), and on most
others in his household, including Karlotta (the governess, played
by Dorothy Gould).

the educational background of Leko (played by Jeffery Kissoon), who
had an M.B.A. paid for by Lulu's husband and represented the new
"black bourgeoisie" in South Africa. Leko (Lopakhin) can, on the one
hand, recoil (with his own racism) against marrying the "colored"
Maria (Varya), who is a child of Johan and a black servant, and, on
the other, show his hand tortured by white police to Pitso Thekiso
(Piotr Trofimov). Leko's education in this household gives a new slant
to the famous *The Cherry Orchard* bookcase (very prominent on
Suzman's act 1 stage); and when we first see Leko asleep at the beginning of act 1, he has a copy of *Hamlet* on his knee. Leko, then, via his
white-supported education-for-power strategy and in his continuing (black) racism, represents both the optimism and pessimism of
this version of *The Cherry Orchard*. As Suzman described it in the
program notes, Mandela's "benign and non-retributive influence will
inevitably wane, and then the window in time that marked the apogee
of his reconciliatory mood may seem like a dream. This play is
intended to celebrate that moment in history. It might not have its
feet firmly in the mud of hard realities, nor is it intended to document probability, but it urges harmony and exudes a benign optimism" (2000, 12). Her celebration is of that charmed Mandelian
"non-retributive" circle via the charmed circle of *The Cherry Orchard*,
with the absent liberal-radical Johan at its heart. Beyond and outside
that lies the "otherness," the "mud of hard realities."

Pitso (James Ngcobo), the radicalized black student who had been educated in Moscow as an underground worker for the ANC. Suzman
replaced the motif of Trofimov's lost galoshes (so often used in
British productions to represent the hopelessness of the "eternal
student") with a Russian fur hat, which Maria (Esmeralda Bihl)
throws at him near the end. The hat is a more active motif in its
South African context because of its revolutionary associations.
Pitso and his new generation liberal-radical white lover, Anna
(Patricia Boyer), *assume* (in their relationship) the new racial equality dream of South Africa. It is Pitso who, in act 2, speaks to those

hard realities. "Everything has changed here and yet nothing has changed. Liberation has come, but the real revolution hasn't even begun!. . . I tell you, 'out there' [the whites] bolt their doors to the real world, while in their own backyards vast numbers of people still struggle for every crumb. They squat in tin townships, they're crammed into hovels — no food, no heat. It's degrading, it hurts me!" (*The Free State* 2000, act 2, pp. 40–41).

Maria (Varya), who, though avoided, partly for racist reasons, by Leko, still leaves stage positively as a "new woman" in South Africa. Her final words in act 4 are "(*a sudden smile*) 'I'm, like, free.'" Like Kele (Dunyasha), she represents the strength among black and colored women that has been lost by the white woman, Lulu (played, in a deliberately restrained way, by Suzman herself).

Leo Guyver (Leonid Gayev), Lulu's brother, who strives for the liberalism of his father's household but, despite his gentle, easygoing nature, finds it hard to avoid politically incorrect comment from time to time (thus exasperating to a new edge his niece Anna, who loves him). Suzman says of Leo (and also Pik/Pischick, played by Peter Cartwright): "When the old boys make political mistakes, like 'He's unusual for a . . . ,' and can't complete the words, you know, there's a moment of frisson in the room. . . . Sometimes that got a laugh. Certainly, if there were South Africans [in the audience], they would laugh. The more uptight, English audience . . . would gasp a bit" (personal interview, June 2000).

The Free State Audiences

I conducted long (in-depth) interviews with thirteen audience members who had seen both *The Free State* and the English Touring Theatre's *The Cherry Orchard* at the Theatre Royal, Bath (some of them had also seen the RSC *The Seagull*). A number of people who responded in questionnaires had deliberately *not* gone to *The Free State* because they said they didn't want to see Chekhov's plays "messed around" or because they wanted to see the "original" *The Cherry Orchard* first. (*The Free State* played in Bath from 8–11 March and *The Cherry Orchard* in mid-June.) Others had gone to both productions, wanting to compare the two versions. We have also seen that the particular theatrical event that audiences made of *The Cherry Orchard* could be a different one for the Chekhov fans, the star fans, the special event or doing culture audiences, and so on.

In the interview, I began with general comparative questions about the ETT's *The Cherry Orchard*, *The Free State* (and, if they had seen it, the touring RSC's *The Seagull*), asking interviewees to enlarge on their questionnaire responses to these productions. I then asked more specific questions about *The Free State* (particularly set design and acting) in the context of Suzman's directorial emphasis of these aspects of the production in relation to the racial politics (and old and new risks) of South Africa. Suzman's own "reconciliatory" (Chekhov) history and geography could then be compared with the responses to it of some among the charmed circle at the TRB.

Among the key indicators of Janet Suzman's political slant on Chekhov were the portrait of Lulu's husband, Johan; the educational background of Leko; Pitso, the radicalized black student who had been educated in Moscow for the ANC; Maria, Leko's racist failure to marry her, and her "I'm, like, free" at the end; the politically incorrect yet humorous Leo, Lulu's brother.

I asked interviewees about all of the major (white and black, owner and servant) characters in *The Free State*. Of the thirteen responses, only one was negative about the production, and she was unable to comment "because the characters were so vastly unmemorable." But all twelve of the other long interview respondents were able, in discussion, to recall many of the characters and performances in some detail. This is how they interpreted the Suzman "key indicators."

Of those who noticed the portrait of Lulu's father, more (60 percent / 40 percent) of the interviewees read this as an image of apartheid, not liberalism. As David put it, "He must have been of the generation of Vervoort and all the people who were so rabidly anti-black and so on, the original white settlers if you like.... I actually felt that if you had gone back by ... only one generation or one and a half generations, then you would have found the absolutely standard South African situation with the blacks as the down-trodden people and the whites as the masters." Only two interviewees had any sense of this being a *liberal/radical* head of the household (husband, father, or grandfather), and of these two, one had heard Janet Suzman talk about it on the radio before the performance, and one had done a production workshop with Janet Suzman. This overall lack of understanding of a key aspect of the set symbolism (since over three quarters of the interviewees either read it incorrectly or "didn't really notice" the image) is important. Suzman's focus on a progressive part of the white intelligentsia was crucial to her positive, pro-Mandelan sense of a white-black reconciliation and what she called "nondoctrinaire" constructions of the present and potential future of South Africa. But hardly any of these very positive interviewees read the production quite that way. One interviewee, Mr. D, did, as we will see, come to see the Mandelan "gentle way of doing things" and that it was a "play about reconciliation." However, he didn't come to that conclusion by seeing the play but, rather, after reading Suzman's program notes when he got home.

Probably it was not surprising, given the response to Johan's portrait, that Leko's educationally embedded role in the inner circle was not noticed much either. Most interviewees "didn't quite know where he was coming from," other than that he was convincing as a streetwise new generation of black businessmen. Alternatively, they compared him as more or less "plausible" with the businessman (Lopakhin) in *The Cherry Orchard*. Ruth, for example, enjoyed the sensory "warmth coming from him" and found him physically "big and cuddly" in comparison with the "more scrawny" and much more ruthless businessman in the ETT *Cherry Orchard*. Because her mother came from Yorkshire, Ruth had grown up to resent the image of Yorkshiremen as all "servant class on-the-make." So she had disliked the ETT Lopakhin's Yorkshire accent, which she ascribed to the attitude, "How are we going to make all these people common and lowly?" The only respondent to mention Leko's M.B.A. was Marjorie, who saw Leko as being "experienced in the world" and without "a strong emphasis on education." For her, the M.B.A. was symptomatic of his pragmatism — "education for a vocation." She did not interpret it as a sign of the white family's liberalism. There was also very little recognition among the interviewees of the past political experience of Leko (i.e., his tortured hand).

In contrast, the black student, Pitso, was read more closely as Suzman intended him to be, particularly through his relationship with Anna. Liz found him "more politicised because he was the African who had been educated in Russia, I think at Moscow University. I met people in Zambia that had done that." Even without having this personal experience of Africa, three quarters of the interviewees read Pitso as much more positive than the usual "eternal student": he "knew how to get there," "seeking education for change," "not feckless like *The Cherry Orchard* student," "political — coming out of the ANC." For Gill, this positive representation took him closer to Chekhov's original student, who "I always connected with Lenin." For Christine, Pitso was "very keen to improve himself and learn more, and was *thwarted* in his attempts" by being chucked out of different universities. Enid "liked his passion. He got his ideologies over that he believed in. I liked the pair of them, because Anna is excited by his ideas. When they leave that house they would have become a powerful pair."

Anna, too, was remembered by most interviewees as "knowing life," being "*naturally* comfortable with all shades of opinion," "capable and modern," "very animated in her philosophical discussion with the student." Rosemary compared Anna with the Anya of the ETT's *The Cherry Orchard*, who was "very simple and innocent.... I mean when Anya comes in and says 'here is my bed and oh I'm so tired I'd like to go to bed,' it was all very much ... like a little girl coming home and reacting. Whereas in *The Free State* I thought ... although Anna was excited and it was fun being home, there was also definitely a sophistication behind it." Though Clair preferred *The Cherry Orchard* presentation of Anya, she made a similar point. "That was very clear in *The Cherry Orchard*, the use of Anya and her complete naivety and innocence. Especially when she is going to bed and you can see her getting undressed, ready for bed, whereas all the adults in the front of the stage are being mature and having a complex conversation, she is just there in her sort of white gown. That was a young image." Being used to this kind of Anya in *The Cherry Orchard*, Gill found *The Free State*'s Anna "very difficult to fit in with the rest at the beginning. She was the most modern of all." But "as the play progressed, her complete lack of prejudice became very important. Whereas the older generations had to work consciously for that sense of equality, she *assumed* it. Maria, in contrast, is more aware of prejudice because she has lived it." Gill particularly liked the "picnic scene" relationship between Anna and Pitso, where they were "relaxed" and communicating as natural equals.

Only two interviewees said they consciously noticed the issue of Maria's color while watching the play. (One or two others said, in response to interview probing, that "maybe they had been half-conscious" about it.) Stephanie did respond to Lulu's direct question to Leko about whether it is because Maria is a "colored" that he hasn't married her. "It's a question that stops you dead.... I thought 'my goodness yes ... he is a true African and she's got white blood at least, not in the previous generation but several generations back. So she is never going to be a true African.'" (We note, though, that Stephanie did not pick Lulu's husband, Johan, as the father.) Gill was also struck by the line about color by Lulu to Leko. "I thought 'how clever' and 'too slick.' But it worked because she is on the cusp between different races.... From that line, it felt clear that was *why* Leko and Maria didn't marry. The whole play was politicised [by that].

But it worked." Otherwise, most interviewees looked for other reasons for the failure of Maria and Leko to marry. One interviewee thought about her own, still-unmarried forty-year-old son; another thought there was perhaps a class issue here; and the actor David read it via his own recent performance in *The Cherry Orchard*. For him, Lopakhin is, "for some reason, not the marrying kind," and Varya "is probably the sort of person who at that era would have seen marriage as, you know, hope for consequence in life. But of course it doesn't happen, does it, and she never actually gets there. And I always think that at the end, it's incredibly sad because what is life going to be for her after the play is over? Very, very sad." In fact, this "sad" interpretation of Varya/Maria was quite contrary to Janet Suzman's direction of the part in *The Free State* and Maria's final lines, "I'm, like, free." But neither David nor any of the other interviewees noted the "I'm, like, free" Maria at the end of the play.

The parts of Gayev (John Quentin) in the ETT's *The Cherry Orchard* and Leo Guyver (Jack Klaff) in *The Free State* were played very differently. Gayev appeared as an affable eccentric, with mannerisms that irritated some of the audience. But Clair particularly liked this performance. "I think in *The Cherry Orchard*, he felt a lot more part of this whole group of people. . . . He was quite a friend. . . . He was bullying them, sort of, making sure things were working. Whereas in *The Free State*, I don't remember him quite as much. He was more businesslike, possibly. . , . He was the one who was trying to sort things out and thinking logically through things." Ruth didn't agree, finding Gayev's "eccentricity distracting and too much . . . without rationale." The more politically active Enid summed up what a number of other Bath "liberals" in the audience may have been feeling. "Leo was a character who *felt* real in *The Free State*, whereas the actor in *The Cherry Orchard* was not — he was very conscious of his acting. In *The Free State* all of our innate racism felt so real and you had to admit that it is *in you*." Whether or not they empathized with him experientially like Edith, people certainly understood Leo. For Gill he was "louche, taking the easy way, not on the same political level as his sister — opportunistic and lazy. He also wanted to *say* the right thing because of the family." For Stephanie the actor was "very good indeed — this man had *experienced* the things he had mentioned." Rosemary found "Jack Klaff very good as Leo — he perfectly portrayed a man brought up in that situation, never having to help himself." For Marjorie there is "no way that he is coping with acceptance of the black characters." Christine found him "a likeable character who had outlived his time, but couldn't adapt. Unlike [Gayev in] *The Cherry Orchard* who was a complete waste of space — in that he came across as not having any function at all, no redeeming features at all."

Whether it was because audience members recognized him as an intuitively long-term racist or as closer to the "outmoded" *The Cherry Orchard* characters, few interviewees spoke of Gayev or any of the other ETT performances with much passion. This is in marked contrast to their description of the last scene of the *The Free State*, where Putswa (Firs) is left sitting in the chiaroscuro, black/white effect of the huge closed shutters that he has tried, and failed, to open. As he sits there, tiny in front of the big windows, the play ends not with his last few words, which are omitted, but with an extremely loud sound of chain saws and trees crashing.

> Oh I thought it was shattering, shattering. I mean I, you know people start applauding and everything at the end of a play but I just felt that I just wanted to sit there quietly for a little while. I was very affected by the end of it. Much, much more so than the later production of *The Cherry Orchard*. My heart wasn't breaking for the dear old retainer in *The Cherry Orchard*, but it was for the dear old servant in *The Free State* (Rosemary).

> I was almost *paralysed* by the sadness of it — the ending of an era, which didn't mean the next era would be O.K. . . . I liked the stage lighting then. It conveyed something of dying — the dying of the day as redolent of the dying of an era (Enid).

> Well, his being in the house for so long and his, sort of feelings toward the house. I found, he was a character who I started to sort of pick up on stage as the play was going on. I'd see him and notice him quite strongly on stage, whereas with *The Cherry Orchard*, I didn't do that as much. He wasn't a character that I was looking out for, and at the end when he was left in the house, it wasn't quite so harsh in *The Cherry Orchard*. . . . But in *The Free State* I thought he was going to listen to the trees being cut down and die then. Well, he had lost his strength, he was losing something that meant a lot to him. . . . But I liked the way at the end . . . it was left open, that he was there and you didn't know. He might have got out, he might have been found . . . and gone on to live a bit more life. . . . The deafening sound — that was what *really* got me, that end. There was this old man, left alone in this huge house and this deafening, this really, really loud noise everywhere echoing around the whole theatre and around the stage. It was a very powerful and well-done moment for me (Clair).

This last scene with the old abandoned retainer achieved a powerful "in the gut" feeling among many of the interviewees, while hardly anyone mentioned responding to Suzman's man from "out there," the vagrant in act 2. One respondent, Liz (who had been in Australia as well as Zambia), did say that she found the vagrant very threatening, "very African, I would even say an Aboriginal out at Cooper Pedy — more frightening than usual because you see people like that today." But she, too, responded more directly to Putswa, seeing in him the master-servant relationship of her houseboys when she lived in Zambia.

So if there was a liminal moment (in Turner's sense) for these audience members, it came less from the out there of act 2 but rather from the in here at the very end of the play, when the peaceful location of Bath and its theatre was shattered by noise, breakdown, and (as Enid said) no definite sense that "the next era would be O.K." In that respect, The Free State was, of course, very different from The Cherry Orchard, where we know, or think we know, "what happened next." In The Free State there was no obvious return from liminality out there in South Africa — although, of course, there was the return of the Bath audience to the heritage foyer, the festival flowers of the city streets outside, and then the country drive home.

Still, for some among that audience at least there was that lingering, "shattering" ending, and it seems that it was this particular combination of sound, set, lighting, and performance rather than either Johan's portrait or the vagrant that conveyed to the audience members interviewed some of Suzman's symbolic meaning about the fragility of the Mandelan dream. That moment represented, above all in this performance, the "no, no, don't do it!" emotionality that one interviewee, Rosemary, described as so central to the "liveness" of the theatrical event. Putswa's death was a moment of the "bad" emotion between performer and audience that helped lift this play to *being* a theatrical event in a way that Stephen Unwin's *The Cherry Orchard* clearly was not for many among its audience.

Why, then, in the conjuncture of perception, cognition, emotion, and communication that make up the "theatrical event" (Eversmann, forthcoming) did the ideological meaning of Suzman's "reconciliatory" play get read this way by some in the audience? The emphasis on audience analysis in this chapter is, of course, strongly qualitative (even reflexively individual), with my references to "many" or "few" among the members interviewed having very little generalized status methodologically . Still, among those who consented to be interviewed, there was a distinct sense of shock over this ending.

Risk and the Sublime: The Case of Old Putswa

We may be helped in understanding this by returning to Scott Lash's analysis of "aesthetic reflexivity and the sublime" within risk culture. In the introduction I mentioned Lash's example of a photography exhibition by Robert Mapplethorpe, who was dying of AIDS, that focused on the homoerotic male body. Lash makes the point that to "consider AIDS through probabilities and statistics is a way of looking at risks via determinate judgments. The more aesthetic consideration of AIDS through the existential meanings of Mapplethorpe's images instead involves reflexive judgment" (2000, 53–54).

When audiences failed to understand the logic of Janet Suzman's white liberal family history via the photograph/portrait of Johan onstage or the racist "reason" for Leko not marrying Maria, it is determinate judgment they were lacking. Thus, they also missed the contextualizing narrative for Leo Guyver's, Lulu's, Anna's, Maria's, and Leko's various actions. But some did — particularly through the performance of Jack Klaff as Leo (but also through the assumed equality of communication between Pitso and Anna) — have a sense of white complicity in the continuing risk of racism. And, in the case of at least one audience member who admitted to it (and probably many more, judging from the kind of awkward "knowing" audience laughter that responded, on the two occasions that I watched this play, to Leo's continuing social and racist gaffs), there was a reflexive sense of embarrassed self-identity with this ongoing racism. As audience members responded to the racism of South Africa via their own experiences, for example, with houseboys in Zambia, there was some intuition of a synthesis between personal and theatrical (and then South African) experience. As Liz said, "With the good old man [Putswa] . . . He was great. . . . Again it could be because of me being out in Africa. It's also a stereotype with the old American Negro and things. . . . When I worked in a hospital out in Zambia, you know, we had houseboys, which was absolutely ridiculous. But it did remind me of that. You know he is the 'faithful servant' — you know, houseboy."

Lash describes this kind of reflexive judgment as aesthetic reflexivity, which engages with the "beautiful." Here "the imagination, objects and events are intuited through, not logical categories, but the 'forms of time and space.' It is the imagination which synthesises or produces through . . . schemata . . . 'representations' or 'presentations.'" In my interview, Liz made her own "presentation" in relation to Putswa's end. She described her time in Africa in terms of the "schemata" of stereotyped American movies but also houseboys and her personal experience of apartheid. "It was when Rhodesia had declared UDI . . . and I had problems with black people and white people and 'you, white, can sit here' and 'black sit there.' . . . I mean . . . it *was* apartheid as there were three prices for everything — a price for the English, a price for the Indians, and a price for Africans."

The narratives of cultural artifacts, says Lash, "are the configurations, the forms through which we judge aesthetically, judge reflexively the risk events, the objects that we encounter and from which we produce other cultural artefacts, other configurations, other forms, other meanings" (2000, 56). Liz produced her own narratives and representations of the "good Negro," houseboys, and apartheid in Zambia in response to what she called the "great" part of the old retainer, Putswa. Her imagination, as Lash puts it, synthesized the "distinctions" of the United States, Zambia, and South Africa, of Chekhov, *The Cherry Orchard*, *The Free State*, and American movies.

But Lash goes one stage further, beyond the "determinate judgement" of cognition and beyond the "aesthetic reflexivity" of imagination, to sensation and the "sublime." Here "sensation is raw. The body takes in the world through sensation. . . . Aesthetic judgements of the sublime expose bodies with lack, expose open bodies to the ravages of contingency, to darkness, to 'fear and trembling.' Hence we also experience this as confirming our finitude" (Lash 2000, 57).

This "gut-wrenching" (Eversmann) directness of the "aesthetic of the sublime" is close to what our interviewees were describing as they watched the last scene of *The Free State*. "I was almost *paralysed*"; "it was shattering, shattering. . . . People start applauding . . . at the end of a play but I just felt that I just wanted to sit there quietly for a little while." And mixed with this "shattering" conjuncture of noise and image on the "live stage" was the sense of finitude. "I liked the stage lighting then — it conveyed something of dying — the dying of the day as redolent of the dying of an era."

As Eversmann would predict, it seems that audiences can work with all of the cognitive, imaginative, and sensational constituents of risk culture. When audiences speak of "a theatrical event — at its best," I think they are referring to their blending of determinate understanding, reflexive imagination, and the "terrible sublime." But it is the last of these that probably has a special effect in theatre as compared with other media which respondents regularly described as "more sanitized." Live theatre, interviewees emphasized, is "experience raw," and it is that special "raw" event of theatricality that seems to have affected our interviewees most in the final scene of the play. For the rest, their particular pleasure in Janet Suzman's *The Free State* seems to have involved a personal negotiation of "determinate understanding" (the recent/current politics of South Africa, which, some interviewees said, were "nearer" and more "known" than Chekhov's Russia), "imaginative synthesis" (with Leo, with Putswa, with Pitso and Anna together, with Janet Suzman herself as Lulu), and the "terrible sublime" of that "shattering, shattering" finale.

8

PLAYING CULTURE
PLEASURABLE PLAY IN
THE FREE STATE AND
THE CHERRY ORCHARD

In the arts, not only is something played, but it is
played for someone, who is not the player.... Theatre
becomes theatre by being an event in which two
partners engage in a playful relationship.
—Willmar Sauter, forthcoming

Playing culture is central to Sauter's communicative model of
theatre research and to his definition of a theatrical event as "the communicative mutuality of performer and spectator, the elements of play,
and their dependence on the surrounding contexts" (2000, 14). Theatre
audiences do not respond to a "political" play like Janet Suzman's *The Free
State* as though it is a political speech, though some Theatre Royal, Bath,
audience members chose not to go to the play, fearing that is what it would
be. Rather, audiences are composed of a variety of leisure conventions
(chapter 6) and social experiences (chapter 7) with which they approach
actors' embodied performances, sets, and so on as they "play culture"
(often *other* cultures, as in Suzman's case) with those on the stage.
According to their positioning as one or other leisure formation in relation to a particular theatrical event, they may respond to a play's "politics" via different routes. Each of those routes is *as a theatre audience*, with
particular perceptual, emotional-aesthetic, cognitive, and communicative responses to the event.

For Sauter, that aspect of the theatrical event that he maps as "playing culture" focuses on the importance of skills and style in a
performer/spectator's pleasurable play, which distinguishes this behavior

from both "the trivial experiences of everyday life" and religious rituals. Yet, as we have seen already, there is a continuity as well as distinction between theatrical event and everyday life. This chapter explores further this relationship between the "playful relation" in the theatre and "everyday" frames in the audience by comparing pleasures in "skills and style" that my *The Free State* interviewees found between this production and the ETT's *The Cherry Orchard*. Here the long interview method, based on comparing two Chekhovs that respondents had seen recently, proved a useful way of articulating issues of production skills and style and audience pleasure.

The first extract from my interview with Stephanie Nailor illustrates clearly the playful relationship (or lack of it) between actors and audience.

Stephanie Nailor

JT: Let's pick up one or two things from your questionnaire response. Just looking at it, you clearly weren't hugely convinced with the recent *The Cherry Orchard*.

SN: I'm afraid that I left at the interval. . . . I had fallen asleep twice. . . .

JT: Whereas in your questionnaire, you felt Suzman's *The Free State* was "superb"?

SN: Yes. Absolutely. They were very convincing [in it]. I think she is a brilliant actress herself, and she is obviously a very good writer to be able to transform it in that way. . . . I heard her on the radio saying that she chose South African actors (with I think one exception) because their voices and way of speaking have the right rhythms, and I think the whole thing hung together so brilliantly.

There are three points to make here. The first is methodological. By beginning each long interview from the point in the interviewee's earlier survey questionnaire where they responded to liking or not liking the ETT's *The Cherry Orchard*, it was possible to compare in discussion their pleasure or displeasure in the two performances by way of specific questions about acting styles, skills, and their sense of place in relation to these plays' settings. These latter — the introduction, for example, of black actors and sets that indicated vast spaces — represented Suzman's own theatrical approach to the politics of South Africa in her play. By employing a structured interview in this way, it was possible to compare the very different everyday responses of the interviewees to the embodied and visual theatrical politics of Suzman's play. It also allowed the interview to move between the highly individualized, affective response (often to individual actors) and the more global and cognitive responses evoked by "ideas," landscapes of place, and embodied ethnicity — in other words, to map the interview across Eversmann's perceptual, cognitive, emotional, and communicative dimensions of the theatrical event.

Second, the interview extract illustrates the dramatic difference in pleasure for this audience member, Stephanie Nailor, between the ETT's and Suzman's Chekhovs and, in particular, the importance in this response of the "skills and style," as Sauter puts it, of Janet Suzman and her black actors. Stephanie Nailor took pleasure in Suzman's skills as an actress but also in her skills and style as a director and writer able to "transform" Chekhov in this way.

Third, like myself as researcher, Stephanie has gone directly from her pleasure or displeasure in these performances to Janet Suzman herself, via a radio talk, to explain cognitively what she had experienced perceptually and affectively watching the play.

> JT: Did you see this as Chekhov or as something different?
>
> SN: I think I saw it as a version of Chekhov. I don't think anybody else could have written it — that sort of attitude to the rich landowners, to their servants, was highly emotional. But I suppose it is very much South African in a way, isn't it? With the white attitude to the blacks, [like] the Russians' attitude to their serfs. They were very affectionate, very fond of them very aware of all that they did for them but also could treat them like dirt without a second thought.
>
> JT: So are you seeing a real parallel there in the social histories of the two countries, then, that you feel Janet Suzman drew to our attention?
>
> SN: Yes, it made it all the more pointed as the servants were all black or colored, not white, anyway.
>
> JT: Whereas you didn't feel that in *The Cherry Orchard* you saw — that relationship?
>
> SN: Nowhere near in the same way. . . . It didn't seem to me as if any of the actors were taking the part seriously. . . . And Prunella Scales seemed to float through it somehow. . . . This was the

disappointing thing. They were all good actors, but somehow it didn't come off in that production for me.

It was as though there was an unspoken contract between performer and audience member to be "serious" and not "float through" this highly cognitive matter of social interaction and cultural play in other cultures. Watching the ETT *Cherry Orchard*, Stephanie felt like someone at a dance whose partner is in some other sphere. It was a matter of betraying the sense of "pleasurable play . . . in which two partners engage in a playful relationship" (Sauter forthcoming).

JT: The next question is about the sets of *The Free State*. Did you like them or not?

SN: Yes, I did . . . because the landscape was foreign to us, and so were the feelings and problems of the people on the stage. Something like that could never have happened in this country. . . . And so it held it all together. . . . You did get an impression of space around the place. . . . They were *conscious* that the world was changing in a way that the people in *The Cherry Orchard*, I think, weren't. . . .

JT: The African actors, the black actors, anyway. What did you think of them?

SN: I think they are very, very good indeed, and she was so right to select them, the people who spoke the language in the way that it was always spoken. In a different way you can see it in the movements of West Indian boys in the street. Their movements are quite different from a young white boy's movements. . . .

JT: Janet Suzman talked in the interview with me about the sort of bantering interdependence of master and servant. . . .

SN: Yes, they know that their masters and mistresses can't do without them. They depend on the whites for employment, but the whites depend on them for an infinity of things. . . . In [the ETT's] *The Cherry Orchard* we saw, it's almost as if they're in a cocoon, closed off from the real world. They are not aware of any problems that might arise ever, almost, whereas in the Janet Suzman production the problems are around them all the time. And the changes that are happening . . . are affecting them now, and they know they are going to affect them more later.

The problem she had with *The Cherry Orchard*, leading her to leave at the interval, was the sense of homology between Prunella Scales "floating" through her part and the social solipsism of her (and other) characters in their "cocoon." It is clear that she wanted the performers/characters to *act* more in both the theatrical-playful and socially agentive senses of the word.

For Stephanie Nailor, then, the charmed circle of the ETT *Cherry Orchard* remained, in performance, solipsistic. In *The Free State* it was opening up, through body language, ideas, and action, "changes that are happening." For her, there was a playful relationship — conveyed by perceptual, emotional, and cognitive cues in sets, embodied acting, and Suzman's transforming of Chekhov's text — between herself as audience member and the performers of *The Free State*. That was how she absorbed the political affect of the play, and then, as Eversmann points out, she wanted to continue with the communicative dimension of the play, ticking her box on *The Cherry Orchard* questionnaire that she would like to talk further about *The Free State* with the researchers.

Clair Mills

JT: Judging from your questionnaire comments you were reasonably happy with what you saw of all three plays?

CM: Yes, and I actually really enjoyed the set of . . . *The Free State*. . . .

JT: According to your questionnaire, you were coming to Chekhov for the first time, and "with apprehension." But *The Free State* was the first of the three, wasn't it? Your first Chekhov?

CM: Yes. . . . Going in to see *The Free State*, I was very apprehensive, but I found it quite [straightforward]. They had not simplified it, but character-wise it wasn't so cluttered on stage and that sort of thing as *The Cherry Orchard* most recently was. I found the characters quite easy to understand, and I instantly identified with it. Being a more modern performance, I found each character easier to sort of define and see who was who and sort of get the relationships between characters quicker than I did with *The Cherry Orchard*.

JT: Why was that? I mean, after all, they have foreign names, another culture. . . .

CM: Although I don't have clear memories of all the things that happened in South Africa, it was something that you are taught about . . . and see on TV . . . and you do grow to understand what happens in South Africa. Whereas my knowledge of Russian history is very vague, to be honest, and I don't know much about it. So I could put the play *The Free State* into context. I could put it into *where* it was performed. . . .

JT: What was that knowledge that was with you when you went into the Bath Theatre Royal and enjoyed *The Free State*? What were you thinking about in relation to current-day South Africa?

CM: It was the time factor. It was a sort of troubled time in South Africa, where they had the problem with apartheid. . . . I'm not quite sure if apartheid had ended, but it was around that sort of time. . . . So it had this sort of tenseness that was in the country, and it came through in the performance. It sort of helped me see where this tenseness was coming from. . . . It helped bring the atmosphere from that whole country into the play.

Clair Mills was much younger than Stephanie Nailor. She was a late-teenage school student with a passion for theatre. Two things are notable in this extract from Clair's interview. First, she was nervous of a "great playwright" that she had heard was "complicated," so she used *The Free State* both perceptually (the "uncluttered" set) and cognitively (the "easy to understand" characters) as a bridge to her understanding of the "real" Chekhov performed by the ETT. Second, her comments illustrate convincingly Philip Auslander's point that the "liveness" of theatre always occurs in a world dominated by what he calls "mediatization." Not only did her television watching over the years of the situation in South Africa make her feel less apprehensive of understanding her "first Chekhov," *The Free State*, but she also carried that television knowledge with her to Chekhov's Russia, since her "knowledge of Russian history is very vague." Her cognitive understanding of Chekhov (on which some of her confidence and identity as a competent theatregoer depended) was deployed as a causal chain, from TV and school accounts via *The Free State* to *The Cherry Orchard*.

JT: So, okay, . . . then you went to another Chekhov, which was presumably *The Seagull*, and then *The Cherry Orchard*. . . . Did you feel you were coming to a totally new play when you saw *The Cherry Orchard* again or — and you saw *The Seagull*, which you also hadn't seen at all before — was there a carryover of some kind?

CM: I found *The Seagull* quite different to *The Free State* and *The Cherry Orchard*. It was a lot simpler. It was quite a relaxing play, I didn't feel like a tenseness of everything inside that. . . . Whereas with *The Cherry Orchard* I came in with an idea of what it was about [because I had seen *The Free State*], which was quite nice, . . . and then when I started watching it, it did take awhile to understand the relationships between characters and that sort of thing because it was quite complicated. They had a lot of people onstage at one time. . . . But having a knowledge of roughly what was going on did help with that. . . . I was trying to pinpoint who was who in relation to who I saw in *The Free State*. . . . And when I got to grips with doing that and working out who was who, it sort of started to click, the actual plot of it started to come easier. . . .

JT: So actually seeing *The Free State* helped as a plot device?

CM: Yes, it was a help, so I could say, "Oh, he is the old man at the end, and she is the magician lady," sort of creating like a link between the two plays. . . . Then I found myself wanting to know a lot more of what was happening in Russia, and I wanted to know . . . where it was set in Russia, because I mean I know nothing about Russia at all. Never been there, I don't know what it looks like. I could have some sort of visual image of South Africa because it's been on television and that sort of thing. But I had no visual image of Russia at all. So it was quite hard to put it in its place and put the characters where they should be in this sort of big image.

JT: Did you feel you got any more sense of Russia in *The Cherry Orchard* or not?

CM: I did get some sense of it, although not . . . as sort of a whole country. . . . Class systems are roughly, from what I gather, around about the same sort of ideas [as in *The Free State*]. So I had some idea of what the class system was. Although some of the relationships between characters that actually were in different class systems interested me. . . .

JT: Do you remember the sets at all for *The Free State*?

CM: Yes. . . . I liked them. . . . It was quite a heavy, large set compared to *The Cherry Orchard*, which was ever so simple. I thought that they both worked very well. As *The Free State* was quite simple, having a large set wasn't a problem, whereas in *The Cherry Orchard* . . . they used a simple set for quite a complicated production. They complemented each other nicely. . . . I preferred *The Cherry Orchard* set, I have to say. I thought it worked wonderfully. . . . The simplicity of it, and its versatility. The way it was moved around the . . . stage to conjure up different images, different rooms, and different places in the house. . . .

JT: Some people . . . said, . . . "Given how minimalist it was, they took an awful long time changing it." And some people didn't like the changing of sets in full view.

CM: The changing of sets did take awhile. But I think the minimalist sets really worked nicely. . . .

JT: Well, with *The Free State* set, then, what was it about it that made it look so "large," as you put it? . . .

CM: I found it a very . . . big sort of *scope*. This big landscape with these small characters in it. And I remember the very end, the very last scene. . . . There's this huge, huge house and this tiny little man. And that is what we're left with. . . .

JT: And what was the emotional feel of that for you then?

CM: The very end . . . was . . . a sort of harsh feeling, and then when you heard the chain saws cutting the trees down and this man lying in the house, it was . . . quite a painful thing. It was . . . very upsetting that this man was sitting there listening to the cherry orchard being destroyed. I thought that was a very harsh moment. . . . There was also a vastness of the whole country that you did feel, especially at the beginning, quite a vastness. And then when they were talking about leaving, there was this huge vastness of this whole country and it being this, this special place.

Like many of *The Free State* interviewees, Clair Mills experienced the "gut feeling" of what Eversmann calls the "embodied emotion" of a theatrical event, which was created by her perception of the internal and external sets, the "very harsh" noise of the chain saw, and the acting of the old man at the end.

JT: What about the actors?

CM: At the beginning of *The Free State* I found that there was quite a relationship between the characters onstage. . . . Leko is doing very well for himself as a businessman, and Kele is a servant, and I thought their relationship very interesting. . . . There was this element of a friendship possibly. . . . This is one of the things that I found hard about *The Cherry Orchard*, some of the subtler relationships that were in *The Free State* didn't come through as strongly. . . .

Though she was one of the interviewees who thoroughly enjoyed *The Cherry Orchard*, Clair Mills came to this enjoyment mainly via the cognitive pathway of *The Free State*. But during that process she came to a powerful emotional involvement with the big spaces out there and the novel, small relationships within the charmed circle of the house. The constituents of her "pleasurable play" were different in each case. With *The Cherry Orchard*, for example, it was to do with the versatility and virtuosity of both acting and set creation, whereas in the case of *The Free State* this seemed more like border territory, leading her more surely toward both the complexities of Chekhov's characterization and toward his Russia, of which she knew so little.

David Wright

Another of my interviewees, Rosemary Morris, said she got a real sense of place from *The Free State*, with the vastness of the sets paradoxically making her feel "more comfortable, more at home" (in part because of her direct experience of the South African landscape) than the sets of *The Cherry Orchard*, which "didn't give me a feeling of anything very much at all." Similarly, to her the performances in *The Cherry Orchard* seemed routine and disappointing ("just a play") in contrast to the sense of people and place achieved by the bantering interaction of masters and servants in *The Free State*. Far from being "just a play," *The Free State* stayed vividly in her memory. "Every single individual actor as I think back on it even now, I can remember them so clearly, and everyone somehow really affected me very deeply." She felt that some of this was due to her experience in South Africa and with South African friends. But she felt her difference in response to the two productions also related significantly to the fact that she was an actor who understood the sense of pleasurable play between performer and audience when theatre was "working." My next interviewee, David Wright, was also an actor.

DW: I am a theatre practitioner too, in a modest sort of way. . . .
Personally, I like to go along and make comparisons, particularly,
of course, with *The Cherry Orchard* and *The Free State* because
we were doing *The Cherry Orchard* ourselves in Bath and Bristol
and out at Hartham Park, which is up near Corsham, and we did
a rerun of it the week before last at the Abbey House in
Malmesbury. . . .

JT: Judging from your questionnaire responses, you seem to have
liked both of these *Cherry Orchards* at Bath. . . . Is that right?

DW: Yes. I think probably *The Free State* was better, although it is, of
course, an entirely different play in the sense that to me *The Free
State* was a political play, and it seems to me that Chekhov really
wrote something that you might call a social play. It's more about
events that befall the family that fall on hard times, whereas *The
Free State*, it seemed to me, had more of . . . the South African
political situation, which underlay . . . most of the production. I
think that is why I liked it, because it was different. I thought
there were some problems with the English Touring Theatre,
which I've heard a little bit more about recently. Apparently they
had difficulty with lines, and apparently they were having
rehearsals till very late. I happened to know . . . somebody who
knew somebody that was in the cast, and they told me that, and it
was showing up a little bit to be honest. . . . And it also really did
depend, for me, on whether you could suspend the disbelief
about the age of Prunella Scales, who is one of my great favorites.
But Madame Ranyevskaya is really supposed to be forty-two or
forty-three, and Prunella Scales was pushing it a bit. . . .

JT: There is a bit of a policy at Bath Theatre Royal of bringing stars
in, often from TV and film, isn't there?

DW: Yes, and of course they do tend to put on productions that
have been in the West End and have been successful. . . .
Sometimes they will come through Bath with a big star, and on
they will go to London. To be honest, that is probably why I
reckon this theatre is hugely one notch up from Bristol, where
they tend to use their own company and perhaps not have quite
so many stars.

JT: Do you ever think the stars let you down?

DW: Not often. It's usually more the plays that slightly let down the
star. I remember a play with Suzannah York, years ago, . . . that was

a great disappointment, and another one with Julie Christie. . . .
And by contrast we saw *Letters and Lovers* some years ago with
Maggie Smith, and it was absolutely out of this world, it was so
good. . . . Again, I think Prunella Scales had some problems in
trying to get into the character. It is a very difficult part to play
Madame Ranevskaya because . . . there are lots of emotional levels
. . . that you have got to try and get to. I think that she was
probably finding it difficult to get into them, particularly when she
was talking about the sadness of her life in Paris and how awful
the man that she had met up with was. I wasn't quite sure that she
had got the emotion there really. . . . Then again, I heard that the
director was completely in awe of the fact that she was playing the
part and therefore had difficulty in directing her very precisely. So
they may have spent a little too much time looking on detail and
not necessarily looking at the broad emotional sweep that they
might have needed.

The dominant discourse in David Wright's comparison and interpretation of the two plays at this point of the interview was clearly that of an
actor "insider" ("I happened to know . . . somebody who knew somebody
in the cast"). His response to Prunella Scales in the part of Ranevskaya was
similar to Trevor Griffiths's response to Judi Dench in the same part: the
worry that star charisma can influence the overall ensemble. Interestingly,
it turned out that he had just been acting in Trevor Griffiths's version of
The Cherry Orchard, and so his response to the ETT production (and
Suzman's *The Free State*) was tempered by this experience as well.

JT: Coming on to *The Free State*, it's interesting that you've made
this point about the classic version of *The Cherry Orchard* and
. . . what you see as Suzman's political version. Did you, as you
watched, think this was Chekhov or something totally different?
DW: I suppose knowing the play already you can't fail to realize that
it is based on the Chekhov play. But I really did think it was very,
very nearly a different play, because the balance between . . . the
parts really is very different. . . . The brother in it was not really
the Gayev that I think of, who is described by Lopakhin as an old
woman. . . . I have been playing Firs . . . in our production, and
the translation that we used was the Trevor Griffiths one, which
was the late 1970s, early 1980s, . . . which of course gives Firs a
slightly more battered and batty perspective for an actor. But I

really thought that in, for example, *The Free State* there was nothing to the Firs part at all. He vanished completely. And indeed . . . the guy who played Firs a couple of weeks ago in the Prunella Scales version . . . was just playing as not really terribly old at all, still very much in possession of all his faculties. . . . I think that was played as a very robust part, whereas, as the Chekhov play was very definitely *written*, he is actually supposed to stagger over, he puts the footstool beneath Ranevskaya's feet, and he can't get up again. . . . I mean, that is what it says in the original Russian, you know, he staggers up again and totters back to his place, which I don't think particularly happened a couple a weeks ago in *The Cherry Orchard*. So I thought that *The Free State* was almost a new play. . . . I think going from a social play to a political play is quite a long leap, although I think it was brilliantly done, and I thought Janet Suzman was fantastic. . . .

JT: Of course, Trevor Griffiths has been accused of politicizing Chekhov. So what do you think about that, having played Firs in Griffiths's version? . . . At the end Firs is . . . almost recognizing that he has blown it. He is half recognizing, he is sort of saying, "What did I do wrong?" Not quite, but almost.

DW: It's sentimentalized, isn't it, really? . . . His last line, "It's gone, it's over, almost as though it had never happened" . . . which I think is maybe a little bit of a Trevor Griffiths-ism. But, to be quite honest, I thought his translation was not as far from the Russian as necessarily supposed. Yes, I agree that "up yours, butterballs" . . . is so brilliantly modern that it shocks the audience every night, or it seemed to every time I gave it. . . . They loved the fact the Firs gets one over Yasha. But . . . in the Bath *Cherry Orchard*, he didn't really shake at all, and yet the lines are that he goes around shaking the whole time and muttering to himself. I mean, that comes right from the original Russian . . . so that at the end you have this complete shock when he comes on to close the play and to indicate that a chapter has closed in the life of this particular house and this particular family. . . .

JT: If I'm getting your sense right, when you are saying *The Free State* is "political," you mean political in the sense of party political. You mean Mandela.

DW: Yes, yes, yes, party political. . . . I just have the feeling that there was a little bit more politics with a big, large P, capital P, than politics with a small p, which of course applies to the whole of life anyway.

By this point in the interview another major discursive source of authority in David Wright's discussion had become apparent: the repeated reference to *The Cherry Orchard* in "the original Russian." David Wright had been senior languages master in one of Britain's more eminent public schools, and his "negotiation" with the politics of Trevor Griffiths (and, correspondingly, of Suzman's *The Free State*) was mediated by this. Griffiths was "not as far from the Russian as necessarily supposed" and so was a worthy writer of the part of Firs, which David had just played.

JT: Did you like the sets?

DW: I thought the set for *The Free State* was very, very good. I liked the ballroom scene where they are actually outside and going back in as the ball is going on . . . and the homecoming right at the beginning of the first act. I thought that looked as if it could easily have been a homestead. . . . There was a really nice scene when they are out in the garden and you have got the vista of South Africa . . . the tower and the fields in the distance and so on. . . . You can see the land, and you can . . . feel the South African fields in the background. That was . . . the impression that I got, that it was a big land, and there was a lot of space there. . . . So I wouldn't criticize the sets for *The Free State* at all. I probably would have done for *The Cherry Orchard*, which I thought was surprising, really, because they made no use of the fantastic stage that they have got at Bath, and they actually carried everything on and carried everything off. I really thought they should have been well past that.

JT: Why was that good for you in *The Free State* production? Why did it work?

DW: Well, going back to the Chekhov, if you think of some of these huge estates that there were in Russia in the late nineteenth century, they really did cover mile after mile after mile. And of course Russia itself is a massive, massive country, and we can hardly really get any conception of it at all here. . . .

JT: Actors? . . .

DW: I thought that the girl playing the maid Kele was absolutely fantastic. She really did a great performance. . . . It's certainly normally suggested that black people will move much more fluently than whites, and I suspect that therefore onstage that is going to come through as well. I also can't remember the last play I've ever seen with a nearly wholly black cast. . . . I loved that. . . . It definitely gave it an entirely different perspective and a different view. . . . It started right at the beginning. . . . There was a different feel to it. . . . I'm not so sure if the original Chekhov would have been a bit more distant in terms of the relationship between the master, mistress, and the servants, whereas in the South African one it definitely . . . did feel much closer and therefore a difference.

As a former head of language teaching, David wants always to return to the original Russian. As an actor, and particularly playing Trevor Griffiths's version of *The Cherry Orchard,* he was able to blend his knowledge of Russian into his performance experience in the part of Firs and then make comparisons with *The Cherry Orchard* and *The Free State* at Bath. Like others interviewed, he was convinced of place and time by both the sets and the performances in *The Free State,* and by redesignating this play as "political" Chekhov, he was able to find it convincing and enjoyable, partly because of his recognition of the parallel in vastness between Russia and South Africa. Like Suzman, he acknowledged that English people can have little experiential sense of that space of *The Cherry Orchard* people. His pleasurable play was certainly more with *The Free State* performers (who, as with a number of other audience members, including myself, were enjoyed early in a sensory way because of their movements) than with *The Cherry Orchard,* about which he believed he had insider knowledge. Interestingly, though, neither production gave him pleasure through his own part of Firs, largely because he saw both of them as losing touch with the original Russian. If Chekhov's Russia was the end point of Clair Mills' pleasure in these plays, for David Wright it was the starting point, and it was from his own authoritative (acting and language teaching) discourses that he derived his political position and his pleasure in *The Free State* as comparable to Chekhov's Russia but also different as a "political play."

Liz Waterhouse

JT: Judging from your questionnaire . . . you don't seem to have liked the recent *The Cherry Orchard* too much, and you loved *The Free State,* as far as I can see.

LW: Absolutely. It was just brilliant. I think that fact that it had been brought up to date made it a lot easier, you know, because their Leko, a black man, is the owner of the land. Plus also Janet Suzman, I think she was just, she just affects me. I think she is the most brilliant actress. You know, she can just walk onstage, she doesn't even have to say anything. . . . It is some kind of aura. I didn't like the one with Prunella Scales in it. It was done more classically, you know, at *that* time. . . .

JT: With *The Free State*, you were saying that it somehow made it easier being current. . . . Did it relate to recent South African things? Was that working for you, or was it something else?

LW: Absolutely, because of now that apartheid, in theory, is gone. You know, blacks have now got the vote and got the power and things. . . . It was a lot . . . more forceful. It was more obvious as well to see, "Well, yes, this *is* an end of an era." You know, and this new era was coming up.

JT: Did you still see it as Chekhov?

LW: Yes, absolutely . . . because Chekhov had this society in change also.

JT: With *The Cherry Orchard* . . . your feeling [in the questionnaire] was that . . . Prunella Scales was . . . "insipid"? And you didn't like the set?

LW: Yes, I didn't like it. I'm not a Prunella Scales fan anyhow, but it so happened that *The Cherry Orchard* was coming to Bath, and we thought Right, we'll see that.

Even more than Stephanie Nailor, Liz Waterhouse had an immediate affective response to Janet Suzman as actress. She was affected instantly by the "aura" of Suzman when she came onstage. This is Sauter's sense of "histrionic history: the natural disposition of the performer, the impact of natural gifts, the dependence upon such things as the form and size of . . . body, the scope of . . . voice, the relation between given conditions and acquired skills — all adding up to what we sometimes call the aura of an actor, the radiation emanating from an actor, the basic facilities which make the spectators listen to and observe the stage actions" (2000, 125). In contrast, as "not a Prunella Scales fan anyhow, but . . ." Stephanie Nailor seems to have half made up her mind about Scales before the performance, and the production of *The Cherry Orchard* "confirmed" her view. In addition, she had a preference for Chekhov "done now" rather than "classically . . . at *that* time," which made it even harder for Scales to convince her, given the deliberate mix of naturalism and minimalism in the ETT's set design.

JT: If you didn't like the sets [in *The Cherry Orchard*], what about *The Free State*?

LW: The set was brilliant . . . and particularly the outside . . . and you could see the cherry orchards. That is what I liked . . . and I liked that big landscape, interestingly enough, actually, because I used to work and live in Zambia for two years. . . . That might have something to do with the fact that I liked the picnic scene, because that was "Africa" . . . absolutely!

JT: What did you think of the actors in *The Free State*?

LW: I thought they were all brilliant . . . with the good old man [Putswa]. . . . He was great. . . . Again, it could be because of me being out in Africa. It's also a stereotype with the old American Negro and things. . . . When I worked in a hospital out in Zambia, you know, we had houseboys, which was absolutely ridiculous. But it did remind me of that. You know he is "the faithful servant" — you know, "houseboy."

JT: Well, it's interesting, though, the actual way that the master and servant class relate in *The Free State*, in a much more bantering style. . . . Is that something that related to your experience in Zambia?

LW: Yes, certainly that is more "Africa," because it's certainly not master-slave as in America with the Negroes — a completely different relationship there.

Liz Waterhouse found herself negotiating racism in Britain after the Stephen Lawrence case. There had been a time when she used (and called) black servants "houseboys" quite unreflexively. Now, though, she returned to check her language ("You know, 'houseboy'") and think a bit, along with others in the audience, about the "humorous" racial gaffs that the Gayev character was making, trying to be liberal in postapartheid South Africa.

Like Clair Mills, Liz Waterhouse spoke of the comparative difficulty of understanding *The Cherry Orchard*, particularly in the ETT version. In contrast, by bringing Chekhov "up to date," *The Free State* was easier to understand while still being "true to Chekhov." Again, like other interviewees, two key factors in her obviously much greater enjoyment of *The Free State* were the specific African landscape (*containing* the cherry orchard) and the performances. Though she spoke at one point of Firs in the context of the black American servant stereotype, her own experience of "houseboys" in Zambia and the bantering style of performance made it "more 'Africa,' because it's certainly not master-slave as in America with the Negroes — a completely different relationship there."

Pleasurable play for Liz Waterhouse had especially to do with a long-term attraction to Janet Suzman, an "affect" that she certainly didn't share with Prunella Scales. This actor affect combined with the historical/political positioning of the production ("It was done more classically, you know, at *that* time") and her own personal experience of Africa combined to create one "brilliant" piece of theatre for her and one "insipid" one.

Mr. S. Docker

JT: From your questionnaire, it seems you liked *The Free State* but not *The Cherry Orchard*?

SD: With [*The Cherry Orchard*] with Penelope Wilton some years ago . . . I felt enraged, you know. "You stupid woman, fancy doing a thing like that!" But with Prunella Scales in this *The Cherry Orchard* production, I thought, Well, there we go. You know, "She doesn't matter. . . . Totally inconsequential." . . .

JT: Penelope Wilton was also, of course, in *The Seagull*.

SD: In the recent one? Yes, I think she was. . . . Well, I was terribly disappointed with that as well. When they opened the stage, I expected to see the distant view of the lake and the moon shimmering in it . . . and the musicians were coming from the other side of the lake, from somewhere else. Because you were told that the lake was behind the theatre, and the music was coming from somewhere else.

JT: What about *The Free State*? You said in your questionnaire that "it wasn't Chekhov, but I enjoyed it."

SD: Well, it was a jolly good yarn, you know. That's what I go to the theatre for, to listen to and see a jolly good yarn. . . . My memory is such that a week later I have to think very hard about what I saw last week, you know.

JT: When you say "it wasn't Chekhov," is that because it was set in South Africa?

SD: Well, yes, and from my recollection of other Chekhovs, it had a different ring to it. The chap who was playing the subsequent landowner, you know, the purchaser, I can't remember his name . . . he came over as such a "so please do something about it as I don't really want to buy it but I will if I have to." And I thought, That wasn't how it was before [in *The Cherry Orchard*].

JT: How do you think he would have been in the original Chekhov?

SD: Well, the one part that I can remember, he was, well, "I'm not really bothered if you do anything much about it but if you don't it's mine." . . . In *The Free State* I thought, He's going to do his best for the family, but in the Chekhov, "Well, if you don't do something about it, I will." . . . And *The Free State*, it wasn't like an updated Shakespeare. It wasn't an updated Chekhov. It stood very well in its own right, I thought. . . . Updated Shakespeare, to me, they can't do it. There is too much of Shakespeare in a Shakespearean play that it cannot be updated. I'm going back here to *A Midsummer Night's Dream* I saw where all the fairies were punks. And that was ridiculous.

JT: Okay, so you feel that you cannot do an updated Shakespeare but you can do an updated Chekhov, or not?

SD: Well, yes. It's still, I mean, Chekhov. . . . When did he die? Early in the century, wasn't it? . . . I think he was alive when my father was alive, you know. So it doesn't need much updating. It was a situation which was, what shall we call it? We can't call it topical. . . . But when I came away and read the program notes . . . then I saw the light, and Mandela's gentle way of doing things, and that is the way the play came over, a sort of play about reconciliation.

JT: Right, so you had two experiences then, really. You enjoyed the play, and then you read the detailed notes by Janet Suzman, and you got an extra spin on it or something?

SD: Yes, it had an extra dimension then which I hadn't appreciated by watching it.

Mr. Docker was by far the oldest of the interviewees. He lived in a retirement home and, because of his "bad memory," was very doubtful about his value to the research program, even though he had ticked the questionnaire box that he would like to talk more about *The Free State*. The *longue durée* of his own and his father's life together made him feel much closer to Chekhov, and therefore this new variant set in South Africa was not "updated" like the "punk" Shakespeare. Still, the length of Mr. Docker's life had also exacerbated his "problem" when going to the theatre, which, he kept emphasizing, was his memory.

> JT: What did you think of the sets in it?
>
> SD: I'm glad you asked me that. I thought, What the hell are they doing with the railway arch in the middle of the expanse of South Africa? ... It was always there [onstage], wasn't it? ... The only image I have of *The Free State* is the railway arch. As I live near Stroud in Gloucestershire and there is a railway arch just like it, I felt like writing to the designer and asking why he had transposed the railway arch in Stroud to South Africa.
>
> JT: I think they were trying to get a sense of South African landscape, actually. Did you get any of that?
>
> SD: No.
>
> JT: I mean the background, the big landscape?
>
> SD: I don't remember any of that. . . . I got fixed on the railway arch.
>
> JT: And you saw it all the time right through the play?
>
> SD: Yes. . . . It didn't go offstage, it didn't move.
>
> JT: I'm trying to work out which one you mean. . . . I remember in the third act, you know, the ball scene, you get these big arches and then the veranda, and then you look out at the landscape.
>
> SD: Yes, it's coming back to me now.
>
> JT: Was it those?
>
> SD: Yes. . . . But do you know, all that I can remember is this arch, this bricked-up arch, and if anybody would have asked about *The Free State* design I would have said, "That's it, I can't remember anything else." . . .
>
> JT: So did that bother you?
>
> SD: Yes, because I was waiting for it to go away. . . .
>
> JT: Okay — a question about the actors. . . .
>
> SD: I was surprised there were so many from South Africa. I thought it was a very good ensemble.

JT: Did you feel they were different somehow from the actors we are used to seeing in Chekhov?

SD: It wasn't Chekhov that I was looking at. . . . No, it was a story about what was going on in South Africa, and if I hadn't seen a Chekhov before, then it was really a good play. But knowing that it was based along the same story line as *The Cherry Orchard*, you kept getting the references back.

JT: What did that do for you? Was that a problem?

SD: Not at all. No.

JT: So you were happy with making the references back to the Chekhov?

SD: Yes, because it was right for the play.

JT: *Why* do you think it was, though?

SD: Don't ask!

JT: Well, they are a century apart, aren't they? . . . Although you did say earlier that you felt that because he's pretty modern, it's much more relevant than Shakespeare.

SD: No, I didn't say it is more relevant than Shakespeare. I said Shakespeare is still very relevant, but you can't put him into modern dress . . . because the words are so strong that they negate anything that you are looking at. Like I went to one of the . . . history plays, and I had to come out in the interval because soldiers came in on bicycles, in army greatcoats and hats and with swords strapped to themselves. We saw *Macbeth*, they were all rushing around in what looked like police armed-unit uniforms with revolvers, and then they had a sword fight!

Despite his anxiousness about his usefulness to the research program, Mr. Docker was, in fact, one of the sharpest of the interviewees in putting me right about what he had or had not said earlier. This encouraged me to probe a little further.

JT: So . . . with *The Free State*, on the one hand you say that you saw it as a free-standing play, on the other that, nevertheless, you kept thinking back to *The Cherry Orchard*, that's what I'm trying to puzzle out. . . . So there must be . . .

SD: It's only because I had seen *The Cherry Orchard*. It's like, how can we say . . . ? No, sorry, can't help you there. . . .

JT: Well, one thing that I was interested in was the way in which the masters and the servants interacted in *The Free State*. Was that something that appealed to you? I mean, from the start there was . . .

SD: They didn't register quite as strongly as they had done in previous Chekhovs, shall we say. You know, how lonely they were down in the hierarchy of servants, and it didn't come over that clearly to me. It didn't *jar* that much.

JT: So as you said before, you weren't really kind of seeing current problems in South Africa throughout this play.

SD: No, because I wasn't looking for that. . . . But I can't remember the bloody stuff. It really is awful. If my wife would have been alive she could have talked to you forever, and the lady I meet there, her husband was at college with my wife, and they both had this incredible encyclopedic memory for anything. . . . And see, throughout my married life for the last thirty years I had never bothered, because if I wanted to remember anything I would ask my wife . . . and she would remember every detail, oh, so much, so much. . . . Now, I'm sorry, but all I can remember is this bloody railway arch.

JT: Well, yes, okay, that is pretty strong. Are there any other things about the three plays? You saw *The Cherry Orchard* fairly recently, and you said you couldn't quite put your finger on it, it didn't quite seem right.

SD: Well, yes . . . Prunella Scales was playing the thing. How can we put it? Oh, she just didn't care . . . and so I couldn't be bothered with her. Particularly after I had experienced Penelope Wilton, when I was so angry with the woman for spending her money when she needed it so badly, you know, and the whole play was swung in a totally different way. . . . Oh, I hated her [as a character]. But I would go and see Penelope Wilton again, but I won't bother with Prunella Scales. Not her fault — it was the way it was produced.

JT: You've talked about Penelope Wilton and Prunella Scales, but what about Janet Suzman in her part?

SD: Yes, I felt the poor lady [that she played] was worn down by it all, what is going to happen, but "I will do my best." . . . Oh, yes. Yes. I thoroughly enjoyed it. . . . Suzman had my sympathy,

Prunella Scales couldn't care less, and I just hated Penelope Wilton.

It seems that Mr. Docker did notice the bantering, less "down in the hierarchy of servants" relationships of *The Free State* but conceptualized that more in terms of previous English *The Cherry Orchards* he had seen than in terms of Janet Suzman's knowledge of white-black, master-servant relations in South Africa. Though he could not remember details of many earlier theatre productions that he had visited, two things he certainly did remember. One was his anger over at least four Shakespeare productions that had "updated" the sets, props, and costumes. The other was the contrast between his pleasurable play with actors he had seen play Ranevskaya in *The Cherry Orchard*. He would go and see Penelope Wilton (who made him "hate" Ranevskaya) and Janet Suzman (who had his "sympathy") but not Prunella Scales, who "couldn't care less." It was the affective part of his relationships to the actors that he remembered so well.

In these *The Free State* long interviews, I was trying to ask questions that tied in systematically to aspects of the production's cultural contexts that were important to Janet Suzman (South African politics, the actors, the sets). But I also allowed the interview to "wander" to try and capture how these Chekhov plays were experienced in terms of the everyday preoccupations of these particular audience members. In this respect, then, I was interested in Mr. Docker's obsession with his railway arch at Stroud but then also the deep sadness that he can no longer remember as he could when his wife was alive; Stephanie Nailor's great disappointment with *The Cherry Orchard* against all expectations, a disappointment she returned to like a motif in the interview many times; the young school student, Clair Mills's apprehension about going to Chekhov, made easier for her by going to *The Free State* first because she felt she could experience *The Cherry Orchard*'s "tension" much better via her knowledge of troubles in South Africa; David Wright's working through as a practicing actor of his pleasures in *The Free State* and *The Cherry Orchard* and his inside knowledge of the production of the latter (as well as his knowledge, as former head of languages at a public school, of Chekhov's Russian stage instructions); Liz Waterhouse's almost visceral attraction to the acting of Janet Suzman but then also her longer memories of her time in Zambia and so her own place in a history of British racism.

All of these respondents (except Clair) preferred *The Free State* to *The Cherry Orchard*. On the one hand, this had a lot to do (as Sauter would predict) with their perception of the skill, style, and enthusiasm with which each play was presented. Mr. Docker expressed this sense of the actor / audience member's "playful relationship" most clearly. "Prunella Scales was playing the thing. . . . Oh, she just didn't care . . . and so I couldn't be bothered with her. Particularly after I had experienced Penelope Wilton, when I was so angry with the woman for spending her money when she needed it so badly. . . . I hated her [as a character]. But I would go and see Penelope Wilton. . . . I won't bother with Prunella Scales." On the other hand, they had also come to that comparison of the performers in various Chekhov plays via their own daily (and long-term) sets of preoccupations.

These preoccupations were at once local and personal (Mr. Docker's worry over his memory and the railway arch; Liz Waterhouse's attraction to Janet Suzman; Clair Mills's apprehension about Chekhov being "too difficult" for her; David Wright's acting at Malmesbury) and, more broadly, social and political (such as Liz Waterhouse's experiences in Zambia). It was by way of these personal/social preoccupations and their actual experience — perceptually, emotionally, and cognitively — of the events onstage (as well, sometimes, as hearing about them on the radio beforehand or reading about them afterward in the program notes) that they came to the inner circle / "other" relationships of *The Free State*.

This particular audience research methodology had focused on the relationship between respondents' expressed pleasures or displeasures in their ETT *The Cherry Orchard* questionnaires and by way of long interviews structured in relation to Janet Suzman's particular emphases on place and occasion in her South African Chekhov. I avoided asking interviewees their personal details at the beginning of the interview to try to avoid these cuing their responses directly rather than via their sense of pleasurable play at these productions. At the end of the interview, however, we did talk a little more about these personal histories and preoccupations.

Social Audience Positions

Mr. S. Docker, who was now "over-70," had been encouraged by his father to study engineering at university just after the war in order to "be in the re-building of the world" (which gave him an additional interest in the Suzman notes on South Africa). Instead he joined the Royal Army Ordnance Corps as a "let out" from his father's vision and then, after two years of intensive overseas army traveling, became a photographic assistant at the Theatre Royal, Bournemouth, which is where he met his wife. "We married because we both loved the theatre." After her death, he still goes to the theatre a great deal, eschewing holidays so that he can afford it. Because he is relatively poor now, he costs everything precisely. He complains that in 1951 the theatre "cost me ... 6.48% of my salary; and I worked it out that to go ... still in the cheaper seats, it would cost me about 20% of my salary, a great deal more." He repeated what he had emphasized earlier in the interview, how much he missed the discussions about plays that brought him and his wife together in the first place. But now at the Theatre Royal, Bath, "I always do my best to meet the widow of the chap who was at college with my wife, which does make a difference." The day after the interview he was planning to go to Stratford to see *As You Like It*. "I just wish Stratford was just a little bit nearer and they'd stop doing 'modern' Shakespeare, or as I say, mucking about with it. I chose to see *As You Like It* because, they tell me, it's in traditional style. But when they try to update it, it loses so much."

Liz Waterhouse, who was now age fifty-five, "escaped" her very academic girls boarding school to see the theatre. This school made even girls on the science side, like herself, "read all of Shakespeare," and it bored her "because we *just* used to read." But, to compensate, there were theatre trips that "got us out of the prison-of-war camp" and "brought it alive." "Bringing it alive" included "bringing it up to date," and, like Clair Mills but not Mr. Docker, this helped her understanding. It was that sense of the "live aura" of Janet Suzman (and, even more, her real acting idol, Vanessa Redgrave) that still brought her so much excitement in some of the theatre she saw. She had been a medical radiographer in Zambia and also trained as a TV sound technician in New Zealand, so she was not just a theatre fan. She also enjoyed "updated Shakespeare" on film and television such as Kenneth Branagh's films and the Baz Luhrmann *Romeo + Juliet*. She liked the latter in particular because of its appeal to younger people, whom she said she would like to draw away from the Spice Girls and into the theatre. "I think they have got to encourage younger people, because when I go I seem to be one of the younger ones!" Later in life she had taken a law degree (still cycling from Warwick University to Stratford for the theatre!), and, as a solicitor, she could now afford to pay more than Mr. Docker for seats. "I don't think theatre tickets are expensive. . . . If I want to go to a production . . . I usually ask for the best seats available, you know, center, front stalls. It's not 'Oh what's the price — oh £30, no, I'll have the £22.' I think it is a good night out, and I do like to see live theatre, you know, and support them instead of your Spice Girls that earn millions."

Clair Mills was one of the theatregoing teenagers Liz Waterhouse would have liked. She had just done her GCSEs and was starting her A level. She had "been really passionate about theatre since I was about nine, and then I started going regularly. For about two years now, and as part of the youth theatre in Bath I can go for £3. So really the theatre has done a lot for the youth theatre to encourage us to go. And so after going once, I got a job and spent all my money going basically weekly, because . . . I really enjoy going. . . . It's something that I want to do for the rest of my life. . . . I'd like to work in the theatre backstage. Well, I would like to act. But I am hopefully going to do stage management for a degree when I finish my A levels. . . . And I go to the theatre as much as I can to see . . . different ways of doing it. I saw the *Clockwork Orange* in Bath last year and then, having seen Chekhov, it is such a mix of different things that I really enjoy it all. . . . There are very few young people who go, which is a shame I think, as I get such enjoyment out of it." As we hear about Clair Mills's interest in stage management, we can begin to understand her particular pleasure (unlike most respondents) in the clever use of the traveling set in the ETT's *The Cherry Orchard.*

Stephanie Nailor, who was now over sixty-five and retired, left school early because her steelworker father was always being moved during the war. "So I finished up in a poor school in Stockport and couldn't wait to leave. Instead of taking school certificate I left. Without higher school certificate . . . I could never afford to stop work and go to university. So I was sort of a secretary all my life, and I suppose my last ten years when I wasn't a secretary was the most interesting. I was one of two-and-a-half typists for twenty-seven barristers in chambers in Bristol, which was absolutely fascinating. But I've done various courses since I retired." One of these was a part-time course in literary theory, which she took up when she had to nurse her husband through terminal cancer and then again for a time after he died. "Some of the literary critics I thought were . . . making up methods of criticism to get themselves published. Frankly, I thought a lot of it was absolute nonsense." Terry Eagleton, though, she did like. "I found some of his attitudes very irritating, but . . . I could put up with the things that I disagreed with in his criticisms as he wrote it so well" — and she was "absolutely sure" that, like her, Eagleton would have enjoyed *The Free State*. But far more than any literary theory, Stephanie Nailor was attracted to the "liveness" of theatre. She finished the interview by returning to her main theme, her disappointment in *The Cherry Orchard* (which was the first Russian play she had ever walked out of), and contrasting it with her experience of the "compelling performance" of *The Seagull*. "I thought it was a marvellous production. And, interestingly — going to the matinee performances a lot of the audience are even older than I am — when there were silences onstage, there were silences in the audience as well, and that doesn't always happen in Bath, I have to say. Some of the little old ladies are a bit twittery, and they start coughing and getting a sweet out when there is a pause. But it wasn't just my reaction that it was a compelling performance, everybody else felt the same thing. And I think when that happens with an audience the actors play . . . better."

These interviewees came from a variety of different social and experiential backgrounds (e.g., David Wright has taken early retirement after a successful teaching career, whereas the other actor, Rosemary Morris from Swindon, who once came second to Diana Dors in a poetry-reading contest and had gone on to study music, gave up her singing career when she married, "as many young woman did back in the 1950s"). Most of my interviewees were retired, but not all were, and not all were "comfortably off." Mr. Docker and Clair Mills were examples at different ends of the age spectrum of people who did not have a lot of money but who put much of what they did have into theatre tickets.

There was, however, one response common to all of these interviewees, of whatever age and background: their "pleasurable play" in live theatre.

The Live Theatrical Event

In the case of *The Free State* long interviews, the methodology began in a highly structured way (to flesh out earlier questionnaire responses about pleasure at the various productions of Chekhov at the TRB). Later — and prior to my biographical wrapup with each interviewee at the end — they were encouraged to talk about theatre generally via more open-ended questions. The common theme of all of them in this part of the interview was their equation of "theatrical event" with "live theatre."

Living on my own, I'm alone with television, and I think some television plays are very good, but somehow there's an *immediacy* in the theatre. I mean, I saw *The Madness of George III* [*sic*] by Alan Bennett a few years ago. I think that is the most moving and most brilliant play that I have ever seen, and I don't want to see the film because it would open it up too much. . . . In the film I believe a lot of the scenes take place out of doors, which of course they can't do that on the stage. So there is nothing in the play to distract you . . . from the horror of the king's situation. I mean, when they were wrapping him into a straight-jacket I wanted to shout, "No, no, don't do it." You know, I was conscious of other people feeling it as well. . . . On the stage you are seeing it happening live in front of you. I mean, occasionally you're conscious of people forgetting their lines or making a slight slip. . . . [With television] even though the action is equally emotional . . . somehow it is more artificial. . . . All the difficulties that you see onstage are somehow smoothed out on film. . . . You see it at thirdhand. You are seeing almost at firsthand with the actors. . . . That is an event in itself (Stephanie Nailor).

I just think that the adrenaline flows more when I see a live production. . . . There's something between an audience and actor. And I am fascinated to talk to other people and to hear their reaction to a performance or a play and note that mine is perhaps different (Rosemary Morris).

Both my wife and I would probably say that we are *fans* of the theatre. . . . It's live, it's there in front of you. The liveness aspect I personally think is enormously important. I agree that they can obviously produce the most amazing effects with film these days. . . . But nevertheless there is still something about the theatre . . . that provides you with an intimacy, a closeness, a surprise . . . that will catch you out far more than a film (David Wright).

I like the liveness of it compared to the cinema. You *relate* to the people onstage, and then it's sort of easier to take on what they are saying, and the plot and so on. You are drawn in much more to the performance if you are there. . . . I'm drawn in to the event of it. I get absorbed in something that isn't just everyday life (Clair Mills).

Having it live, in front of a real audience, is important. And audiences for matinees are totally different from the evening, the old gray cells don't work as well. But there's a wholeness onstage, whereas with TV they only give you bits (Mr. S. Docker).

I like theatre because it's live . . . as opposed to watching a play on the television or a film. I would rather be there, you know, with actual people (Stephanie Nailor).

I got a similar response, with only slight variations, from all of the people I interviewed. The "liveness" of a theatrical event was about "immediacy," not "thirdhand" experiences like film and television. Another interviewee, Gill Meyrick, expressed this feeling as a "passion." "I'm passionate about plays. . . . The interaction between audiences and performers is crucial. Liveness is crucial, whereas actors on TV and film are *a)* often not in sequence, *b)* not responding to an audience. . . . I could have touched Lear's foot from the front row. All that awareness of actor and actor, and actor and character, is airbrushed out on film and TV."

As well as "an intimacy, a closeness," liveness was also about "a surprise . . . that will catch you out far more than a film" (David Wright). Sometimes that surprise is visceral, an "embodied emotion" (Eversmann), as in Stephanie Nailor's "No, no, don't do it" response to the stage version of *The Madness of King George.* "Liveness" was also about the communication of understanding. Virtually every school student interviewed in any of the audience research projects for this book agreed with Clair Mills's point: "You *relate* to the people onstage, and then it's sort of easier to take on what they are saying, and the plot and so on."

Many interviewees also talked, like Mr. Docker, of live theatre as a "wholeness," compared with TV, "where they only give you the bits." Another interviewee, Enid Watson, said, for example, "It's a more holistic experience than cinema or TV, where you are seeing thirdhand. There's the camera, and the editing. Film's like a sanitized product, whereas in certain theatres it's an event." The experience of theatre is, as Eversmann says, multimedial and multiaffective, encouraging audiences and actors to play between perceptions, emotions, cognitions, and the wish to communicate, as did each person who responded to the survey question: "Would you like to talk more about your experience of *The Free State*?"

"Theatre's in the raw!" said one interviewee, Ruth Ennard, and it seems clear that for many people the "social-political event" of Janet Suzman's *The Free State,* her ostended relationship of inner circle and out there, was strongly mediated by the pleasurable play of this "raw" theatrical event of live theatre at the Theatre Royal, Bath. The liveness of it incorporated, of course, the frisson of a white Bath audience seeing a largely black cast embodying in a new way a play that many of them were familiar with and others (like Clair Mills) hadn't seen but were a bit daunted by. But the liveness could also incorporate their own experiences of the very different landscape (via set design) and personal interrelationships (via the "bantering" style of performance).

What seems clear from most of these interviews is that they didn't feel that the ETT's *The Cherry Orchard was* really "live" in these ways at all. For them, it would not take risks, tried little that was new, was "just a play." There was none of the surprise that David Wright looked for in live theatre, none of the heightened sense of risk, even horror, that made Rosemary Morris want to shout out in her seat. Nor was there the actor-audience intimacy that most interviewees ascribed to the event of live theatre. Pleasurable play between actors and audiences, as Sauter says, requires *engagement* between them. For many of them, *The Cherry Orchard* was "just a play" because it did not achieve that. As Mr. Docker saw it, "Oh, she just didn't care . . . and so I couldn't be bothered with her."

THEATRICAL PLAYING

MUCH ADO, MEDIATIZATION, AND "LIVENESS"

Theatrical playing . . . is a quality of theatrical communication, which has to be carried by all participants—the performer as well as the spectator!
—Willmar Sauter, forthcoming

Because live performance is the category of cultural production most directly affected by the dominance of the media, it is particularly urgent to address the situation of live performance in our mediatized culture.
—Philip Auslander, Liveness

Theatrical playing, in Willmar Sauter's historical example, has three aspects: "[F]rom many reviews we can learn that Sarah Bernhardt always was present as stage personality, as artist, and as role. In other words, she functioned simultaneously and with equal strength on the sensory, the artistic, and the symbolic levels." So in Bernhardt's case, the sensory was represented by the kind of reaction to her recorded by D. H. Lawrence when he professed to "love her to madness" after seeing her in *The Lady of Camelias*. That particular part was also constructed artistically according to historical, regional, international, and professional conventions of the time. And the symbolic aspect of Bernhardt's parts depended on audience's imaginative work, for example, in translating "Bernhardt's gestures, movements, utterances into the fictional significance of Phèdre . . . as Greek woman" (Sauter, forthcoming). Sauter's emphasis in his example of Bernhardt is on the artist, whereas the focus of this chapter — remembering Sauter's point that we should focus on the spectator as well as the performer — is on how these different aspects of "theatrical playing" relate to audiences' pleasures in live performance.

In an audience member's talk about pleasures in performance, sensory, artistic, and symbolic discourses are constantly in use with "varying degrees of discursive authority" (Kuhn 1987, 347). Liz Waterhouse's relationship with Janet Suzman in *The Free State*, for example, was clearly sensory (chapter 8). "Janet Suzman . . . just affects me. . . . I think she is the most brilliant actress. You know, she can just walk onstage, she doesn't even have to say anything." But even in the short extract printed from the interview with Liz (chapter 8), she also emphasized artistic levels of pleasure (in playing between international and filmic conventions of "blackness") and associated symbolic meanings ("that is more 'Africa,' because it's certainly not master-slave as in America with the Negroes").

This chapter will consider how audience pleasures of theatrical "liveness" relate to Sauter's three levels of theatrical playing, sensory, artistic, and symbolic, and also to Lash's divisions of aesthetic risk response between determinate judgments, imaginative reflexivity, and the "raw sensation" of the sublime.

Liveness and the Postmodern

When we examine audience responses to events like theatre, we tap into very particular pleasures around liveness that media and cultural studies scholars seldom explore except as a postmodern effect of a world of endless simulation. Postmodernist accounts of contemporary cinema, for example, often emphasize its surface iconography and spectacle, focusing on film's (and indeed the current world's) "style and stylishness" rather than its narrative complexity, character "depth," or style of interplay between live performer and live audience member. Thus Brooker notes the "blurring together" and "heteroglossia of inter-cultural exchange" in postmodernism "as idioms discourse across the arts and academy, and across . . . popular or mass forms" (1997, 20).

Taking these broader theoretical themes as a starting point, chapter 2 focused on the Railway Street Theatre Company's production of *Much Ado about Nothing* because it was all about the "heteroglossia of intercultural exchange" (situated in U.S./Italian iconography of the 1950s). And this production certainly "blurred together," in typical Gifford manner, idioms from the arts, the academy, and popular cultural forms. But in making this selection, the chapter also followed Philip Auslander's agenda that liveness must be examined "within specific cultural and social contexts" (1999, 3). As he says, we need to "describe both live performance's cultural-economic competition with other forms and the position of live performance in a culture for which mediatization is a vehicle of the general code in a way that live performance is . . . no longer" (Auslander 1999, 5, 6). In both of Gifford's Shakespeare productions (chapter 2) the sense of a prevailing culture of mediatization was central. Gifford's entire (and potentially last) season at the Q Theatre was heralded in her brochure as "better than the movies," and this comparison of "live" and "media" was not only emblazoned verbally on the *Much Ado* posters, it also helped determine the film noir style of these posters and to some extent the performance style and lighting of the Dogberry and Verges subplot in the production itself.

In Auslander's view theatre performance theorists who seek in liveness a "resistance" or "opposition" to dominant cultural economies are misguided. The influences of other media on theatre is not a matter of "contamination" (Pavis). Rather, the relationships of "mass" media and "live" theatre are always locally situated and historically contingent. How "live and mediatized forms are used is determined not by their ostensibly intrinsic characteristics but by their positions within cultural economy" (Auslander 1999, 51).

Auslander does not explore liveness empirically at the audience level, nor does he engage with risk (as against post) modernity, whereas Gifford's productions certainly do. In fact, postmodern readings of Gifford's work are doubly problematic. First, her plays *A Midsummer Night's Dream* and *Much Ado about Nothing* engaged with intimate, sexual, and economic risk play, both onstage and offstage, between their performers and their audiences (chapter 2). Second, audience surveys and interviews with young people consistently revealed that Gifford's boundary-crossing mix of high art and popular cultural styles was most appreciated for exactly those qualities that postmodernists claim are absent from contemporary response, that is, because of its aid to understanding narrative, its complexity of characterization, and its success in "bringing [not blurring] together" its different high or popular cultural units. For example, the following questionnaire responses as to why they liked *Much Ado* from school students in New South Wales illustrate the importance to their pleasure of Gifford's narrative drive, her depth characterization, and her multiple role-play. "*Much Ado* had an interesting interpretation, the Shakespearean language was overcome by physicalisation so that it was easy to understand." "I . . . loved . . . the cast and how effectively they were used to portray an array of complex yet wonderfully presented characters." "I liked this production because the acting made it easier for those who don't understand the language. I also liked that the actors played multi characters but made it work." "I love this play . . .

particularly the . . . characters' . . . subtle transitions." "They really made the play easy to understand. It's good how each player changed person (multiple characters)."

The repeated emphasis among these students was on the way in which the mix of popular and high culture with the multiple-role acting made this not only a "fun" production but also an understandable narrative via "subtle" and "complex" characters. This was an emphasis on what Lash calls "determinate judgment." Further, the pleasure in *Much Ado*'s more "understandable" language and narratives related directly, in very many students' perceptions, to the *liveness of the theatrical event.* "It was really funny! It was easy to understand (the Shakespeare) because modern songs were also included. . . . I like seeing the plays live, and experiencing the play at the moment, rather than video, or at the movies" (Emma, age sixteen, Arcadia, Sydney, NSW). "It was exciting to see real people live performing . . . a very amusing, light-hearted, personal atmosphere" (Miranda, age sixteen, Arcadia, NSW). "It's really exhilarating and exciting to sit so close to the actors, not like the movies" (Sarah, age sixteen, Arcadia, NSW).

These NSW students were displaying key aspects of what Sauter calls "theatrical playing," involving the sensory, artistic, and symbolic levels communicated between an actor ("as stage personality, as artist, and as role") and audience member. Questionnaire responses indicated that the "blurring" of popular culture (the Elvis music, etc.) with the Shakespeare text and the fusing of sensory ("exhilarating"), artistic ("multiple parts"), and symbolic ("modern songs") dimensions were mobilized substantially on behalf of determinate judgment ("understanding") of the HSC text. But how extensive were these feeling across a wider audience? And which other of Lash's risk aesthetics may have been in theatrical play here?

Methodology

The earlier analysis of Gifford's *Much Ado* (chapter 2) was primarily structured around theories of text, performance, spectatorship, and social audiences' response to risk. This chapter focuses more on methodology, exploring ways of accessing what the pleasures of liveness mean to audiences when they emphasize it as a key aspect of theatrical play. Postmodern accounts of cinema will not help us much here because they are particularly weak methodologically, ascribing pleasures and affects to audiences with little or no empirical analysis of actual audiences.

It is important not to replicate this problem here. Large claims, for example, were made in chapter 8 about the theatrical event, liveness, and audience pleasures from just thirteen long interviews. But in the case of Gifford's *Much Ado* there was the opportunity to survey much larger audience numbers than with Suzman's *The Free State* and via a much wider range of methodologies. Would the liveness factor still be seen as central to the enormous popularity of this production? Would it hold for different age, gender, and socioeconomic groups among theatre audiences? Would it always be strongly related to determinate judgments, as with the school students studying for their final examinations? Given that we might expect students doing their HSCs to look for "understandable" performances of a difficult text, how would quite different audience groups and individuals relate, cognitively and emotionally, this liveness effect to their own, different, everyday lives? How would they talk about sensory, artistic, and symbolic aspects of theatrical playing? Would different methodologies draw attention to different levels and kinds of response to liveness and mediatization? Would there be any continuity of theatrical playing across different methodologies and different audiences?

In February 2001 several hundred questionnaires were distributed at performances of Gifford's *Much Ado about Nothing*, both in Penrith and during its country tour, and six focus groups of about forty school students who had just seen the play were conducted. In April 2001 a preliminary analysis was conducted of 273 questionnaires that had been returned by both Q Theatre and country theatre audiences, and long interviews took place with a number of audience members who had indicated they were willing to talk about their experiences of the performance. A follow-up survey of 129 school students from the Western Suburbs of Sydney was also conducted in April to see whether the strong "liking" effect of *Much Ado* that was evident in February immediately after the production was maintained up to two months later.

The *Much Ado* questionnaire contained a number of "Did you like it? Yes/No. Why?" questions relating to the overall performance as well as to different aspects of the semiotics of production (sets, costumes, music, acting, interpretation). It also contained a multiple-choice question (developed from the earlier Theatre Royal, Bath, audience research).

Why did you personally come to see *Much Ado* today? (the following are comments by other theatre-goers in answer to this question: Please tick the relevant one(s) and put a 1 next to the *most* relevant): (i) "Just love seeing Shakespeare"; (ii) "Haven't seen much Shakespeare — wanted to catch up on him"; (iii) "Haven't seen this play — wanted to catch up on it"; (iv) "Some star actors in the cast"; (v) "Love going to this theatre"; (vi) "It was a special day for me" (birthday, anniversary, etc.); (vii) "I'm studying the play for HSC"; (viii) "Just chance"; (ix) "Read good reviews in the papers"; (x) "The poster/leaflet attracted me"; (xi) "Friends saw it — said I should go"; (xii) Other reason: say which reason.

There then followed questions about live theatre: "Is there ever anything 'special' about going to the theatre for you? Yes/No. In what way?" and "Was *Much Ado* a special event in this way?" As the intention here was for the respondents to construct what (if anything) was a "special event" about theatre for them, neither the word "live" nor "media" was mentioned in this general survey question. The opportunity was taken, however, with school students who were not completing the questionnaire to ask more focused questions (to be completed on one sheet of paper). These included "Is there anything about theatre that you particularly like, compared say with TV or film?"; "Compare this production of *Much Ado* with *a*) reading it at home or school; *b*) seeing Shakespeare on film or TV (name the ones you have seen)"; "If all theatre productions were like the Q Theatre's *Much Ado about Nothing*, would you like to go to the theatre again?" The questionnaire concluded with demographic questions, a question at the request of the Railway Street Theatre Company as to how often respondents would visit the theatre were the Q Theatre to close, questions about cinema and TV viewing habits, and finally an open-ended "any other comments" section.

Before looking at the results from the variety of methodologies employed, there is an initial reflexive point to be made about the methodology overall that can be illustrated from a few questionnaire responses from a broad regional and socioeconomic range of young people in NSW.

Although I'm not a fan of Shakespeare, I really enjoyed this adaptation of *Much Ado about Nothing.* . . . The music gave you a good break from the text. The acting was amazing. . . . I love Q Theatre productions, haven't missed one for the last 3 years, and I couldn't miss it for the world. The theatre is amazing, it has an amazing atmosphere, I love it. Every time I go to the Q is a special night for me (Sally, age seventeen, Blue Mountains, NSW).

It was a very enjoyable, engaging, emotional, humorous and stunningly acted performance. The actors really brought *Much Ado about Nothing* to life much better than the actual book. The atmosphere is amazing — I love the connection you have with the actors, being so close (Josh, age sixteen, Arcadia, NSW).

It was clever and well acted. . . . It is really cool because it is easier to relate especially to the actors (Jayne, age sixteen, Sydney, NSW).

It was a unique experience of Shakespeare! (It had nothing to do with the fact that Claudio was playing guitar in front of me!!?) . . . It gave new meaning to *Much Ado about Nothing* (Grace, age sixteen, Hazelbrook, NSW).

These responses suggest something beyond the determinate judgment of "better understanding" the HSC text. Of course, survey questionnaires have their own modes of address, especially if they are completed in the classroom, as the above comments were. Certainly, my own experience of the teenagers at the Q theatre itself and afterward at Penrith railway station confirmed that they "loved the play." But were these elaborated responses (to "Did you like the set/costumes, music, acting, interpretation — Yes/No. Why?" type of questions) what they "really" felt? What clues were being offered here? And what about Grace, whom I had happened to overhear at Penrith Station after the show commenting on the "hot" Benedict playing his guitar right in front of her, "within touching distance"?

Neither Grace nor I had known she would be in a focus group interview I conducted with school students a couple of days later. When we did discover it, it caused some embarrassed good fun (and elicited the personal questionnaire message to me quoted above). One answer to my question is, *of course* these survey responses were the students' "real" reasons for liking the production of *Much Ado*. But it was also the case that the survey questions tended to tap into only some audience subjectivities, and perhaps they emphasized some of Sauter's theatrical playing levels more than others. Grace really did love the "new meaning" (Sauter's symbolic level, Lash's determinate judgment) that director Mary-Anne Gifford gave to Shakespeare. Grace went on in the questionnaire to discuss how and why she did enjoy the "new meaning": in terms of her pleasure in the "50s Italy" sets and costumes; the 1950s rock music, which "set the comedic mood"; and the "professional and interesting acting" (artistic level), which together meant that the interpretative "challenge was pulled off exceptionally well."

Not to accept Grace's (and the other students') intelligences in explaining why they liked *Much Ado* would be worse than patronizing, especially in the context of so much researcher-led interpretation in cultural studies of young people's so-called resistant readings.

Still, there is something in that sense of a living intimacy of space, as between Grace and "Claudio" in her (and others') comments, that also suggests the sensory (and Lash's imaginative-reflexive) level of audience-actor communication. Like Sally, quoted above, Grace found the Q Theatre, as Lash would put it, a "memory grounding institution" where judgments of "the beautiful are a sort of 'feeling' as we intuit . . . through *imagination* . . . through, not logical categories, but the 'forms of time and space.'" This layering of actor-audience interaction needs further exploration empirically.

Results

To try and access these difficult questions empirically, the remainder of the chapter will deploy findings from a range of methodologies employed: quantitative survey data, focused (qualitative) survey responses, long interviews, postcoded (qualitative) survey responses, individual audience case studies, focus group discussions, and the follow-up survey. The strengths and weaknesses of each of these methods will be noted in passing.

Quantitative Survey Data

Survey questionnaires are helpful, at least, in indicating the extent to which Grace's "artistic," "sensory," and "symbolic" pleasures were shared by her age group, by other age groups, by theatre audiences who saw the production in country towns (compared with audiences in the city of Penrith), and so on. For example, in response to the "why I went to this production" multiple-choice question, Grace ticked first "friends saw it — said I should go" (conceivably these friends also told her about the actor Don Hany, playing Claudio!); second "love going to this theatre"; and third "just love seeing Shakespeare." Although she positioned "I'm studying the play" only seventh of her salient reasons for coming, her age group in fact placed "studying" first, followed closely by "love going to this theatre" and "love Shakespeare." The high ranking of "love going to this theatre" and "love Shakespeare" proved a potent mix for their pleasures and meanings generated around *Much Ado*. Of this age group ($N = 51$),

91 percent liked the production, 88 percent liked the set and costumes, 84 percent liked the use of music, 97 percent liked the multiple-role acting, 86 percent liked the interpretation, and 91 percent saw theatre as "special." And this high ranking of "love this theatre," "love Shakespeare" was also a feature of all the other audience age groups. (They were placed first and second, in fact, by all the age groups: >17, 18–25, 26–35, 36–45, 46–55, 55+.) Overall, of respondents across age categories, 96 percent liked the production (89 percent on tour and 99 percent at the Q Theatre in Penrith), 87 percent liked the set and costumes, 92 percent liked the use of music, 98 percent liked the multiple-role acting, 92 percent liked the interpretation, and 97 percent find theatre "special." When asked what made theatre "special" for them, 51 percent up to age 17, 63 percent 18–25, 68 percent 26–35, 64 percent 36–45, 59 percent 46–55, and 70 percent 55+ emphasized liveness.

But why was liveness in the particular Q theatre space so "loved" by the whole range of its audiences? To explore this it was necessary to turn to more focused qualitative responses.

Focused Qualitative Survey Responses

The following comments were elicited by a different methodology, where school students who were not being surveyed by questionnaire were asked to "write up to a paragraph" (after seeing *Much Ado*) in answering focused questions relating to Gifford's specific "better than the movies" scenario: "Is there anything about theatre that you particularly like or dislike (compared, say, with TV or film)?" The following was a symptomatic response: "I like the way the actors manage to bring the audience into the scene so the audience can feel what the character is feeling. And I also like the way you can look around the rest of the stage and see the other actors' reactions instead of just having to focus on whatever was captured on the camera." The emphasis here was on the way live interaction between actors and audiences position spectators "holistically," with enough personal space available not to feel "pinned" by the camera. This led to a "reality" effect. "You get to interact with the actors and see the audience's reaction. It's more real." "It makes you feel more like you are a part of it because it's live and up close." "I like the closeness of the characters that you don't get when watching TV." "Reality" also related to the pleasure in the risk of live performance. "Theatre is more exciting, there is always the risk something could go wrong. It's more interesting to see real people perform for *you*."

Clearly, these focused questions generated very similar answers to the questionnaire, only slightly more explicitly using "live theatre versus TV or film" as their frame. A common sensory theme was emerging of theatre being live and up close, allowing for a more personal relationship with actors "so the audience can feel what the character is feeling." This, and the live interaction between actors and audience in an unedited performance, led to a risky sense of it being "more real because they are right in front of your eyes." We have, in fact, heard comments like this before in response to *The Free State*, particularly the "No, no, don't do it!" adrenaline rush or risk aspects of the "raw sublime" and the "imaginative synthesis" of interacting between actors' schemata and our own. As one respondent to the focused question said, "Compared to TV and films theatre is more involving and enjoyable, draws more on personal experience, and is much better emotionally."

Long Interviews

The "more real because right in front of your eyes" pleasure in liveness was given a more precise dimension in the long interviews conducted. These were with fourteen audience members from all age groups. To examine the generalizability of the liveness effect across different age groups rather than complicate this with other demographic variables, the interviewees chosen for analysis were all female. One major advantage of a long interview was that it enabled more probing of how the liveness factor related to an individual audience member's pleasures. Interviewees, for example, regularly spoke of their liking of *Much Ado* in contrast to their other, more everyday leisure activities like cinema or television.

The long interviews quickly revealed a particular sensory pleasure in live physical proximity, even a sense of personal invitation, between actor and audience member. Nicole, like other audience members quoted, spoke of the emotional intimacy of feel, where she could almost touch the performer.

> I think theatre is a lot better than the movies, TV and things like that because it's a lot different. Like, with a movie, the actors, they've done their bit. . . . You can't do anything to change it. But when they're on stage, they, like, *respond* to the audiences, whether they're laughing, whether they're upset. . . . At a movie you can sigh or cry. But [onstage] the actors can . . . play off that a bit. . . . It's like you can get more involved as a person, like you can *feel* and you're *there*, rather than . . . [in movies]

it's just a screen. . . . 'Cause the actors are real people . . . they're *there*
. . . like you could reach out and touch them. They're not just a pro-
jected image. . . . I think *Much Ado* also worked well when they had the
monologues, when the characters actually talked to the audience. It
looked like they were talking to *you* instead of just . . . into a camera
(Nicole, age sixteen, Glenbrook, NSW).

This begins to elicit more clearly those other "non-HSC" sensory pleasures in theatre that Grace's "He's so hot!" hinted at. As Nicole spoke of the
actors as "real people . . . they're *there* . . . like you could reach out and
touch them. . . . It looked like they were talking to *you*," we were beginning to get a sense of the pleasures of what one respondent called the "intimate gaze" of theatre.

This intimate and personalized aspect of live performance was something that all age groups emphasized, both quantitatively in the survey and
more specifically in the long interviews. For example, eight-year-old Lillian
said that the thing she most remembered about *Much Ado* was that Benedick
had expressed his love for Beatrice directly to *her*, sitting in the front row
next to her mother. For little Lillian this was an embarrassing experience in
a performance she otherwise loved, and she was cross with her mother for
raising it with the researcher during her interview. She probably felt too
young for that sensory kind of "imaginative synthesis" with an adult actor.
Nevertheless, with different levels of pleasure in the intimate address of live
performance, members of all age groups said much the same as sixteen-
year-old Nicole. Twenty-year-old Johanna was quite open about how the
liveness of theatre related to her own personal relationships.

It is *live*. It is more interactive than movies, a good atmosphere. . . . And
you're so close to the actors and what they are showing . . . romance,
marriage, and a cynical woman who eventually lets down her guard
and falls in love. . . . So we like Beatrice and Benedick because it's something we can relate to, in that probably people do want love but then
they put up veils and make jokes about it. Like you don't need [love],
and yet then you see the barriers come down [onstage]. So you —
everyone wants to be independent and strong and pretend like they
don't need anyone. But you do (Johanna, Glenbrook, NSW, 18–25 age
group).

Johanna went on to talk of the imaginative synthesis between the life
schemas of Beatrice, who "wants to be independent and strong and pretend

like they don't need anyone," and her own. Natalie, who was a little older and went to the theatre a lot, talked about this actor-audience "bouncing off each other's feelings" as the "magic" of theatre.

> Theatre's special because of the atmosphere created by the audience-actor relationship. It's a shared enjoyment.... You lose that "I'm watching something, I'm following something" to where you sort of become involved in the play. And you're enjoying being entertained by the actor, and you can feel that relationship whereby *they're* really feeling the audience's reception, and they play back to that, where they're really enjoying entertaining the audience. . . . And you can really feel that magic then, when they're enjoying performing to us, and we're enjoying the performance. So you get this lovely kind of circle happening, where you're just bouncing off each other's feelings. . . . It's got to be *live* for that to happen. . . . It's different to watching a movie. [In the theatre] you're watching the performer respond to your attention and loving it (Natalie, Woodford, NSW, 26–35 age group).

Along with many other respondents and interviewees, Natalie was describing what Lash calls aesthetic reflexivity and Sauter refers to as the aesthetic dimension of theatrical playing, enjoying the game of conventions between actors and audiences, which goes well beyond formalized role-play to a personal "synthesis" of intimacy. This is an emotional bond beyond the "determinate judgment" of "understanding" the play better, which school students talked about. Julie was even more explicit about this, suggesting that "perving" on actors allows us to see more clearly into ourselves. "Theatre's one of the very few events where you get to sit and *really watch* people relating and get to watch them in an intimate way. . . . You get to sit there and totally analyze someone and look at all their faults and their idiosyncrasies and their frailties, and where else do you get to do that? . . . Like metaphors they parallel our own experiences, and so in a way it causes us to relate situations to our own lives and get right into it. . . . We wouldn't be able to see it if it wasn't 'us'" (Julie, Woodford, NSW, 36–45 age group).

This intimate chemistry between actor and audience member was, Ingrid suggested, crucial to the sense of fusion that allows the audience member, too, to feel "life size" in acting out "the scene." "Theatre's live productions have got that special quality lacking in TV because it's *there*, it's in front of you, it's life size, and you can just virtually touch the people onstage. With the background being all dark and the stage being all

brightly lit you become more a part of the *scene*. You are there, alive —
and it's different from watching the square screen. . . . You're actually there,
on the spot, hiding behind the shrubbery and watching it all happening,
and suddenly you're *part* of the characters, in their garden with them. . . .
It's the *liveness*" (Ingrid, Glenbrook, NSW, 36–45 age group).

Theatre's spectator positions offer the sense of being in community
with the actors, "*part* of the characters, in their garden with them." This,
then, was the "real high" that Susan explained (chapter 2) as "using more
senses" than in her routine media use or even in her everyday life, where
she spent much of her week ferrying her children to and from football.

Theatre's a real special event for me. It's time out for me and my girlfriends. You need time out from taking the children here, there, to
school, to their soccer and sports. . . . You use more *senses* than at the
movies. There's more intimacy. It's three-dimensional. You can get a
bond with the actors. You feel they are looking straight at you, and you
feel how they feel, and you don't get that in movies. There's an audience bond too — I talked with the lady next to me at the interval who
was a relation of one of the actors. I usually talk at the interval or afterward with my girlfriends. It's interesting getting feedback, with different opinions on the play. . . . Theatre's important for me emotionally.
It gives me energy. I left *Much Ado* on a real high (Susan, Valley Heights,
NSW, 36–45 age group).

Perceptions, emotions, cognitions, and communicative dimensions
(Eversmann) were blended in this close bond with actors and other audience members. And energy, a "real buzz," was the payoff, as we saw earlier
with our Belvoir Street audiences. For Eleonor, the real buzz was in this
intimate, *invited* (via direct eye-line) sharing of exploratory experiences
between actor and audiences. It is this fact that made theatre *less* removed
from daily life than cinema or television. "Theatre is special. Cinema is
quite different. For us it's a commoner event when you get out the film
[on video]. . . . It's not as special as going to the theatre and seeing the
actors onstage. . . . The *liveness* is important — look what they can make
an audience feel, make *you* feel, whereas in the television it's much more
distant and on the movies much more removed from everyday life. We
were sitting right in the center in the front [at the Q Theatre], and there
were occasions when we had *direct* contact with the actor, and I suppose
it's a real buzz. We get a lot out of that" (Eleonor, Glenbrook, NSW, 36–45
age group).

Contrary to Sauter's opinion, part of the "eventness" of theatre is in this direct contact with everyday life. Finally, as Mary argued, this everyday sharing of the actors' emotions could then be shared again socially, with a live audience, and even communicated beyond the theatre. "*Live* theatre is special, and enjoying it with a group as part of an everyday audience adds to this. . . . The informal atmosphere seems to give permission to laugh at the humor or react to actors' situations, so the audience can share the actors' emotions and enjoyment. I do enjoy that live aspect — the interaction with the acting, the staging. . . . I definitely feel more part of it than with films or TV. . . . It's not distant like a film. . . . There's an element of improvisation every night in live acting. . . . The audience is obviously important. And there's an external social bonus that you can meet up with friends and connect that up to them afterward" (Mary, Thirroul, NSW, 46–55 age group).

These differently aged female interviewees all agreed that live actor-audience closeness is so intimate that for a while, as actors' and audience's eyes meet, the look invites you on to the stage to inhabit the actors' bodies as they try out scenarios that are also close in a sensory way to your own personal life. For example, Johanna said, you "pretend you don't need anyone" and "put up veils and make jokes about it," but on the stage you see those "barriers come down." Because of the lighted stage / darkened auditorium close-up relationship, Ingrid said, "you become more a part of the *scene*" with these so intimately known (because, as Julie said, so closely scrutinized) actors/characters. And then, having explored alternative scenarios on the stage, you have the bonus of comparing your personal experiences of this, as Mary said, with others in the audience. This is seen as a live spectator position.

Postcoded Qualitative Survey Responses

What proportion of the Q Theatre audience did feel this way about the live actor-audience relationship? By postcoding open-ended "in what way?" responses to the survey question "Is there anything 'special' in going to the theatre for you?" it was possible to examine the liveness effect quantitatively in relation to other special "buzzes" in going to the theatre. A significant majority of my respondents and interviewees (in all age groups) did — like Susan, Ingrid, Julie, and the others — get this special "buzz" out of live performance.

These quantitative data revealed the following reasons across the sample (in order of numerical significance) for the "special" nature of theatre: 62 percent said it was "because it's live" (this was linked to issues of intimate atmosphere, personalization, rapport between actor/audience and audience/audience); 20 percent said it was the social event of going to the theatre (going with family, friends, "a rare night out"); 11 percent liked the "escape into complete fantasy" away from everyday life; 6 percent had a professional interest in the theatre, admiration for the actors' art, and so on; and there were 6 percent "others." In addition, the open-ended written comments in this "in what way?" section strongly reaffirmed the cluster of pleasures elaborated in the long interviews. But whereas long interview respondents interwove their reasons as a narrative, these focused survey responses offered a more generalized and layered set of answers. Thus we could isolate, via postcoding, the following "levels" of pleasure.

Live/intimate/personal sensory pleasures: "I love the intimacy of live shows at this theatre." "Very intimate atmosphere, I love seeing Shakespeare performed live — and just seeing the 'raw' acting in front of you." "It's more intimate than film, a refreshing change — I love live performances." "I love the intimacy of live theatre — I feel part of the action." "I love the intimacy and realism of life versus film." This sense of spatial intimacy then related directly to a feeling of "imaginative synthesis."

"Being there" in a live actors/audience community: "The atmosphere is amazing — I love connecting with the actors you have, being so close." "The attraction is the 'live' element and the interaction actor/audience and vice-versa." "I love the way the audience reacts, how real it all is. You can look an actor in the eye and feel king of the world." "The actor/audience relationship — it's a shared enjoyment." "The contact between actor/audience is an active pleasure, not passive as in films/TV." "I just love the 'live/life' experience."

These kinds of response were ubiquitous. One respondent's comment, "Inclusion within scene, by proximity delivering actuality," might have seemed somewhat hermetic but in the context of the other responses was in fact quite precise. It was the "real" and "intimate" ("by proximity") relationship with live actors (the sense of sharing experiences) that allowed for the audience's "inclusion within [the] scene" and thus produced a "more immediate and intense experience than film, which is more narrative and effects based." Thus, despite some postmodernist accounts, these theatre audience members thought it is *film* that is (still) narrative based, whereas in theatre they "feel part of the 'action,' acting 'live' — magical." There was clearly, here, in the "immediate," "intense," and "intimate" relationship shared with individual actors a strong element of what Sauter calls the "emotional" and "sensory" aspect of theatrical playing and, in particular, Lash's sense of the imagined synthesis (of your schema / my schema) that is central to aesthetic reflexivity. This sense of an individually shared, symbiotic community between actors and audiences that so many respondents referred to led also to an appreciative recognition of what Sauter refers to as the "artistic" level of theatrical playing.

Artistic pleasure: This was evident in the specific audience pleasures in the energy, crafted talent, professional enjoyment, risk taking, and hard work of the actors that together made for a unique experience for each audience member. "Theatre is magical — I marvel at the actors' ability. Theatre is unifying — there's a certain energy in good performances that generates an audience I don't find in cinema or sport." "I love the energy of live productions." "I enjoy the live performance by people who obviously enjoy it themselves." "It's the close action I enjoy, the great actors, and knowing how much work's been done." The risk taking of theatre performers was strongly emphasized by audiences as a pleasurable "artistic" aspect of good theatre. This composite experience of spatial immediacy with live actors and audiences, each "working artistically" and "riskily" to give an "entirely different" performance each night, led to the buzz of the symbolic real.

Symbolic pleasure: At this level respondents emphasized their pleasure in the real of theatre: "It's immediate and real with real actors — not TV." "Theatre is much more realistic than TV or cinema." "It's better than the movies because it's real, and right in front of you."

Clearly, there are a number of different kinds of pleasure in liveness apparent in these many responses, and we can see already that they recur whatever the methodology and whether or not the methodological approach focused comparatively on theatre, film, and television. But using different methodologies also helped take us further in understanding Sauter's theatrical playing. For example, the postcoded survey questions generated single responses at the different (sensory/artistic/symbolic and determinate/imaginative/sensational) levels, in contrast to the long interviews, which revealed how audience members wove these levels together to offer *associative logics* explaining their pleasures at their theatrical event.

The perceived time-space coordinates of theatrical events (in the mediatized context of film and television) is a here ("real," "right in front of you") and now ("risky," "not edited") performance. And the perceived communicative relations are where images and schema involving repre-

sented participants (the characters in a play) are seen to merge reflexively with images involving interactive participants (actors and audiences) in a playing that is at once sensory, artistic, and symbolic. What
the actor-audience interactions did for my theatre audience respondents
was set up new (mutually constructed) understandings of and attitudes
toward the represented characters and their relationships, which were
thus "participated" in, often via audience members' own experiences.
This is why Julie commented in long interview, "We wouldn't be able to
see it if it wasn't 'us'"; and Johanna said, "It is more interactive than
movies. . . . So we like Beatrice and Benedick because it's something we
can relate to, in that probably people do want love but then they put up
veils and make jokes about it."

Most particularly, it was the intimate gaze of audience-actor relationships that was mentioned again and again in long interviews and occasionally in questionnaire responses. For Susan, "you can get a bond with
the actors — you feel they are looking straight at you, and you feel how
they feel and you don't get that in movies." For Eleonor, "the *liveness* is
important. . . . We were sitting right in the centre in the front, and there
were occasions when we had *direct* contact with the actor, and I suppose
it's a real buzz." For Ingrid, "you're actually there . . . and suddenly you're
part of the characters, in their garden with them. . . . It's the *liveness*." For
Natalie, "you can really feel that magic then . . . where you're just bouncing off each other's feelings. . . . It's got to be *live* for that to happen." For
Nicole, "it felt like they were talking to *you*," and for a survey respondent,
"you can look an actor in the eye and feel king of the world."

It was this intimate gaze of theatre spectatorship that led so many
respondents to blur together notions of it being real with being magic
and to treasure the sense of live participation that "'we' can relate to" and
yet enjoy escapist fantasy at the same time, as in these survey responses:
"Some performances give a real life — a wonderful escape." "I love the
magic, escapism and imagination needed for live theatre. . . . This [*Much
Ado*] is a time 'we' can relate to." "The live performance is a window into
other worlds." This is what audience members meant when they talked of
loving "the 'live/life' experience," "the personal interaction," "connecting
with the characters in a live way," and "feeling part of the 'action,' acting
'live' — magical." It was the sense of "live people onstage doing it just for
those present" and the "shared experience between actor/audience" that
led respondents to say, "Theatre doesn't just wash over you like music and
some films — there's a higher level of participation."

Other live leisure forms may be successful in doing the same. But it was the particular aspects of the theatrical institution (Eversmann's transitivity, collectivity, multimediality, and ostension) that the audiences I surveyed and interviewed perceived as central to its special event. It is not just, then, the playful relationship between performer and audience *but also the reflexive relationship between the everyday and the theatrical event* that clearly gives so many people so much pleasure. For many audience members the theatrical event is both a unique and spontaneous occasion (a sense of another world or fantasy) and part of both the performers' and audiences' everyday life within a particular, live, immediate, and intimate co-working place. It is this combination (around liveness) that makes audiences refer to film and television (not theatre) as outside the pleasures of the everyday.

Case Studies

Most of the methodologies employed have focused on the "within the theatre" experience. But individual case studies via long interviews could also relate the magic inside the Q Theatre with everyday reality outside in more detailed, specific, and negotiated ways. This method could also explore alternative approaches to cultural meaning when interviewees could not afford regularly to visit the theatre. Susan has been mentioned before for finding theatre special because it was "time for myself and my girlfriends" away from the routines and rituals of being a single mother with kids and not a lot of money. Susan exposed quite clearly the double playful relationship between everyday and theatrical event. "The children accept that now — that I go to the theatre every couple of months or so, if I've got the money. But there's no money around, my daughter's just had braces on her teeth."

Susan was having to negotiate locally the relationship between a body-centered, image-saturated globalization (her daughter's braces) and her own everyday pleasures, including an escape into fantasy-reality. As a result, she couldn't often afford the theatre, so she had constructed an alternative fantasy-reality space. She had recently set up a book club with her girlfriends. This was an alternative place where, without much cost, they could achieve some "fantasy, like reading a novel in an hour and a half." Novels aren't, she said, as "live, three-dimensional, and realistic" as theatre. Still, like theatre, the novels she brought to her book club did relate, in fantasy, to her everyday life. Recently, she presented her views at the book club on *Chocolat*, the story of another single mother, more mobile than Susan, who (also with little money) started a chocolate shop and constructed her own community out of a religiously and socially conservative village in France.

As Susan noted, religious conservatism in Italy also dominated Mary-Anne Gifford's *Much Ado about Nothing*, signified by the huge crucified Jesus on the back cloth. So it was possible to also consider the symbolic by way of these alternative leisure paths of book club and theatre. Susan had noticed the huge crucifixion image and recognized what it signified. "It indicated the religion of the time — everything run by the church, so women had to be 'pure.' That was the way of life, which was why it was so devastating when Hero was betrayed." As a single mother, Susan was well placed to interpret the gender politics of Gifford's interpretation. For Gifford, these *Much Ado* men were, first and foremost, understandable as soldiers. Susan also commented on "a lot of betrayal in it" not of Claudio by Hero but by the men. She also saw how the soldiers doing Presley interpretations were still playing "men." "The music matched their feelings and temperaments and needs perfectly. . . . The men [impersonating Presley's *Surrender*] were cocky. They were men letting their hair down, entertaining personality-wise. . . . It put a different feeling into the play . . . men coming into the soft life of women. The music really made that — it expressed their personalities and emotions."

This small case-study analysis of Susan restores the discussion of theatrical event and liveness to the familiar cultural studies territory of resistant (political) meanings (as in the case of the teenage girls at the Barbican Theatre, chapter 1). This is important. But we should not forget that Susan's main pleasure in this performance, her reason for "leaving the theatre on a high," was not mainly to do with this symbolic level. It was related to the "fantasy . . . intimacy, three-dimensions, reality" of the production's intimate gaze. And this related directly to Gifford's offer (which Susan willingly accepted) of the energy (and personal memories for both Gifford and Susan) of Elvis Presley. Susan said, "I just loved the music. I grew up with rock and roll. I used to go to rock and roll dances. I've still got an Elvis LP. The music made you feel good . . . and it complemented the speeches perfectly. . . . It was well acted, very funny. It left me on a real high."

In the midst of her single-mother routines, Susan (in fantasy/reality at the theatre) recalled memories and pleasures of an earlier reality when she herself was a teenager. It was that conjuncture of memory then and pleasure now, of reflexive imagination and sensation, that the intimate gaze of the Q Theatre had offered her. This was why she walked from the theatre "on a real high."

Focus Group Discussion

The case study of Susan has revealed an extra dimension to the sensory relationship of theatrical playing that was hinted at earlier. This is the audience play between past and future histories that Gifford's *Much Ado* encouraged and that in chapter 2 was examined in terms of issues of risk. So what of teenagers not then (like Susan, who was remembering her teenage years) but now? Most of the teenagers discussed in chapter 2 also loved the Elvis scene but for different reasons. Focus group discussion was a useful method in extending the dynamic of discussion that clearly went on immediately after the performance and allowed respondents to agree (forcefully sometimes with a multiple "yes"), to offer supportive laughter, to contradict others' points of view (sometimes urgently enough to interrupt the interviewer), to adjust their opinions, and, in the case of the interviewer, to probe and inquire.

Whereas the long interview with Susan extracted her memories of being a teenager with Elvis as a kind of nostalgic golden age, the focus group discussion provided much more of a sense of the teenagers as a set of social audiences interacting now. In part, this filled in some of the ellipses in Susan's account. She, too, probably struggled over Shakespeare's long sentences, "big descriptions," similes, and metaphors in school. But these forgotten years of determinate judgment were not the aspect of her teenage years that the Elvis scene related to now as it did for the Springwood students. Yet as Susan and these high school students sat in the theatre together, they were, despite their other differences, the same social audience in one key respect. The Springwood focus group students responded as follows to the question as to whether theatre is "a special event as against film or television." "You can never experience the same thing on TV and be a part of it." "You forget you're 'watching.'" "They're working with us, we are part of the experience, we're not just spectators." "And they play it to how the audience is reacting. . . . If they've got a good audience they might take a few more risks, there is that sense that very much you are doing it together, you're creating that experience for each other." "And it is a whole. . . . Like at times when they do make eye contact, it's amazing. You're there watching these people onstage, and it's like their lives are unfolding in front of you, and they are good enough to share it with you." Thus while in their questionnaire responses the school students profiled their pleasure in their determinate judgments of understanding Shakespeare better, focus group interviews tended to reveal a broader range of what Lash calls aesthetic reflexivity, just like all the other age groups interviewed after *Much Ado about Nothing*.

Follow-up Survey

The figures of a more than 90 percent approval rating for *Much Ado about Nothing* may seem surprisingly high, particularly among school-age students. The Springwood High School students, for example, might be seen as almost a self-picked sample insofar as these were HSC drama students at a school that had a special relationship with the Q Theatre. And both the questionnaires and focus group interviews at Springwood (and the other schools surveyed) took place within a couple of days of the performance, when the event was still fresh in memory. What would the response be from school students a couple of months after the production?

In late April 2001 I surveyed 125 Year 9 students doing general English from Catherine McAuley High School near Paramatta. Nearly all of these students answered the "Why did you personally come to see *Much Ado* today?" with an "under orders" response: it was a "compulsory school event," a "school excursion — we had to go," "they made us," "I was compelled to go with the school," "it was a school excursion — therefore we had no choice," "we were forced to go," "we were only given 2 choices, stay at school and do work or go and watch *Much Ado* at Penrith, near Penrith Plaza where you could go shopping after." These were certainly not self-defined fans of Shakespeare or of theatre more generally. At best we got the response: "I just go for fun — when I'm forced to."

Yet even among this large group of "under orders" students, favorable responses to Gifford's *Much Ado* (87 percent) and its actors (89 percent) were still remarkably high two months later, though there was a significant fall-off in approval ratings for sets and costumes (66 percent), music (68 percent), interpretation (74 percent), and theatre as special event (52 percent). It is arguable, though, that even that lowest figure of 52 percent — students who, after seeing *Much Ado about Nothing*, rated theatre as a special event in their lives — is unexpectedly high for a large bunch of Western Suburbs students dragooned to the Q Theatre in Penrith!

Moreover, examination of the qualitative responses for "liking" the play indicated a significant continuity with the main sample.

Live/intimate/personal sensory pleasures: "It was interesting because it was very in your face.... I felt part of the play because they were so close and upfront." "It was very personalised being so close to the actors." "It was ... a different experience to the movies having to see the actors performing live and feel more involved." "It is much more personal than the movies. ... The small theatre helped make it that way."

"Being there" with live actors/audiences: "I absolutely loved it. ... The theatre is a great place to go. It's really fun and exciting." "I liked the way they were able to perform in front of a large group of students who don't really appreciate plays; but *Much Ado about Nothing* made teenage plays enjoyable and entertaining."

Artistic pleasures: "Everybody played their part with enthusiasm, and it was great." "It ... looked well-rehearsed and much worked on." "It was well organised and you could tell that the actors knew what they were doing and saying." "I especially liked the actors because they did a great job."

Symbolic pleasures: "It was interesting and yet funny — romance, believable characters." "It's like going to the cinema, but this is real." "It seems more realistic and actually like it is happening."

The combination "interesting and yet funny — romance, believable characters" was repeated many times by the follow-up group. For the girls at Catherine McAuley High, the event and the real came together by way of that mix of comedy, romance, and the believable. In the process, their school HSC text also became more understandable, and what Eversmann calls the multimediality of theatre was pressed by them into the service of this mix of levels of pleasure and need. So, for example, when asked whether they liked the sets, music, actors, and interpretation, a typical questionnaire response was "I liked the sets because they were so realistic. I liked the music because it suited the scene. I liked the acting — the actors showed expression. I liked the interpretation — the play was clear and understandable."

The acting in *Much Ado* was almost universally praised by these students for its feeling and expressiveness, enthusiasm, confidence, risk taking, professional style, preparation, experience and talent, use of the whole stage, believability, "reality," and good multiple role playing. When, however, actors were not seen as able to differentiate these multiple roles, students found the interpretation "hard to understand," and some of these then said they did not like the production. Finally, among those (over 50 percent) who found theatre is a special event, it was liveness, as in the main sample, that was the compelling reason for this pleasure. "I love seeing a story come alive in that way." "I love the live acting, something you can't get from TV." "I just get a buzz seeing girls pash onstage." And if the girl who enjoyed seeing two female actors kiss onstage was perhaps unusual in her particular response (a few more conservative students said this was the one thing they *didn't* like about the play, which was the result of Gifford's multiple-role production), one has the feeling that it was still the risky blend of intimacy, proximity, and liveness that excited her.

It was very evident, from both quantitative as well as qualitative measures, that the "compulsory school excursion" students from Catherine McAuley High much enjoyed what some called the "school event" of visiting the Railway Street Theatre Company in Penrith for *Much Ado about Nothing* and indeed still remembered their pleasures in detail two months later. One student from this school can have the last word, because her overall questionnaire response typified not only her school colleagues but much of the overall response to *Much Ado about Nothing* across age groups. She said that she liked the production because "it was entertaining all the way through, the actors did a great job and there were funny sections along the way." She liked the sets because "they displayed the exact time frame well and suited the characters." She enjoyed the music because "it was loud, made people start bopping in their chairs, and set the atmosphere." She liked the actors because "they were believable." She enjoyed the interpretation because "it was original and out of the ordinary." She thinks theatre is "special" because it's different from "the everyday of television and movies — it's live" and "they take risks." *Much Ado* was a very special event in this way for her, particularly "because the audience were my friends and it was fun to be watching."

10 CONCLUSION

This book has tried to bring together two ways of mapping the theatrical event in terms of audience research. The first has been to examine the issue from a production approach, exploring the situating of spectator positions (or, in Pertti Alasuutari's term, the process of audiencing) during production. Part 2 of the book, drawing on the "Chekhov: In Criticism, Production and Reading" project, explored this part of the map. The second way has been to draw on recent theatrical event theorists, in particular, Willmar Sauter's overlapping, four-part map, on which I have drawn extensively in part 3.

Both maps have, of course, overlaid each other. In the previous chapter, for example, I emphasized the importance of examining live performance not only in the context of a mediatized culture but also in terms of theatre's own particularities as an institutionalized form of transitive, collective, intermedial, and ostended live production. It is in this context, I have suggested, that we will best understand social audience pleasures in the intimate gaze spectator position established by the Railway Street Theatre Company's *Much Ado about Nothing*. To push cultural studies another notch along the way here we need to go much farther, to explore, in precisely situated performative conditions, the relationship between an audience's everyday and the theatrical event, the cinematic event, the television event, the art event, the sports event, each of which will have its own global (mediatized) and local places and occasions.

This is not to forsake traditional media studies enterprises — far from it, as the sketchy description in chapter 9 of Susan and the Springwood students on gender, music, and meaning in *Much Ado about Nothing* was meant to suggest. I do not want to reduce the "pleasurable" to the "political" (Alasuutari), but we must not ignore the political (and the economic) either. Nor must we forget, in all this discussion of localized liveness and theatre's intimate gaze, that a globalizing mediatization is also integral to these meanings and pleasures. That is why I chose Gifford's *Much Ado* for this particular analysis at the end.

By way of conclusion, bringing the two maps of production study and theatrical event analysis together in their focus on audiences, I will return to the data from chapter 9, which can, in fact, summarize all of Sauter's segments of the theatrical event. Every individual audience member engaged with each synchronic (multimedial) segment in this live (transitive) performance process. To conclude with an individual and local case study of what we now know to be a much broader matter of liveness, mediatization, and risk modernity, I will focus on the responses of Nicole, a Springwood drama teacher in her midtwenties.

Playing culture: As she spoke with me in long interview about why theatre is a special event for her, Nicole linked together many of the issues of magic, the everyday, the spontaneous, the real, and the intimacy of skilled actor-audience communication that we have seen mentioned separately in questionnaire responses and elaborated in long interviews.

> The thing I love about going to the theatre is you're never quite sure what's going to happen. . . . How are the performers going to connect with me? And even if it's a fourth wall type of production or there's no direct address to the audience, just every now and then the actor's eye looking out into the audience can seem to catch yours. You're in the space there with them, when they're making the magic happen, instead of having it recorded on film . . . where you know that they've done seventy-five takes to get it right. And it can sometimes be as exciting when something goes wrong, to see how they'll deal with it. . . . You *know* that it's real, you know that it's there and then, that it's live. That's the special part of theatre. . . . For me, when I say "real" I'm thinking of the actors' craft as much as anything else. And I'm thinking of the fact that they're up there, if they make a mistake they don't have the chance to go back and rewind the tape and cut it and re-edit it out. That's the comparison with cinema. When I say "real" it is probably a simplified way of saying, "They are there in front of me. I know they have to have rehearsed hard. . . . I'm hoping that they're living in the moment and giving the best performance that they can." . . . The magic and reality of it is, then, that the actors did certainly seem to be enjoying the production of *Much Ado* and, therefore, so did we. . . . The audience will respond more to a good play than a good film, because . . . it's give and take. They know the actors can hear them laughing, can hear

them applauding, can hear their gasps of amazement.... So in theatre you know that your appreciation is being registered on some level by the performers as well as by everyone else in the crowd.

Notably, Nicole, without any prompting from me as interviewer, used the grammar of mediatization to articulate her love of theatre. The live and the real and the actors' craft and skill are sharpened in the context of what happens in the cinematic "other," where producers "have the chance to go back and rewind the tape and cut it and re-edit it out." This is not to say that Nicole did not like cinema or television. She was a regular viewer of both. But it does indicate that "playing culture" is embedded also within its own institutional determinants, in this case, the transitive nature of theatre linked to the interactive collectivity of skilled production and live reception.

Cultural context: As an English and drama teacher who had lived and taught in a remote rural New South Wales town (where she felt that the only "market" in intimacy for a young woman teacher was in relation to other "visitors," mainly, police and hospital workers), Nicole had experienced the conservatism of Australian macro- and micropolitics at first-hand. Professionally, this had expressed itself in a lack of local interest or facilities for her students to see HSC theatre. She recalled vividly the expensive trip to Sydney to see a Shakespeare play. Because of the distances involved in getting to Sydney and the lack of railway facilities in much of rural New South Wales, and because of the considerable travel cost, she and the teenage girls spent the night in a sleazy hotel, where she was seriously concerned for her students' safety from some of the men hanging around there. Experienced in this context of both pleasure and risk, Nicole was thus positioned personally and professionally to recognize (now as a resident of the Blue Mountains) the importance of Mary-Anne Gifford's efforts to save the Q Theatre for Western Sydney as well as for remote country New South Wales. "The variety on offer has particularly impressed me. I would be devastated if the Q shut down, both for myself and my students. It is simply too difficult to get into Sydney with the frequency that I visit the Q." In the absence of a live theatre nearby she would have to resort more to video "because it's cheaper." She likes film and TV (and, as we will see, played between the Kenneth Branagh *Much Ado about Nothing*, Baz Luhrmann's *Romeo + Juliet* film, and the Q Theatre's *Much Ado* in interpreting the latter). But for Nicole, seeing films and videos was certainly not as good as playing culture at the theatre.

Contextual theatricality: Mary-Anne Gifford responded to the political and economic risks of running a touring theatre in an era of minimal state subsidies through an interplay between different high and popular cultural artistic conventions, which included her critical use of the energizing and audience-broadening devices of mediatization. In her 1998 *A Midsummer Night's Dream* at the Q Theatre, Gifford deployed 1920s and 1930s Hollywood costumes, character devices, and music to signify symbolically the F. Scott Fitzgerald long party atmosphere of the victorious powers after 1918, an atmosphere from which Germany awakened violently. In parallel to the theme of the captured Amazon queen, Gifford's production played across a powerful and sometimes violent comedy of gender and class, with a strong sensory deployment of the working-class mechanicals' exuberantly comic 1930s routines. In *Much Ado about Nothing* Gifford symbolically situated her tale of men as war machines returning to *La dolce vita* in 1950s Italy. Politics was certainly a "long perspective" for Mary-Anne Gifford, but it was always mediatized for a wide audience. For the school English teacher Nicole, Gifford's mixed political, organizational, and artistic conventions worked perfectly.

[T]aking the typical Shakespearean themes of love and confusion to Italy in the 1950s . . . seemed to work. It gave the play a whole *Roman Holiday* sort of feel — the fashions and so on. . . . And taking it to that era following the Second World War added to it. . . . The first time we saw the men, it was a moment of stillness, and it was like, "These people have been in a war. These men have witnessed terrible things, have been through horror." And I just watched the film version again recently and noticed the contrast in the Kenneth Branagh film when they came back from war. They're all excited and happy and "it's wonderful to be here," whereas [in the Q *Much Ado*] . . . sure, they *became* happy and carefree, and they celebrated [in the Elvis impersonation scene]. But when we first saw them [in the town gateway] it carried that sense of "we've really been fighting." . . . It seemed like such a long moment, that scene. . . . Their expressions were stern, exhausted, almost grief-stricken . . . but then, I also thought the music really worked. . . . The Elvis impersonation worked artistically because they were supposed to be disguised at that point [in the Shakespeare text]. So it was a logical disguise to choose, given the era it was set in. And I really felt it added to the whole entertainment value and interest value for the audience. . . . It's quite appropriate to use music in Shakespearean comedy. . . . I think that . . . using the setting and the costumes and the music of that era did broaden the appeal. It did take it away from, you know, the "authentic Elizabethan look," which can sometimes put people off and can add to the fact that they think it's too hard for them to understand.

Clearly, Nicole drew on her drama teacher competence in theatrical and Shakespearean conventions several times in these comments, but she drew also on film and media contexts. Many among the *Much Ado* respondents did this, and there were plenty of other audience members who were not drama teachers who felt that the Elvis impersonations and other music were perfectly appropriate to Shakespearean comedy. While perhaps few had Nicole's close understanding of the interplay of gender, popular cultural, and "bums on seats" conventions in Gifford's work (or, rather, could express this so articulately), a very large number of respondents did find the setting and music appropriate to Shakespeare and were fully aware of the importance of these connections in keeping the theatre alive in a market economy.

Theatrical playing: At this level, as Sauter says, the artistic, sensory, and symbolic aspects of what Nicole describes as the "magical/real" of the theatrical event connect with the audiences' everyday lives. In long interviews I focused on three semiotic systems (music, set/image, and gender characterization) at play within the multimediality and ostension of the Gifford theatrical event. It is the familiar cultural studies quest for "meaning" that we are engaged with here but within the playing culture aspect of liveness. Nicole's response to these semiotic systems in the production indicated the way in which meaning, play, and everyday identity worked for her.

Gifford placed the huge image of the crucified Christ very centrally, at the back of the stage, to emphasize not only the (Catholic) Christian morality dominating the supposed *dolce vita* of Shakespeare's Italian world of women but also the controlling masculinity of this world of fathers as governors and soldiers as killers. For Nicole, one of the major interests of Gifford's production was the initial focus on the "long moment" of men as stern "we've really been fighting" soldiers. She felt the power of these wordless men in a strongly sensory way. While she did not relate the crucified Christ image directly to this tale of masculinity, she did perceive this continuing through the male display of the Elvis impersonations and the music. She also recognized the connotation of the looming Christ figure for the Hero narrative — though, interestingly, initially did so via a mediatized intertextual reference. "The Christ figure actually reminded me a little bit of the Baz Luhrmann version of *Romeo + Juliet*, because that was a common image used throughout that film. So that was the first thing that occurred to me. Then, apart from that, I thought, Well, Italy, strong Catholic society — there's more than an element of that there. Within the play itself there's the wedding, the supposed betrayal, and the force of religion in their lives comes through strongly."

Nicole drew significantly on her own personal feelings of identity and her everyday experience of relationships, past and present, in enjoying the interaction of Hero and Beatrice.

> This is where your everyday experience gets involved. I'd just sat and had word games with a friend, so you appreciate the fact that Beatrice and Benedick had word games between themselves....You can appreciate what's going on, onstage ... through your own relationship.... I think some of the things Beatrice says are fantastic, and, yeah, I've definitely got a *personal* admiration for her, getting one up on Benedick every now and then. She's an interesting, strong woman who won't follow what her uncle is telling her to do, whereas Hero does..... There is a sense of Hero being a little bit at the mercy of her father ... or husband-to-be. And there's definitely still a male power in the world that *exists*. But I don't see a lot of Hero in myself now, not anymore. I respond emotionally more to Beatrice.... I do see Hero in my friends because of their situation and personality, in terms of *their* current partners or fathers. I like to feel I'd got beyond that when I reached eighteen. But it *was* there for me, definitely it was there.

It was in that intimately playful relationship between actors (playing Beatrice and Hero) and herself as an audience member and between the theatrical event and her past and present everyday life that the politics and the pleasures of Mary-Anne Gifford's *Much Ado* were both *sensed* and *symbolized* by Nicole. She, like many others at the *Much Ado* production, enjoyed a special relation of intimacy established between theatre audiences and actors in performed situations (when the "skills and style" of the latter were seen to be at their peak) and between the production's leisure industry mediatization (as in the Elvis scenes) and her past and present daily life. Like others, Nicole talked about these pleasures as a social audience member by way of different discursive constructs (Kuhn 1987, 347).

In this book, the agenda and discourse of analysis has been more risk than postmodernist. For example, the place and time of the Railway Street Theatre that performed *Much Ado about Nothing* derived from the economic risks to a small, local, touring theatre company trying to communicate about current personal and political cruelty in a market economy. The liminal and transgressive spaces provided by that theatre as live event allowed, for example, young people to negotiate the age, gender, and sexual preference risks in their everyday lives. The analysis of this book has emphasized the blurring of fantasy and reality, just as postmodernists do. But it has sought to place these in the *social action*, as intimate gaze, of an audience member's (and performer's) everyday leisure and working life. In the repeated audience references, among the *Much Ado* audience responses, to other "images" (e.g., Baz Luhrmann's *Romeo + Juliet*), as in the production's own reflexive presentation of Elvis Presley, *La dolce vita*, and other 1950s media images, there was evidence for both Baudrillard's world of simulacra and for Auslander's mediatization.

But these were, I have argued, multiple and locally embedded images and significations. If Trevor Griffiths's "enlightenment project" (chapters 3 and 4) was indeed dead (and the popular reception of other theatrical work described in this book, of Mary-Anne Gifford and Janet Suzman, has suggested otherwise), then the project of individualization within risk modernity seems a more convincing transgressive alternative than postmodernism's celebration of infinitely repeatable simulations.

Yet if, as both postmodernist and risk modernist theorists observe, there is a current deterritorialization of identity as direct spheres of contact are lost, the audience data discussed in this book (derived from a wide variety of age groups and cultures) suggest that liveness in theatrical events is one place and occasion where people still find active pleasure and performativity in direct spheres of intimate contact. Others may find this in sports, festivals, carnivals, or a variety of other "liveness" events and inflections, each of which needs its own analysis in the context of mediatization. In particular, we need to look further at these in terms of Lash's sense of anti-institutions, or "disorganizations," which "bond through intense affective charge" as "reflexive and flexible communities, enduring only a short while and then forming once again" (2000, 59). In the sect, says Lash, trust lies in the "mediated face-to-face of the affinity group" (2000, 59). This trust seems to be especially strong in the theatre at those times when audiences begin to experience what one respondent called the "real event" in a synthesis of cognition, imagination, and the sublime.

REFERENCES

Abercrombie, Nicholas, and Brian Longhurst. *Audiences: A Sociological Theory of Performance and Imagination.* London: Sage, 1998.

Adam, Barbara, and Stuart Allan. *Theorizing Culture: An Interdisciplinary Critique after Postmodernism.* London: UCL Press, 1995.

Alasuutari, Pertti, ed. *Rethinking the Media Audience: The New Agenda.* London: Sage, 1999.

Allen, David. *Performing Chekhov.* London: Routledge, 2000.

Armfield, N. *The 1997 Book.* Sydney: Company B, Belvoir Street Theatre, 1997.

Ang, Ien. *Living Room Wars: Rethinking Media Audiences for a Postmodern World.* London: Sage, 1996.

Auslander, Philip. *Liveness: Performance in a Mediatized Culture.* London: Routledge, 1999.

Australian Vice-Chancellor's Committee. *Report of the Academic Standards Panel: English.* Canberra: AVCC, 1994.

Bain, Keith N. *Hyperartificial* "Cinema and the Art of Cool." Ph.D. diss., University of Stellenbosch, 2001.

Barthes, Roland. *S/Z* . Trans. R. Miller. London: Jonathan Cape, 1975.

Baudrillard, Jean. *The Ecstasy of Communication.* New York: Semiotext(e), 1988.

Beck, Ulrich. *Risk Society: Towards a New Modernity.* London: Sage, 1992.

Bennett, Susan. *Performing Nostalgia: Shifting Shakespeare and the Contemporary Past.* London: Routledge, 1996.

———. *Theatre Audiences: A Theory of Production and Reception.* London: Routledge, 1997.

Bennett, Tony, and Janet Woollacott. *Bond and Beyond: The Political Career of a Popular Hero.* Basingstoke: Macmillan, 1987.

Brooker, Peter, and Will Brooker, eds. *Postmodern After-Images: A Reader in Film, Television and Video.* London: Arnold, 1997.

Broude, Norma. *Impressionism: A Feminist Reading.* New York: Rizzoli International Publications, 1991.

Bukatman, Scott. "Who Programs You? The Science Fiction of the Spectacle." In Peter Brooker and Will Brooker, eds., *Postmodern After-Images: A Reader in Film, Television and Video,* 74–88. London: Arnold, 1997.

Carlson, Marvin. *Performance: A Critical Introduction.* London: Routledge, 1996.

Collins, Jim. "Television and Postmodernism." In Peter Brooker and Will Brooker, eds., *Postmodern After-Images: A Reader in Film, Television and Video,* 192–207. London: Arnold, 1997.

Davies, Bronwyn. "The Concept of Agency: A Feminist Poststructuralist Analysis." In A. Yeatman, ed., *Postmodern Critical Theory,* 42–53. No. 30, 1991.

De Marinis, Marco. *The Semiotics of Performance.* Bloomington: University of Indiana Press, 1993.

Denzin, Norman K., and Yvonna S. Lincoln. *Collecting and Interpreting Qualitative Materials*. Thousand Oaks, CA: Sage, 1998.

Dick, Leslie. "Magnolia." *Sight and Sound* 10, no. 4 (2000): 56–57.

The Dictionary of Painting and Sculpture: Art and Artists. Mitchell Beazley Library of Art v. 4. London: Mitchell Beazley, 1979.

Elam, Keir. *The Semiotics of Theatre and Drama*. London: Methuen, 1980.

———. "Text Appeal and the Analysis Paralyis: Towards a Processual Poetics of Dramatic Production." In T. Fitzpatrick, ed., *Altro Polo Performance: From Product to Process*, 1–26. Sydney: University of Sydney, 1989.

English Touring Theatre. *The Cherry Orchard Education Pack*. ETT Education, 2000.

Eversmann, Peter G. F. "The Experience of the Theatrical Event." In Cremona, Anne, Peter Eversmann, Hans von Maanen, Willmar Sauter, and John Tulloch, eds. *Theatrical Events, Borders, Dynamics, Frames*. Amsterdam: Rodopi, forthcoming.

Fischer-Lichte, Erika. *The Semiotics of Theatre*. Trans. Jeremy Gaines and Doris L. Jones. Bloomington: Indiana University Press, 1992.

Gifford, Mary-Anne. "Better Than the Movies." Penrith: Q Theatre, 2001.

Griffiths, Trevor. Lectures at Birmingham University Theatre Masters Program, coordinated by David Edgar. 1989, 1990, 1992.

Hallett, Bryce, and Peter Gotting. *Sydney Morning Herald*, February 27, 2001:14.

Holderness, Graham. *Shakespeare Recycled: The Making of Historical Drama*. Hemel Hempstead: Harvester Wheatsheaf, 1992.

Holland, Peter. "Chekhov and the Resistant Symbol." In J. Redmond, ed., *Drama and Symbol*, 227–42. Cambridge: Cambridge University Press, 1982.

Jameson, Frederic. "The Nostalgia Mode and Nostalgia for the Present." In Peter Brooker and Will Brooker, eds., *Postmodern After-Images: A Reader in Film, Television and Video*, 23–35. London: Arnold, 1997.

"Jozef Israëls." In *Encyclopaedia Britannica*, 5:463, 1973.

"Jozef Israëls, 1824–1911." In *The New International Illustrated Encyclopedia of Art*. 1981. 12:2368–69.

"Jozef Israëls 1824–1911" and "Hague School." In *The Dictionary of Painting and Sculpture: Art and Artists*. 1979. 4:92, 93.

Kuhn, Annette. "Women's Genres: Melodrama, Soap Opera and Theory." In C. Gledhill, ed., *Home Is Where the Heart Is: Studies in Melodrama and the Woman's Film*, 339–49. London: BFI, 1987.

Lash, Scott. "Risk Culture." In B. Adam, U. Beck, and J. Van Loon, eds., *The Risk Society and Beyond: Critical Issues for Social Theory*. London: Sage, 2000.

Loos, W. and G. Jansen. *Breitner and His Age: Paintings from the Rijksmuseum in Amsterdam, 1880–1900*. Trans. M. Hoyle. Amsterdam: Rijksmuseum and Wanders Uitgevers Zwolle, 1995.

McRobbie, Angela. "Dance and Social Fantasy." In A. McRobbie and M. Nava, eds., *Gender and Generation*, 130–61. London: Macmillan, 1984.

Morley, Daivid. *The "Nationwide" Audience: Structure and Decoding*. London: British Film Institute, 1980.

The New Illustrated Encyclopedia of Art. V. 12. New York: Greystone Press, 1981.

Olivier, Bert. *Projections: Philosophical Themes on Film.* Port Elizabeth: University of Port Elizabeth, 1996.

Patton, Cindy. "Performativity and Spatial Distinction: The End of AIDS Epidemiology." In A. Parker and E. Sedgwick, eds., *Performativity and Performance*, 173–96. New York: Routledge, 1995.

Pickering, Michael. *History, Experience and Cultural Studies.* Basingstoke: Macmillan, 1997.

Press, Andrea. *Women Watching Television: Gender, Class and Generation in the American Television Experience.* Philadelphia: University of Pennsylvania Press, 1991.

Radway, Janice. *Reading the Romance: Women, Patriarchy and Popular Literature.* Chapel Hill: University of North Carolina Press, 1984.

Roach, Joseph. "Culture and Performance in the Circum-Atlantic World." In A. Parker and E. Sedgwick, eds., *Performativity and Performance*, 45–63. New York: Routledge, 1995.

Royal Shakespeare Company. *The Cherry Orchard* program (Stratford-upon-Avon), 1995.

Sauter, Willmar. "Introducing the Theatrical Event." In Cremons, et al., eds. *Theatrical Events, Borders, Dynamics, Frames.* Amsterdam: Rodopi, forthcoming.

———. *The Theatrical Event: Dynamics of Performance and Perception.* Iowa City: University of Iowa Press, 2000.

Schieffelin, Edward L. "Problematizing Performance." In Felicia Hughes-Freeland, ed., *Ritual, Performance, Media*, 194–207. London: Routledge, 1998.

Senelick, Laurence. "Chekhov and the Irresistible Symbol: A Response to Peter Holland." In J. Redmond, ed., *Drama and Symbol*, 243–51. Cambridge: Cambridge University Press, 1982.

———. *The Chekhov Theatre: A Century of the Plays in Performance.* Cambridge: Cambridge University Press, 1997.

Suzman, Janet. "Introduction." In *The Free State: A South African Response to Chekhov's "The Cherry Orchard."* London: Methuen, 2000.

Thomson, Peter. "Shakespeare and the Public Purse." In Jonathan Bate and Russell Jackson, eds., *The Oxford Illustrated History of Shakespeare on Stage.* Oxford: Oxford University Press, 2001.

Tulloch, John. "Chekhov Abroad: Western Criticism." In T. Clyman, ed., *A Chekhov Companion*, 185–206. Westport, CT: Greenwood, 1985.

———. *Chekhov: A Structuralist Study.* Basingstoke: Macmillan, 1980.

———. "Going to Chekhov: Cultural Studies and Theatre Studies." *Journal of Dramatic Theory and Criticism* 13, no. 2 (Spring 1999): 23–55.

———. *Legends on the Screen: The Narrative Film in Australia 1918–1929.* Sydney: Currency Press, 1981.

———. "Multiple Authorship in TV Drama: Trevor Griffiths' Version of *The Cherry Orchard*." In J. Bignall, S. Lacey, and M. Macmurraugh-Kavanagh, eds., *British Television Drama: Past, Present and Future*, 175–84. Basingstoke: Palgrave, 2000b.

―――. *Performing Culture: Stories of Expertise and the Everyday*. London: Sage, 1999.

―――. *Television Drama: Agency, Audience and Myth*. London: Routledge, 1990.

―――. *Trevor Griffiths*. Manchester: Manchester University Press, forthcoming.

―――. *Watching Television Audiences: Cultural Theories and Methods*. London: Arnold, 2000a.

Tulloch, John, and Tom Burvill. *Chekhov: In Production, Criticism and Reception*. Canberra: Australian Research Council, 1996.

Tulloch, John, Tom Burvill, and Andrew Hood. "Reinhabiting *The Cherry Orchard*: Class and History in Performing Chekhov." *New Theatre Quarterly* 13, no. 52 (1998): 318–28.

Tulloch, John, and Henry Jenkins. *Science Fiction Audiences: Watching "Doctor Who" and "Star Trek."* London: Routledge, 1995.

Tulloch, John, and Deborah Lupton. *Risk and Everyday Life*. London: Sage, 2003.

―――. "Risk, the Mass Media and Personal Biography: Revisiting Beck's *Knowledge, Media and Information Society*." *European Journal of Cultural Studies* 4, no. 1 (February 2001): 5–27.

Turner, Victor. *From Ritual to Theatre*. New York: Performing Arts Journal, 1982.

van Dijk, Teun. *Prejudice in Discourse: An Analysis of Ethnic Prejudice in Cognition and Conversation*. Amsterdam: John Benjamins, 1984.

Waites, James. *Sydney Morning Herald*, March 6, 1997: Arts 15.

Williams, Linda. "Something Else besides a Mother: *Stella Dallas* and the Maternal Melodrama." In C. Gledhill, ed., *Home Is Where the Heart Is: Studies in Melodrama and the Woman's Film*, 299–325. London: BFI, 1987.

Williams, Raymond. *Drama from Ibsen to Brecht*. Harmondsworth: Peregrine, 1968.

Wynne, Brian. "May the Sheep Safely Graze? A Reflexive View of the Expert-Lay Knowledge Divide." In S. Lash, B. Szersynski, and B. Wynne, eds., *Risk, Environment and Modernity*, 44–83. London: Sage, 1996.

INDEX

Abbey House, 251
Alasuutari, Pertti, 4, 5, 15, 195, 294
Alexander, Marva, 224, 226
Allen, David, 122, 125
Ang, Ien, 9, 17, 20
Armfield, Neil, 155, 157, 159, 160, 164,
	167, 168, 169, 170, 171, 172, 176, 177,
	179; *The Alchemist*, 163, 168, 183;
	Company B, 159, 168; *The
	Governor's Family*, 163–66, 171, 179;
	Lulu, 169; *Night on a Bald
	Mountain*, 170; *The Seagull*, 26, 154,
	155–85; *The Tempest*, 163, 171
Aubrey, Sarah, 49, 52, 56, 58, 60
Auslander, Philip, 9, 247, 273
Australian Research Council, 113
Australian Vice-Chancellors'
	Committee, 121, 122, 125

Barbican Theatre (London), 3, 39, 50,
	211; and *The Tempest*, 3–5, 39, 50, 289
Barker, Trent, 49, 56, 57
Barthes, Roland, 19, 130, 137, 144
Baudrillard, Jean, 26, 27, 28, 29, 300
BBC1 television: *The Cherry Orchard*,
	83–112
Beck, Ulrich, 19, 26, 29, 30, 31, 33, 44,
	219, 220
Belvoir Street Theatre (Sydney), 22,
	26, 113, 128, 155, 167, 168, 283. *See also*
	Neil Armfield
Bely, Andrey, 121
Bennett, Alan: *The Madness of King
	George*, 268, 269
Bennett, Susan, 6–10, 11, 12, 18, 19, 33,
	40, 54, 55, 79, 155, 157, 178, 182, 190,
	195, 201, 216
Bennett, Tony, 16, 18; and Janet
	Woollacott, 16

Berger, John: *Ways of Seeing*, 88, 102, 164
Berkeley, Busby, 50, 54
Bernhardt, Sarah, 13, 14, 38, 271; in
	Lady of the Camelias, 271; in *Phèdre*,
	14, 271
Bihl, Esmeralda, 231
Birmingham Repertory Theatre, 223,
	225
Blanchett, Cate, 160, 171, 175, 176, 177,
	178, 179, 183
Bloomsbury Group, 34, 129
Borghesi, Anna, 159, 162, 166, 167, 169,
	171
Boyer, Patricia, 231
Bradby, David, 127
Branagh, Kenneth, 265; *Much Ado
	about Nothing*, 61, 296
Brecht, Bertolt, 13, 84, 88, 100, 104, 108,
	109, 110, 189, 190, 191; and the
	Berliner Ensemble, 13, 189, 190
Brideshead Revisited (television pro-
	gram), 222
Bristol Hippodrome, 191, 211, 214, 215
Bristol Old Vic Theatre, 191, 215
Brook, Peter, 54, 119
Broude, Norma, 94
Brown, Capability, 229
Brustein, Robert, 137
Bukatman, Scott, 28
Burvill, Tom, 84

Carlson, Marvin, 16
Cartwright, Peter, 232
Catherine McAuley High School
	(Parramatta, New South Wales),
	291, 292
Chekhov productions and audiences,
	83–112, 113–53, 154–85, 189–218,
	219–41

reading formation, 16, 17, 18, 21, 22, 36, 80, 84, 94, 95, 98, 104, 109, 113, 114, 135, 136, 146, 147, 150, 151, 200

Redgrave, Vanessa, 265

Reid, Don, 155

resistant reading analysis, 4, 50, 278

risk modernity, 19, 23, 25, 26, 27, 30, 35, 36, 40, 44, 45, 75, 299, 300; theory of, 22, 27–29, 31, 32–35, 37, 39, 299

Rogger, Hans, 124

Roxburgh, Richard, 171

Royal Shakespeare Company (Stratford-upon-Avon), 22, 27, 124, 128, 189, 215. *See also* Noble, Adrian

Rush, Geoffrey, 159, 160, 172, 179, 183

Sauter, Willmar, 6, 12–15, 37, 38, 50, 60, 72, 76, 87, 189, 190, 219, 230, 242, 245, 271, 294, 295, 298

Scales, Prunella, 191, 202, 203, 206, 207, 209, 210–13, 216, 246, 251, 253, 256, 257, 258, 262, 263, 264

Scardifield, Simon, 206

Schofield, Tess, 159, 168, 171, 172, 173

Scott, Anne, 104, 107

semiotics of production, 16, 201, 232–38, 275, 298

Senelick, Laurence, 113–25, 131, 144

Shakespeare productions and audiences, 3–6, 38–80, 271–93, 295–300

Shapiro, Adolf: *The Cherry Orchard*, 118

Simon, Barney, 222, 223, 230

Sinatra, Frank, 63, 78, 79; *Love and Marriage* (song), 78

Skinner, Cornelia Otis, 14

Smith, Maggie, 191, 252

Spall, Timothy, 109

spectatorship and social reading, 17, 21, 22, 30, 34, 36, 39, 40, 47–74, 80, 83, 89, 92, 93, 95, 110, 113, 114, 141, 151, 182, 185, 264–67, 281–84, 294

Spence, Sue, 88, 91, 93, 101, 102

Springwood High School (New South Wales), 38, 72–79, 290, 291, 294

St. Mary's High School (New South Wales), 73

Stalin, Joseph, 118

Stanislavsky, Konstantin, 115, 118, 119, 209

Stein, Peter, 119

Stella Dallas (film), 56

Strehler, Giorgio, 119, 120, 122

Styan, John L., 137

Suzman, Janet, 10, 26, 191, 194, 206, 219, 220–44, 253, 256, 258, 259, 262–65, 300; *The Free State*, 26, 32, 189, 190, 191, 194, 195, 201, 206, 209, 211, 212, 219–41, 242–70, 272, 275, 280

Swan Theatre (Stratford-upon-Avon), 211

Taganka Theatre, 123

Taylor, Noah, 172, 176, 177, 179, 183

"terrible sublime," 32, 34, 60, 239–41, 272, 300

Thatcherism, 84, 85, 87, 96, 110, 220

theatre collectivity, 10, 294

theatre multimediality, 10, 16, 45, 70, 83, 108, 111, 147, 201, 292, 294, 295, 298

theatre ostension, 10, 294, 298

Theatre Royal (Bath), 22, 128, 189–218, 221, 223, 226, 229, 247, 251, 265, 270, 275; *A Clockwork Orange*, 194, 266; *Popcorn*, 194; *Rocky Horror Picture Show*, 194; *Shopping and Fucking*, 194. *See also* Noble, Adrian; Suzman, Janet; Unwin, Stephen

theatre transitivity, 10, 294

theatrical event, 3, 5, 6–17, 19, 21, 23, 25, 26, 27, 31, 35, 36, 37, 39, 130, 154–85, 210, 218, 219, 221, 238, 242, 267–70, 284–88, 294, 300

theatrical playing, 14–15, 37, 70, 74, 85–86, 271–93, 298

third generation audience theory, 5, 6, 15–16, 158; audiencing, 15, 16, 17, 18, 23, 84, 95, 157, 195, 294

Thomson, Peter, 54

Studies in THEATRE HISTORY & CULTURE